Henry Charles Groves

A Commentary on the Book of Genesis

for the use of readers of the English version of the Bible

Henry Charles Groves

A Commentary on the Book of Genesis
for the use of readers of the English version of the Bible

ISBN/EAN: 9783337100131

Printed in Europe, USA, Canada, Australia, Japan

Cover: Foto ©Lupo / pixelio.de

More available books at **www.hansebooks.com**

A COMMENTARY

ON THE

BOOK OF GENESIS

FOR THE USE OF

Readers of the English Version of the Bible.

BY

HENRY CHARLES GROVES, M.A.

PERPETUAL CURATE OF MULLAVILLY, DIOC. ARMAGH.

MACMILLAN AND CO.
Cambridge:
AND 23, HENRIETTA STREET, COVENT GARDEN,
London.
1861.

Cambridge:
PRINTED BY C. J. CLAY, M.A.
AT THE UNIVERSITY PRESS.

PREFACE.

In the course of the last thirty years much has been done to elucidate the text of the Pentateuch, to clear away the uncertainties and obscurities involving the Geographical and Historical notices contained in it, and to dispose of the objections which the disclosures made by the rapid advance of several branches of Physical Science were supposed to present to the statements of this part of Scripture. But the information on these various points hitherto had to be searched for in a number of works which for the most part are accessible, or of interest, to the scholar alone. To bring it, in some measure, and so far as it bears on the book of Genesis, within the reach of the general reader, is the object of this Commentary; in the formation of which have been consulted the works containing the latest results of the investigations in sacred criticism and exegesis, in Biblical Geography and History, and in Science considered in relation to religion. Throughout it the requirements of the general reader have been kept in view; and yet it is hoped that the student will find much to assist him in the study of this portion of the Holy Scriptures.

The author, while he has taken every care to secure the work from imperfections which may impede its utility, is well aware that from its nature many shortcomings will probably be detected in it. But those who are most competent to discover these defects, will be the most ready to acknowledge the difficulty of avoiding them.

The following are the works referred to in the Commentary: those enclosed in brackets are such as the author had not access to, and for the citations from which he is indebted to some of the other authors made use of.

CRITICAL AND EXEGETICAL WORKS.

H. Ainsworth, *Annotations on the Five Books of Moses.* Lond. 1639.—R. Kidder, Bishop of Bath and Wells, *Commentary on the Five Books of Moses.* Lond. 1694.—S. Patrick, Bishop of Ely, *Commentary on the Hist. Books of the O. T.*, 1694. Reprinted, 1851.—E. F. C. Rosenmüller, *Scholia in Vetus Testamentum.* Pars Prima, cont. Gen. et Ex. Lips. 1795.—F. J. V. D. Maurer, *Commentarius Grammaticus Criticus in Vet. Test.* Lips. 1835.—[P. von Bohlen, *die Genesis,* &c. Königsb. 1835.—Fr. Tuch, *Komm. üb. d. Genesis.* Halle, 1838].—E. W. Hengstenberg, *Egypt and the Books of Moses.* Translated with additional notes by W. C. Taylor. Edinb. 1845. *Authenticity of the Pentateuch.* Clark's Trans., 2 Vols. Edinb. 1847. *Christology of the O. T.* Clark's Trans., 4 Vols. Edinb. 1854.—Otto von Gerlach, *Commentary on the Pent.* Translated by Rev. H. Downing. Edinb.

1860.—*The English Bible divided into paragraphs.* R. B. Blackadder. Lond. 1853.—D. A. de Sola; J. L. Lindenthal; M. J. Raphall, *The Sacred Scriptures*, Heb. and Eng., a new translation with notes, &c., Vol. I. Genesis. Bagster, 1844. —M. M. Kalisch, *Hist. and Crit. Comm. on the O. T.* With a translation. Genesis. Lond. 1858. —Aug. Knobel, *die Genesis erkl.* Leipz. 1852.— C. H. H. Wright, *Book of Genesis*, in Heb., with a critically revised text, various readings, and grammatical and critical notes, 1859.—J. H. Kurtz, *Hist. of the Old Covenant.* Clark's Trans. 3 Vols. Edinb. 1859.—Frz. Delitzsch, *die Genesis ausgel.* Leipz. 1860.

WORKS ON THE GENERAL INTRODUCTION.

H. A. C. Hævernick, *Historico-Critical Introd. to the Pentateuch.* Clark's Trans. Edinb. 1850.— Horne, *Introd. to the Holy Script.*, Vol. II. ed. 10, by Samuel Davidson, D.D. Lond. 1856 (cited as Davidson's *Introd.*).—The same revised and edited by Rev. J. Ayre. Lond. 1860 (cited as Ayre's *Introd.*).—K. F. Keil, *Lehr. d. hist. Krit. Einleitung in die Kanonisch. u. apok. Schriften des Alten Testamentes*, 1858.

GEOGRAPHY.

Edward Robinson, D.D., *Biblical Researches in Palestine.* Sec. ed., 3 Vols. Lond. 1856.— A. P. Stanley, *Sinai and Palestine, in connection with their history.* Lond. 1856.—J. Kitto, *Scripture Lands.* Lond. 1850.—W. M. Thomson, twenty-five years a missionary in Syria and Palestine, *The Land and the Book.* Lond. 1860.— Col. Chesney, *Expedition for the Survey of the rivers Euphrates and Tigris.* 4 Vols. Lond. 1850.

WORKS CITED IN REFERENCE TO THE RELATION OF THE BIBLE TO MODERN DISCOVERIES, EITHER HISTORICAL OR SCIENTIFICAL.

Prof. Sedgwick, *Discourse on the Studies of the University of Cambridge.* Lond. 1850.—W. Whewell, *Indications of the Creator.* Lond. 1846.

—C. Hardwick, *Christ and other Masters*, Pt. I. Camb. 1855.—Cardinal Wiseman, *Twelve Lectures on the Connection beween Science and Revealed Religion*, 2 Vols. 1859.—*The History of Herodotus*. A new English version, edited with copious notes, &c., by G. Rawlinson, M.A., assisted by Col. Sir H. Rawlinson, and Sir J. G. Wilkinson. 4 Vols. Lond. 1858-60.—G. Rawlinson, *The Hist. Evidence of the Truth of the Scripture Records.* Lond. 1859.

INTRODUCTION

ON THE

AUTHORSHIP OF THE PENTATEUCH.

WORKS referred to: ,Bish. Kidder, *Dissertation concerning the Author of the Pentateuch;* prefixed to his *Commentary on the Pentateuch.* —Hævernick, *Introduction to the Pentateuch;* Clark's Translation. Edinb. 1850.— Hengstenberg, *Dissertations on the Genuineness of the Pentateuch;* Clark's Transl. Edinb. 1847.—Davidson, *The Text of the O.T. considered,* forming the second vol. of Horne's *Introd.* Lond. 1856.— Kurtz, *Hist. of the Old Covenant;* Clark's Trans. 3 Vols. Edinb. 1859.—Keil, *Einleit. in d. Kanon. u. apokr. Schriften des Alten Testamentes.* 1859.—Ayre, *Introd. to the Crit. of the O.T.;* a revised and enlarged edition of the sec. vol. of Horne's *Introd.* Lond. 1860.—Delitzsch, *Commentar über die Genesis, Einleitung.* 1860.

Names of the Pentateuch.

The first five books of the Old Testament are throughout the remainder of the Hebrew canon referred to under the name of *The Law, The Book of the Law, The Law of Moses, The Book of Moses, The Book of the Law of Moses.* By the Rabbins they were called *The Five-fifths of the Law;* by the Greeks, *The Pentateuch,* or *Five-volume Book.*

Origin of division into five books.

When the division into five books was made is questioned. Hævernick and Davidson ascribe it to the authors of the Septuagint version; Michaelis concludes it to be older than this, yet not original; while Keil and Delitzsch think that there is internal evidence that the work naturally distributes itself into these five portions, and therefore consider the division to be as old as the composition of the entire work. But as no trace of it is found in the New Testament citations, and as the names now current for the different books were unknown to the Jews, and are of Greek origin, it is most probable that the division into five books is due to the Septuagint translators.

Essential and original unity of the Pentateuch.

But whenever made, the contents of the five books show that they collectively form one systematic and connected work. This unity

AUTHORSHIP OF THE PENTATEUCH. xiii

of the Pentateuch is displayed in its *subject-matter* and *language*.

(i) In the subject-matter, (1) by the inflexible firmness with which the one great aim and object of the history is kept in view. The covenant between the Lord and Israel is the central point of the whole. All that is mentioned before it is preparatory, and the history subsequent to it is but the detail of the full development of that momentous transaction. The Pentateuch commences with the creation; by thus showing the original position of man it explains and prepares the way for the covenant by which in some small measure he was to be restored to that position which he lost by the fall. It terminates with the death of Moses, the mediator of the covenant, when his work was accomplished, and when Israel was about to be instated in the full enjoyment of his covenant relation. In the historical treatment of the interval between these two terminal points the great object is kept steadily in view; minute and otherwise insignificant details are mentioned because they bear upon it; while the most important historical events are omitted as only

displayed,
(i) in its subject-matter, (1) by one object being kept in view throughout it;

(2) by the mutual coherence of details;

obstructing the advance of the history[1]. (2) We discern a similar oneness of conception in the close coherence and relation of the different historical details; in the earlier portions of the history preparing the way for the later, and the later pointing back to the earlier, which they either further develope or supplement[2].

(3) by adaptation of chronology to its plan.

(3) But the essential and original unity of the Pentateuch is perhaps most plainly displayed in its chronology; not merely in the accurate consistency of the different portions of the chronological chain which runs through the work, but also in the adaptation of it in its various parts to the plan of the history. "It is at first chronologico-genealogical, connecting the computation of time with the lifetime of the Patriarchs of Israel, reckoning from the commencement of the same to the birth of the first-born. This plan, which is exactly followed as far as Jacob's history extends, then gives place to another, arising out of an epoch in Israelitish history, the removal of Jacob into Egypt. Then joining on to this, we have

---

[1] Delitzsch, *Einl.* p. 15. Comp. Dean Trench's *Huls. Lect.* pp. 26—29.

[2] Keil, *Einl.* p. 106.

the reckoning according to the second great event, the departure of the Hebrews; and this chronology is invariably continued throughout the last four books of the Pentateuch[1]."

(ii) The minute analysis by which Keil[2] has proved the identity of *language* in all characteristic peculiarities may perhaps be considered as testimony collected by a partial advocate. But it is confirmed by the admission of such witnesses as Tuch, De Wette, and Hupfeld, who maintain the composition of the Pentateuch out of different documents. To account for a similarity of language between portions which they assign to different authors they assert that the supplementalist intentionally copied the style of the groundwork[3]. There may, perhaps, be observed a slight dissimilarity in the general tone of Deuteronomy and the other books, but yet the difference in style is not greater than may be naturally accounted for by the hortatory nature of the book, by the addresses themselves, and by the prophetic character of some of them[4]. Pro-

(ii) In the style.

Admissions of opponents.

---

[1] Hævernick, p. 23; Keil, p. 106.
[2] *Einleit.* §§ 27, 30, 32.   [3] *Ibid.* p. 110.
[4] Hævernick, p. 338; Keil, p. 98.

fessor Davidson, indeed, asserts that a difference of style irreconcileable with unity of authorship may be perceived by every critical scholar. Yet Delitzsch, whose view is supported by Kurtz, maintains that the supplementalist author of the Pentateuch had formed his style on that of Deuteronomy[1].

Authorship.

The essential and original unity of the Pentateuch being thus established, we may next consider what information is presented regarding the authorship of it by the other portions of the canon of the Old and New Testament.

Ascribed to Moses in the N.T.

In the New Testament it is not only appealed to by our Lord and the apostles as part of the inspired canon (Matt. iv. 4, 7; xii. 5; Gal. iv. 21), and as the *Law of Moses* (Joh. vii. 23, Act. xxviii. 23), and as *Moses* (Luk. xvi. 31, Act. xv. 21); but they say in plain words, that Moses *wrote* the Law (Mark xii. 26, Luk. xx. 37, Joh. v. 46, 47; Rom. x. 5)[2]. It is said by opponents of the unity of the Pentateuch, that as our Lord did not come to teach the

---

[1] Delitzsch, *Genesis, Einl.* p. 38.

[2] A collection of passages of similar import may be found in Bp. Kidder's *Dissert.* p. xxvi, or in Ayre, *Introd.* p. 545.

Jews criticism, He might have accommodated in this case His language to a vulgar error¹. But it certainly lowers His Divine character to represent Him as supporting by language, which he could easily have avoided, an error respecting the rule of faith and life.

The writers of the Old Testament use the same language of the author of the Pentateuch; see 1 Kin. ii. 3; 2 Kin. xxiii. 25; 2 Chron. xxiii. 18²; 2 Chron. xxx. 16²; Dan. ix. 11, 13; Mal. iv. 4; Neh. viii. 1³. However, besides this direct, the later books of the Hebrew canon present a mass of indirect evidence which testifies plainly that the Pentateuch in its present form must have been composed in the time of Moses. This evidence we may divide into two groups; 1st, according as it is yielded by the historical facts recorded in the Hebrew Canon; or 2ndly, as it is collected from the literature of the Hebrew nation. *and also in the O. T.*

Indirect evidence of O.T. divided into two groups;

(1) Throughout the whole of the history of Israel, from the death of Moses to the Cap- *(i) as presented by historical facts,*

¹ Kurtz, III. 510.
² Deuteronomy cannot be referred to here, as it contains no laws respecting sacrifices.
³ From ver. 14 it appears that the Law of Moses mentioned here included Leviticus.

tivity, there meet us facts which prove incidentally that the Mosaic institutions formed the recognized basis of religious worship, and of domestic and public life in Israel. These are presented not only in the periods, such as are marked by the names of Joshua, David, Solomon, and Hezekiah, when allegiance to Jehovah was the ruling principle of the nation, but even in the dark and troubled times of the Judges, and of the schismatic and sometimes openly apostate successors of Jeroboam[1]. But while these facts prove that the Law was always, even in the earliest times of the nation, existing amongst the people, we may remark that there is no appearance of its having gradually developed itself out of the religious feelings of the people. Nowhere does it show itself as a system thus gradually moulding itself into shape, assuming fresh modifications as time made them necessary. And the continual opposition it experienced from the inward repugnance of the Israelites manifests it to have reached their nation from without, in other words, to have been given to them by God.

[1] Hengstenberg, *Pent.* I. 169—212, II. 1—122; Keil, § 34.

(2) We might easily deduce from the facts just referred to, the existence of the Law in its present written form at a time previous to the period of the Judges. But it is needless. The whole literature of the nation proves it. In the earliest of the prophets, Hosea and Amos, in the records of the ten tribes separated from the house of David, in the sacred literature of the times of David and Solomon, in the speeches and hymns recorded of the times of the Judges, we have such full and frequent allusions to the expressions, words, turns of thought, and narratives peculiar to the Pentateuch, as prove that in its present shape it must have been familiarly known in all these periods to the twelve tribes of Israel[1]. *(ii) and by verbal allusions.*

External direct evidence thus plainly attributes to Moses the authorship of the Pentateuch; indirect evidence traces it up to the confines of the time he lived in; the office, the character of Moses, point to him as in every way likely to have been qualified to be the historian of the Covenant of the Lord with Israel. Why should not we then give our *Objections to supposition of Moses being the author.*

---

[1] Hengstenberg, *Pent.* I. 107—169; Delitzsch, *Genesis*, pp. 11—15; Keil, *Einl.* § 34; Kurtz, III. 509.

assent to this evidence? Can there be produced anything peculiar either to the time he lived in, or to the circumstances in which he was placed, to make it incredible that he should have been the writer of the Book? Two circumstances of this nature have been alleged. It has been asserted that the art of writing was unknown in the time of Moses. This assertion is refuted by the Assyrian and Egyptian remains. Babylonian inscriptions have been traced back so far as the year B.C. 2200[1]. We have the authority of the eminent Egyptian archæologist Rosellini[2], that before the Exodus writing was practised in Egypt to *at least* as great a degree as it is amongst us. Every transaction of domestic as well as of public life appears to have been committed to writing. The antiquity of the art in Egypt is proved by the number of very ancient papyrus-rolls which have been discovered. Seyffarth, "through whose hands more than 10,000 Egyptian papyrus-rolls have passed," decides that writing on papyrus was practised in Egypt 2000 years

1. Art of writing unknown in his time.

---

[1] Rawlinson, *Herod.* Vol. I. p. 435.
[2] Hengstenberg, *Egypt and the Books of Moses*, p. 88.

before the Christian epoch[1]. And, to use the words of Lepsius, from the then state of things in Egypt, as we are now acquainted with them, and of which the Jews must have been cognizant in the fertile province of Goshen, "it is wholly incredible that they did not possess a running-hand as well as the Egyptians[2]." It has in the next place been asserted[3] that, admitting the existence in Egypt of the art of writing, the rude uncivilized nomadic condition of the Israelites at the time is incompatible with the supposition that the complicated legislation of the Pentateuch was composed for their use. An assertion like this is not unlikely to have a certain degree of weight at the present day, when the Patriarchs and their descendants are too often represented as mere Bedouins, and have thus attributed to them the hopeless degradation of those lawless nomadic hordes, who of choice and not of necessity embrace their vagrant life, and steadily resist the influences of civilization with which they may be brought into contact. Such lan-

2. Rude condition of the Israelites.

[1] Delitzsch, p. 20.
[2] *Tour from Thebes to Sinai*, pp. 88, 89.
[3] By Hartmann and Vater (Hengstenberg, *Pent.* I. p. 405).

guage expresses a conception of the state of the Hebrews thoroughly opposed to the scriptural representations. We find no trace of nomadic rudeness among the Patriarchs. They availed themselves of the conveniences and luxuries which civilization had created for more favoured nations. Judah had a signet; Joseph wore a richly-adorned garment; Abraham paid for the land he purchased in money, and Jacob's sons brought money for corn; Eliezer presented Rebekah with a gold ring and bracelet. It may be plainly perceived that their nomadic life was forced upon the Patriarchs; wherever it is practicable they forsake it. Lot settles in Sodom, and dwells in a house. When Abraham goes down into Egypt, instead of taking up his abode in the pasture-lands on the borders, as nomads by profession and inclination have been in the habit of doing for centuries, he betakes himself to the king's residence. Isaac lives in a house in the city of Gerar, near the king's palace. Jacob builds a house on his return from Mesopotamia. Similarly we find the Israelites represented as having during their sojourn in Egypt conformed themselves to the existing state of civilization there. They dwelt in houses with door-posts and lintels (Ex. xii. 4, 7, 22, 23), intermixed with the Egyptians, so that the destroying angel could pass by one door and stop at another. They devoted themselves to agriculture (Deut. xi. 10). They acquired a variety of arts and handicrafts (1 Chron. iv. 14, 21, 23[1]).

Still, although there is no incredibility presented by the condition of Moses or the circumstances of his times to prevent us from acknowledging him as the author of the Pentateuch, it is alleged that the Pentateuch itself, by containing passages which manifestly were written subsequent to the time of Moses, plainly declares that it was not written by him. A large number of passages of this nature have been eagerly adduced. Each advocate of the late composition of the Pentateuch has his list of passages containing traces of post-Mosaic composition. But gradually these lists have been diminishing in length as passage after passage had to be relinquished under the weight of the convincing arguments by which the learning and searching criticism of writers like Hengsten-

3. Traces of post-Mosaic composition.

---

[1] Hengstenberg, *Pent.* I. 406—413; Kurtz, II. 156—162; Thomson, *The Land and the Book*, pp. 296, 383.

berg, Hævernick, and Keil, showed the shallow grounds on which they were alleged. Thus Professor Davidson alleges only about thirteen out of the many which are to be found specified and answered in the works of Hengstenberg[1] and Keil[2]; while later still, Delitzsch[3] and Kurtz[4] cite only three of these as fairly presenting marks of an age subsequent to Moses, viz. Gen. xiv. 14, where Laish is mentioned under the name Dan, which it received in the time of the Judges, and Ex. xi. 3 and Num. xii. 3, where Moses is mentioned in terms of praise, coming appropriately only from a later historian[5]. As regards Dan, if we bear in mind that the custom of the Hebrews was to revive the old names of places distinguished by peculiar recollections[6], and sometimes with an additional allusion to the circumstances which attended the renewal of the old name[7], we can have little difficulty in regarding Dan as the primitive name of the place in Abraham's time, which was

Dan.

---

[1] *Pent.* II. 146—276. [2] *Einl.* § 38.
[3] *Genesis*, p. 39. [4] Vol. III. p. 516.
[5] Delitzsch, pp. 39, 40.
[6] Compare the case of Hebron.
[7] Compare the case of Beersheba, as thus named first by Abraham, afterwards by Isaac.

displaced for Laish by its Sidonian conquerors, and restored by the victorious Israelites. As regards the two other cases, to say that the language in them is such as could not be used by Moses of himself, is pure assertion incapable of proof[1]. Indeed the quality attributed to Moses in Num. xii. 3 is not generally considered so praiseworthy that a Hebrew panegyrist of the great Lawgiver would have been likely to have enlarged on it.

Laudation of Moses.

The difficulties being thus cleared away which embarrass the claims of Moses to the authorship of the Pentateuch, we may without more delay examine what the Pentateuch itself declares concerning its own author. In Ex. xvii. 14 we find 'The Lord said unto Moses, Write this for a memorial in *a book*, and rehearse it in the ears of Joshua.' In the Hebrew the expression is even stronger, 'in *the* book:' marking a reference to a larger work in which this notice was to be inserted. Only thus indeed, with the definite article, does the passage give an intelligible meaning. Our English translation presents the strange idea that Moses was

Assertions of the Pentateuch regarding its author.

---

[1] Compare the remarks of Hengstenberg, *Pent.* II. 141, and Bishop Kidder, p. lix.

ordered to draw up a special document containing merely, 'I will utterly put out the remembrance of Amalek from under heaven[1].' Again, Ex. xxiv. 4, 7, 'Moses wrote all the words of the Lord ... and he took the book of the covenant;' and in Ex. xxxiv. 27, after another revelation, Moses is ordered to 'write all these words.' A similar order is given to him in Numb. xxxiii. 2. In Deuteronomy several passages occur (i. 5; xvii. 18; xxviii. 58; xxxi. 9—11, 22, 24—26) which Davidson, Delitzsch, and Kurtz take as ascribing the composition of the whole book of Deuteronomy, as far as ch. xxxi. 24, to Moses. Now admitting for the moment that these citations from Deuteronomy apply only to that book, and that they were not intended to apply to the entire of the book of the law, we have even thus a strong presumption in favour of Moses having been the author. He is claimed directly as such by one entire book, and by important portions of two others; throughout the remaining portions of the Pentateuch, although there is silence as to whom they were written by, there is nothing, as we have seen, to repudiate Moses as the author. But there

---

[1] Hengstenberg, *Pent.* II. 123; Hævernick, p. 15.

is positive proof that the passages in Deuteronomy, which speak of Moses as having written *this law*, comprehend in the expression 'Law' the five books, and not Deuteronomy alone. From Neh. viii. 14, it appears that *the law* read in obedience to the command given in Deut. xxxi. 10, 11, comprehended Leviticus; for the direction about making booths is only given in that book. The reading of the entire Pentateuch on this occasion may not be explained away as an irregular proceeding of natural occurrence at the first solemnization of the festival since the time of Joshua[1]. The passage referred to does not support the charge of the neglect of the festival[2]; of the observance of which in the time of Solomon we have direct evidence (1 Kin. viii. 2). And the entire of the Pentateuch could easily have been read by Ezra, as it is written (Neh. viii. 18), 'Day by day, from the first day to the last day, he read in the book of the law of God.'

It is thus seen what firm ground both the Synagogue and the Church had to rest on in asserting that Moses was the divinely-inspired

Unanimity of the Synagogue,

---

[1] Davidson, p. 615, who refers to Neh. viii. 17.

[2] Hengstenberg, *Pent.* II. 132.

author of the Pentateuch. Among the Jews this opinion has been opposed only by Isaac ben Jasos (circ. A.D. 1000), Aben Ezra (†1167), and by Spinoza (1670), who for his atheistic opinions was expelled from the synagogue. Among Christians of various sects, the only exceptions to the unanimity which prevailed on this subject up to the latter part of the last century, were, Carlstadt (1520), A. Masius (1574), Ant. van Dale (1696), Peyrerius (1655), R. Simon (1678), and Clericus (1685[1]).

<small>and of the Church.</small>

But within the last seventy or eighty years a theory has been maintained by many German theologians, which is completely opposed to the view so long and so unanimously entertained by the Church. The first who broached this theory was a Belgian physician, Astruc[2]. He observed that much of the book of Genesis may be divided into different sections, marked by the exclusive use of one or other of the two names, Elohim and Jehovah[3]. Concluding that

<small>The latter interrupted in the last century.</small>

<small>Document-hypothesis of Astruc.</small>

---

[1] Keil, *Einl.* § 35.

[2] *Conjectures sur les Mémoires originaux, dont il parait, que Moyse s'est servi, pour composer le livre de la Genèse.* Brux. 1753.

[3] In the English Bible translated *God* and LORD, not *Lord*, which generally denotes *Adonai*.

this alternate use of the divine names was not accidental, he tried to explain it on the external ground, that Moses had compiled Genesis from different *documents*—two principal documents distinguished by the exclusive use of the two divine names, and ten distinct memoirs which are proved to be foreign to the first two documents by the interruptions to the history and the contradictions which they present[1]. This now notorious *Document-Hypothesis* excited little attention for some years after its publication. At length Eichhorn[2], by adopting it with certain modifications, brought it into general notice. The idea was before long extended to the whole Pentateuch, and the *Fragment-Hypothesis* was introduced by Vater and Hartman, according to which this work was made up of a number of separate fragments possessed of no internal connexion, but composed by different authors, and which were strung together after the Captivity[3]. This view was, however, shown to be so inconsistent with the plan which evidently pervades the Pentateuch, that

Brought into notice by Eichhorn.

Extended to entire Pentateuch. Fragment-Hypothesis.

---

[1] Hengstenberg, *Pent.* I. 220; Hævernick, p. 46.

[2] *Einleitung in d. A. Test.* 1780—1783.

[3] Hævernick, pp. 47, 443; Keil, p. 60; Delitzsch, p. 41.

it was laid aside, and in its place a modification of the old document-hypothesis adopted, which, under the name of the *Supplement-Hypothesis*, is in one form or other maintained by many German critics of the present time. According to this, an ancient document, distinguished by the use of the name Elohim, forms the essential basis (*grundschrift*) of the work, out of which the Pentateuch arose by means of a *supplementary* document, distinguished by the use of the name Jehovah. These two are traced as far as Ex. vi. by this characteristic use of the two names, but there this use ceases, and for the remainder of the work they are traced by internal characteristics of style and phraseology. The two documents were combined by the hands of an editor so skilfully as to render their separation very difficult, in some instances almost impossible[1]. This is but a general, and necessarily therefore an imperfect outline, of a hypothesis which assumes a different form as it passes through the hands of its different advocates. No two of these are agreed as to the portions, even of the one book of Genesis, which are to be assigned to their respective

[1] Davidson, p. 593.

authors; or as to the periods of the composition of the different documents; or as to the time in which the Pentateuch assumed its present shape.

The view brought forward by Delitzsch is here adduced as a sample of the *Supplement-Hypothesis*, not merely because it is the latest revision of it, but on account of its presenting it in its most specious and least offensive form. Ex. xix.—xxiv., the legal section in Ex. xxxiv., and the whole of Deuteronomy to ch. xxxi. 24, were written by Moses. The other laws were communicated only orally by Moses, and were committed to writing after his death by the priests, to whose office it pertained to do so. The composition of the sacred Chronicle was commenced on the soil of the Holy Land after the conquest. Some one, such as Eleazar the son of Aaron, of priestly rank, wrote the great work commencing, *In the beginning God created*. Into this he inserted the roll of the covenant, Ex. xix—xxiv., dwelling very lightly on the last words of Moses, because they had been recorded by the Lawgiver himself. A second historian, such as Joshua, or one of the elders on whom Moses' spirit rested, and

Delitzsch's view.

many of whom outlived Joshua, supplemented this work, and with it incorporated Deuteronomy, on which he had formed his style. Each of them, the priestly Elohist, and the prophetical Jehovist, is the echo and copy of the great lawgiver, their teacher and prototype. The consciousness that the Law was thus composed seems to have occasioned the remarkable passage, Ezra ix. 10—12, where a commandment given in the wilderness is said to have been commanded by the prophets, the servants of Jehovah[1]. Such is the plan devised by Delitzsch. Even Kurtz, once the advocate of the essential unity of the Pentateuch, announces himself a convert to Delitzsch's view, though in doing so he expresses his disapprobation of some important positions in it[2].

<small>Fundamental error of these hypotheses.</small> It is evident that all these plans for portioning out the Pentateuch into different documents rest on the foundation that the divine names are used arbitrarily throughout the book of Genesis. This is certainly a misconception. There is an internal difference in the meaning of the two names which regulates their

---

[1] Delitzsch, *Genesis, Einl.* pp. 37—41.
[2] *Hist of the Old Cov.* III. 516.

use throughout, as will appear from the following considerations.

In Scripture names are evidently formed in the closest relation to things, so that the name is the thing itself so far as it can be made apparent[1]. This is especially the case in regard to God. His name is Himself so far as He is known by, or manifested to His people; comp. Ex. xxiii. 21; Deut. xii. 5; Matt. xxviii. 19; Joh. xvii. 6, 11, 26. The names of God are therefore to be regarded as expressions of His nature and character, so far as men have been enabled to arrive at the knowledge of them. That this is the case with the names of God which are used in Genesis, is proved by the much perverted passage, Ex. vi. 3. This cannot mean that the Patriarchs were not acquainted with that particular name of God. The antiquity of this name is proved from its being formed from a root already antiquated when the Pentateuch was written; and also from its entering into the composition of several names older than the time of Moses[2]. The

Divine names have meaning, and are used according to their meaning.

---

[1] Hengstenberg, *Pent.* I. 279—292.

[2] *Jochebed*, Ex. vi. 20; *Ahijah*, 1 Chron. ii. 25; *Abiah*, 1 Chron. vii. 8; *Bithiah*, 1 Chron. iv. 18; *Moriah*, Gen. xxii. 2.

knowledge referred to is rather that of actual proof and present experience, as in Ezek. xx. 9; xxviii. 23. The Patriarchs had indeed, as the Lord here says, known and experienced Him as the Mighty God, who raised up offspring to the aged Abraham and Sarah; who provided abundance for Isaac in the time of famine; who brought Jacob safely through his difficulties: but under that character in which God was actually known to man when first created, and under which He was to be known to His covenant people, these Patriarchs had not yet by the like actual proof and present experience known Him. This passage alone might show us that by the *import* of the divine names their use in Genesis was regulated.

Derivation and import of Elohim. The name *Elohim*, the plural form of *Eloah*, which is seldom used except in the poetical parts of Scripture, is derived either from a root signifying *strength* (Gesenius, Fürst, Tuch, Kurtz), or from a root expressive of *fear, terror* (Hengstb., Hæv., Keil., Del., ed. III.). By a peculiar use of the plural[1] in Hebrew, to

---

[1] The error that the idea of a plurality of persons was conveyed in the name was first maintained by Peter Lombard (†A.D. 1164). It was opposed by Calvin, Mercer, Cajetan, Bellarmin, Drusius, Buxtorf, and G. Calixtus (*Hengstenberg*).

denote the individual as if comprehending the fulness of all that belongs to each and all of the same class, the plural form Elohim expresses, according to these derivations, either the Supreme Power, or the Highest Object of Awe, in whom the infinite fulness of the divine perfections is centred. But this plural form, as it thus raises and intensifies the conception, certainly in another sense weakens it, by presenting a vague, indefinite, abstract conception of the Deity. It represents GOD more as the Great First Cause, the Source of Creative Power, and Object of Awe, than as the Personal Ruler of the Universe, clothed with His Personal Attributes of Holiness, Justice, and Goodness[1].

It is now agreed that the vowel-points attached to the consonants of the name Jehovah properly belong to the word *Adonai*, which the Jews, through a mistaken reverence, substituted for the former name whenever it occurred in their reading of the Scriptures. There is still some question as to the exact vocalization of the word. Hengstenberg and Keil decide for *Jaháveh* or *Jahveh*. It is properly the

Derivation and import of Jehovah.

---

[1] Hengstenberg, *Pent.* I. 273.

third person singular of the future of the verb *havah*, an antiquated form of *hayah*, to be, to exist. The derivation and import of the name are intimated in Ex. iii. 13—15: 'And Moses said unto God, Behold, when I come unto the children of Israel...they shall say unto me, What is His Name? what shall I say unto them? And God said unto Moses, I AM THAT I AM (*ehyeh asher ehyeh*): and he said, Thus shalt thou say unto the children of Israel, I AM (*ehyeh*) hath sent me unto you. And God said moreover unto Moses, Thus shalt thou say unto the children of Israel, The LORD (*Jahveh* or *Jehovah*) God of your fathers, the God of Abraham,...hath sent me unto you: this is my name for ever, and this is my memorial unto all generations.' From this we may infer: (1) that pure absolute existence is certainly an essential part of the idea conveyed in the name, and, as an immediate consequence from it, perfect immutability. The revelation of this character of the Almighty at this time must have been most important for Israel, longing for a release from bondage; comp. Mal. iii. 6; Rom. xi. 29. But (2) the passage before us forbids us taking the name as meaning merely

The existing One, The Being[1]. The expression, *I am that I am*, is one which, at the same time that it draws attention to the necessary existence and immutability of the speaker, also points to him as a Personal God. There is even more than this contained in the name; for (3) it intimates even more than personal existence; it declares by its very form the personal close relationship which God was about to stand in towards Israel[2]. Neither the personal form of the word Jehovah (*He is*), nor the change of person in the name of God when used by Himself (*I am*), and when used by man (*He is*), should be passed over as meaningless; they point to the close communion,—if the expression may be used—the personal intercourse, which was to exist between God and man. The name Jehovah, therefore, reveals God as the living personal God, who vouchsafes to draw nigh to man, who on his part had been rendered capable of holding intercourse and conscious communion with his Maker by having been created in His likeness and image. As

---

[1] Hengstenberg, *Pent.* I. 262; Keil, *Einl.* p. 69; Fairbairn, *Typol.* II. 29.

[2] Hævernick, p. 61.

the moral attributes of Mercy, Goodness, Truth, and Justice, properly adhere to God considered as the Personal existence dealing with His intelligent creatures, so when God passed before Moses, He declared his character as Jehovah to be 'merciful and gracious, long-suffering, and abundant in goodness and truth, &c.,' Ex. xxxiv. 6, 7. The Creator, who in relation to all other creatures was Elohim, the First Cause, was to man in Paradise, Jehovah, the living Holy Personal God, holding intercourse with man. Man having by sin withdrawn himself from this state of conscious personal intercourse with God, was in a certain degree brought into union with His Maker by the Sinaitic covenant (Lev. xxvi. 12; Deut. iv. 7, 24), by which God once more became Jehovah to him; and this again was the preparatory stage to the perfect restoration in Christ, to whom properly therefore belongs the name Jehovah (Joh. i. 10—14; Eph. i. 10, 11; ii. 18).

Natural distribution of the names in Gen. according to these meanings.

If these explanations of the two names of God be correct, it can be easily seen that different portions of the book of Genesis might be marked by the distinctive use of one or other of them, according to the nature of the subject-matter. To see this clearly we must distinguish between the use of these names by the different characters of the sacred narrative and by the historian himself. A knowledge of God under His character of Jehovah must have been brought by man from Eden, and both recollections of the past and hopes for the future would naturally lead religious-minded men to speak of God by that name, and especially under that name to invoke Him when they worshipped by the divinely instituted rite of sacrifice, which was the pledge of restoration to the state they had forfeited. As religious feeling waxed cool, and faith weak, since "the natural tendency of man's mind is partly to lose itself in a plurality of gods, partly to unite this plurality again, i. e. to form an abstraction out of it[1]," the use of Elohim gradually became universal, and God was thus spoken of by those who had not lapsed into polytheism, as by Abimelech; or He was spoken of under some other name which did not so strongly express His Personal character towards man, as in the case of Melchizedek. Even by the Patriarchs this name would be

[1] Hævernick, p. 59.

used if circumstances occurred which tended to obscure the personal conception of God, as in the case of the required sacrifice of Isaac; or if their conduct gave reason to suspect that their faith in a living, holy, judging, personal God was too weak to raise them above the promptings of the senses, as we see was the case with Jacob, and more especially with his sons. And as advancing years made the revelations granted to Abraham, of God as about to become Jehovah, to retire into the distant past without continual fresh manifestations to revive the name, we might have further reason to expect the more general name to supplant at last the more particular. As to the use of the name Jehovah by the Patriarchs, we might expect it to be used by them after God revealed to Abraham His intention of becoming Jehovah again to his family, especially in cases when allusions would be made to God's leadings in carrying out His intention, as in the conversation with Eliezer about Isaac's marriage, and in the prophecy concerning Jacob's twelve sons. But, on the other hand, references only to the general superintending providence of God would be made under the designation Elohim; or, if distinct allusion were made to the particular earthly blessings and protection which God exhibited to His chosen servants in this life, designations of a more personal character would be used, such as El-Shaddai.

With regard to the use of the sacred names by the historian, it is hardly conceivable that Moses, writing with the manifestation of Jehovah on Sinai and the fulfilment of the promise to Abraham fresh in his mind, should not have framed his application of them in reference to this event. One like him, trained and prepared for his office as Lawgiver, who had been living in a close, conscious proximity to the Almighty not again vouchsafed to men, must have been so thoroughly embued with a sense of the Divine names as to apply them generally, if not always, with a meaning. Yet as, on the one side, we see that the minute adaptation of the name to the subject must have been in proportion to the religious feeling of the author, so, on the other hand, must the ability of the critic to mark the adaptation be in proportion to the religious feeling which enables him to grasp the Divine nature and character so far as they are revealed. We ought not therefore to be surprised if in attempting to trace the reason of the application of the names of God throughout Genesis, we oftentimes fail in discerning the minute shades of difference which may demand the one name in preference to the other, or even at times wander widely from the mark. Nor in this is there any valid objection to the principle; and certainly no such serious objection as to lead us, in despair of a satisfactory solution, to adopt the document-hypothesis, which tacitly acknowledges its inability to account for the use of the divine names in very many places, by suggesting interpolations and corruptions of the sacred text. But a parallel case will show that we cannot expect to account in every passage for the peculiar language of the sacred writer, and that it is sufficient if the principle in general shows its truth. In the New Testament, the names Jesus, Christ, Lord, are not identical, and we see in general that the distinctive use of them is designed and appropriate; and yet even in one single epistle of St Paul it would be impossible to assign in each particular in-

Parallel from the N.T.

stance a satisfactory reason for the preference of one name to the other. It is thus that in the book of Genesis we may discern in general a principle regulating the author's introduction of the names of God. He surveys the history of the past from the point of view he has attained to at Sinai. In detailing the sacred history he appears to have used the expressive name Jehovah, first, wherever it was necessary to represent God dealing with mankind as the righteous Ruler; and secondly, to mark out the line of acts by which God was leading Abraham and his seed to the intended revelation at Sinai. In certain places, e.g. ch. xvii., he appears to have used the more general name for the purpose of preventing any misconception, as if the Revelation on Sinai had been already anticipated; and in others, as in ch. xxxii. 24—32, either for the purpose of expressing the subjective state of the individual mentioned, or because the transaction was not one of those by which the Almighty pointed to the coming Revelation. Where the historian speaks of the ordinary arrangements of God's general providence, or of God's acts in relation to those for whom

He was no more than Elohim, either the material and animated world, or man who had reduced himself to the level of the animal, as in ch. vi. 9—viii. 20, ix. 1—17, he speaks of God as Elohim. Yet even in these sections he is careful to notice where God acts as Jehovah. But to the notes on the different passages the reader is referred for an illustration in detail of the truth of the principle here contended for. Enough has been stated to show that it has some foundation to support it.

No internal evidence militating against the external. It would not be in accordance with the design of this work to enter into an examination of the different allegations by which it has been attempted to establish a diversity of style in the different portions of the Pentateuch. The few cases which can be treated in a manner intelligible to the reader unacquainted with Hebrew, will be found noticed in the Commentary; e. g. Padan-aram and Aram-naharaim. But in fact it is not necessary. The argument for the diversity depends entirely on the truth of the distinction between the Jehovah and Elohim documents in Genesis; it stands or falls with it. Sufficient has now been adduced to show that while the distinction is opposed to *all* external testimony, as well as to the internal testimony, direct and indirect, of the Pentateuch itself, there is good reason for explaining the phenomenon of the use of the Divine names in such a way as to render unnecessary recourse to so empirical and superficial an explanation of it.

COMMENTARY ON GENESIS.

PREFATORY.

The account of the creation with which the book of Genesis opens has been made the subject of much discussion. Whether it is to be taken as literal matter-of-fact history, or as legend, or as myth; whether it was made known to the writer by tradition, by prophetic vision, or by direct inspiration; whether it embraces those successions of life in the world, which, concealed for thousands of years, have been but lately brought to light by Geological research, or merely narrates the sequence and order in which the present system, wherewith man is concerned, was brought into existence:—all these points have yielded matter for earnest investigation and discussion within the last few years.

An examination of the different cosmogonies which are found in the early legends of most nations removes some of the uncertainties which embarrass the subject. The Chaldæans, the Egyptians, and Phœnicians, the Hindoos, Greeks, Etrurians, and Goths, the Chinese, and the tribes of America[1], nations of different races, all have their cosmogonies, which, by various degrees of resemblance, claim affinity with that of Genesis. As, however, there is no reason for considering that these cosmogonies were derived from it, the natural conclusion is that they may be traced up to one common source, namely, a communication received from the first parents of the human race. That Adam received it by divine revelation is rendered probable by the account in Genesis. For since it is there intimated that man's welfare depended upon maintaining his appointed place in the constituted order of creation, it is but a reasonable inference that the Creator communicated to him the necessary knowledge of the relation in which he was designed to stand to God, and to the rest of God's creation[2], especially as it was conveyed in facts the knowledge of which he could not have at-

---

[1] Faber, *Hor. Mosaic.* I. 17—40; Delitzsch, pp. 80—82 Kurtz, *Bible and Astronomy*, p. vii.

[2] Delitzsch, p. 86.

tained to by any exercise of his own reflective powers[1].

Are we therefore to conclude that the author of the Pentateuch prefaced his history with this account of the creation which he had received by tradition from the first man[2]? Such a supposition is incredible. The comparison of the other national legendary cosmogonies with the biblical narrative at once demonstrates it to be so. All of them, without exception, by the dualistic or else pantheistic principle, by the national element, by the degraded and often revolting conceptions, which are found interwoven into their texture, show how grievously the primitive revelation of this important religious truth was distorted as it passed through the hands of man. There is nothing in what is narrated of either the fathers or descendants of Abraham to lead us to think that a tradition would fare better with them than with the other nations. And yet the Biblical cosmogony alone, by its perfect purity from all admixture of what is national, by the simple pure conceptions it presents, by its direct ethical tendency[3], by the contradiction

[1] Kurtz, *Bib. and Astron.* p. xi.   [2] Ibid. p. vii.
[3] Trench, *Huls. Lect.* pp. 24—26.

it gives to the two principles, hylozoism or dualism, and pantheism, one or other of which principles is at the bottom of every heathen cosmogony, proves its freedom from all human modifying influences[1]. No other rational account of this phenomenon can be given than that the author of the book of Genesis received the history of creation therein contained absolutely by divine communication.

How then was it communicated? by prophetic vision[2]? or by direct inspiration of the Holy Spirit? There is nothing in the Bible to support, and there is much in it to oppose, the view, that the author describes what he saw represented to him in a series of prophetic visions, each of which seemed to him to occupy a day's duration. In the sacred narrative itself there is nothing to indicate the visionary nature of the communication, nothing to suggest any difference as to the manner in which this and other facts were revealed. In the remainder of the Bible no instance is found of the past being presented to the prophet's eye in the shape of

---

[1] Delitzsch, pp. 82—84.
[2] H. Miller, *Test. of the Rocks*, pp. 157—191. Kurtz, *Bib. and Astron.* pp. xvii—xx.

vision. In the Pentateuch itself (Ex. xx. 9—11, xxxi. 12—17) the reason assigned for the hallowing of the sabbath is the fact of the creation in six days. But if these six days are only visionary conceptions there is no reality on which to build the hallowing of the sabbath; and indeed the institution, so far from being derived from the fact of the creation, would rather seem to have originated the representation of it in six visions. And, lastly, in the later books of the Bible we find the psalmist (Ps. viii. civ.), our Lord Himself (Matt. xix. 4—6), and the apostles (Heb. ii.; 2 Pet. iii. 5), all alluding to, and arguing from, the narrative as a real historical account.

The passages just referred to from the Old and New Testaments help to a conclusion on another point debated in connection with this subject. By treating the narrative as matter-of-fact history they negative that view which represents Gen. i—ii. 3 to be merely an ideal account of creation, as it unfolded itself in the mind of the Divine Artist, and which was laid before man in this shape, in order to teach him his place in reference to the rest of the Universe, and in reference to God the Creator[1]. This representation has this certainly to recommend it, that it brings into full light the important ethical teaching of the narrative; and also that it relieves us from all the difficulties which embarrass it, when taken as an account of the successive acts whereby the visible external order of things in the material universe was produced. But the very process by which the ethical teaching is made prominent, removes from it the firm historical basis on which it is built:—by it the history of creation becomes no more than an idea embodied in a historical shape. The difficulties moreover, which are only such as, from the nature of creation and the nature of language, must embarrass every account of creation[2], are displaced only to make way for the greater difficulties of accounting for the language of our Lord, and of inspired historians, psalmists, and apostles. As an accessory argument it may be observed, that the computation of time by weeks, common to nations scattered over Europe, Asia, Africa and America[3], seems to point to a

---

[1] Maurice, *Patriarchs and Lawgivers*, Lect. I.
[2] Whewell, *Indications of the Creator*, pp. 111, 162, 172.
[3] Delitzsch, p. 82. Rawlinson, *Herod.* Vol. II. p. 335.

fact and not to an ideal representation as its origin.

If then Gen. i.—ii. 3 is an account of the successive acts of creation communicated by God to Moses, how much of the earth's history does it embrace?

When geological science had advanced so far as to show that this globe had been occupied before man's creation by different successions of organic life, it was not unnatural that inquiry should arise as to the relation in which these conclusions stood to the declarations of Scripture. The view was put forward by Cuvier and Professor Jamieson[1], that the scriptural days of creation represent indefinitely great periods of duration corresponding to the creative periods developed by Geology. To avoid the obvious impropriety of taking days to denote indefinitely long periods, and to smooth away some important discrepancies between the geological and scriptural sequences of creation which the advance of the science had brought to light, the late Mr Hugh Miller modified this view, and represented the narrative to be a description of creation as it was set before the historian in a series of consecutive visionary

[1] Hitchcock, *Religion of Geol.* p. 65.

scenes. On the first day was represented the Azoic period; on the second, the Silurian and Old Red Sandstone period; on the third, the Carboniferous period with its gigantic and abundant vegetation; on the fourth, the Permian and Triassic periods, in which he supposes the heavenly bodies to be no longer hid from the earth by the steaming mist which hitherto rose from its heated surface; on the fifth, the Oolitic and Cretaceous ages of the Secondary period, marked by the enormous monsters of the deep and gigantic birds; and on the sixth, the Tertiary ages, during which the gigantic mammals possessed the earth, and at the close of which man appeared[1].

But the objections to this scheme are neither few nor insignificant. (1) The harmony between the Geological and Scriptural successions of creation can only be maintained by the introduction of the visionary hypothesis, which has been proved untenable. (2) It is inadequate; for it speaks of only three successions of organized existence, while Geology discloses as many as there are strata. (3) It is incorrect. We find the seas throughout the entire Palæozoic period abounding with life, including animals of all the principal

[1] H. Miller, *Test. of the Rocks*, pp. 174—191.

divisions, and even some of the reptile order; and yet, according to this scheme, this period should exhibit only the specimens of the vegetable kingdom. And, on the other hand, it is only late in the period, and after the appearance of animal life, that we trace the fossil remains of vegetable life. (4) According to it the scriptural account would pass over unnoticed the creation of most, if not all, of the animals and plants of the present world, in order to mention the creation of the different species which perished before man's creation. For as very few, if any, of those now existing were contemporaneous with those buried in the strata, they must have been created subsequently and on the sixth day. (5) Scripture evidently speaks of all the animals and plants of the Mosaic cosmogony as having been created for man, "partly for his nourishment, and partly as means of, or aids to, his own peculiar activity[1]." Geology displays to us the various organisms of the primeval world, only to tell us that most if not all of them passed from existence before man appeared. (6) It seems inconsistent with the character of the Sacred Record that it should put prominently forward a statement which, it was not merely possible or

---

[1] Kurtz, *Bib. and Astron.* p. cxxiii.

probable, but actually necessary for man to place a false interpretation on, until the advance of science in the nineteenth century should disclose the true meaning of it.

These objections are so very serious as to cause us to fall back on the long-maintained opinion, that the narrative refers simply to that stage of the history of the earth to which man belongs. This view has been adopted by Dr Chalmers, Dean Buckland, and Professor Sedgwick; and in Germany by Dr A. Wagner, and by Professor Kurtz, who has given an elaborate exposition and defence of it. According to it, in the first verse of Genesis the creation of the Universe is ascribed to God. The Biblical narrative then, passing over absolutely unnoticed all those great pre-Adamite periods of which Geology speaks, proceeds to narrate the succession of creative acts by which the earth was made the fitting abode for man, who, after all things were created for his use, <u>was himself last of all created</u>.

Against this view one great objection has been urged by the late Hugh Miller. It supposes a chaotic gulf of death and darkness between the existing and the pre-Adamite worlds. He asserts that Geology negatives this supposition; that it is an established fact in Geology that many of the existing organisms were contemporary during the morning of their being with many of the extinct ones during the evening of theirs[1]. However, this assertion is contradicted by the eminent Palæontologist, Agassiz. So far from allowing the genetic descent of the living species from the different Tertiary divisions, which have been regarded as identical, he declares them to be specifically different[2]. No other objections have been brought against this interpretation, save such as have been urged against the scientific language of the whole of scripture. No attempt is therefore made to enter on that subject, which belongs more to the general evidences of religion than to a commentary. An exact though brief discussion of it may be found in Dr Whewell's *Indications of the Creator*.

[1] *Test. of the Rocks*, p. 121.
[2] Kurtz, *Bib. and Astron.* p. cxxiv. Comp. Whewell, *Indic. of the Creator*, p. 162.

Chapter I.

ver. 1. IN THE BEGINNING] Lit. *first of all, firstly*. The writer does not mean to define the time when God created heaven and earth; he only declares how God commenced the creation. (*Knobel, Wright.*)—GOD] Heb. *Elohim*. This name, which represents God merely as the Almighty First Cause, is aptly used throughout this portion of Genesis as far as ch. ii. 3, in which the sacred writer treats of the creation of the Universe, and introduces man merely as the highest portion of creation. Even in vv. 26—28 the Creator is spoken of as Elohim, for man is there noticed only as a link in the great chain of created being.—CREATED] Heb. *bara*, a word used exclusively of divine productions (*Kalisch, Delitzsch*). There has been much discussion as to whether the idea of creation out of nothing belongs strictly to the Hebrew word. We cannot, however, expect to find in Hebrew or in any other language a term adequate to express perfectly an act of God's power such as Creation, which transcends all human thought and experience; comp. Phillips, *Life on the Earth*, p. 45; Whewell, *Indic.* pp. 107, 177. The Revelation of this great fact is placed in the front of the inspired record, because the knowledge of it, though essential to true views of religion, could not be arrived at by man independently of Revelation. It was unknown to the heathen. Without exception all the religious and philosophical systems of the heathen were based on the supposition of the eternity of matter; comp. Hævernick, *Introd. to Pent.* p. 94; Burton, *Bampton Lect.* p. 60, and note 21. For this reason the Christian Church has ever made the creation by God *of all things visible and invisible* a prominent article of her creeds; comp. Pearson, *On the Creed*, Art. *Maker of Heaven and Earth;* King, *Crit. Hist. of Apost. Creed*, c. ii. The sacred narrative by declaring the temporal existence of the world in relation to the Eternal God, and the specific distinction between the Creator and the Creature, at once announces the falseness of all the heathen cosmogonies, which invariably were based on either the dualistic and hylozoic principle of the eternity and essential evilness of matter, or the pantheistic principle by which matter is confounded with God. —It is well remarked by Mr Barry, that "the Creation is described with a constant reference to <u>man as its centre</u>. Its various objects are described as seen by him, and as they bear upon his welfare, temporal and eternal. It may be that they have other and even more transcendant purposes; but these, while they are not excluded, are left veiled in darkness, because the knowledge of them is not necessary to him for the fulfilment of his duties upon earth." (*Introd. to the O. T.* p. 50.) —HEAVEN AND EARTH] The Biblical term for the Universe; comp. Deut. xxxii. 1; Isa. i. 2; Ps. cxlviii. 13 (*Kalisch*). The heaven of this verse is evidently not the *heaven* or terrestrial firmament of ver. 8; it denotes the entire expanse of the stellar universe.

ver. 2. Many of the early Christian writers (see Wiseman, *Science and Revealed Religion*, i. p. 283), and many scientific writers and critics within the last few years (*Horsley, Chalmers, Buckland, Sedgwick*), are of opinion that the second verse does not represent the earth as existing then, in the state in which it was first

created in the time referred to in the first verse. They think that an interval of undefined duration elapsed between the epochs marked by the two verses, during which the earth passed through those geological transitions, which the stratified formations reveal. The creation of the heaven and earth is then removed out of the work of the first day. The reference in Ex. xx. 11, does not contradict this view. The comparison of the two passages in the Hebrew will show that in the latter passage when it is said that in 'six days God made the heaven and the earth, &c.,' allusion is made merely to the six days' work of constituting the earth in its present state, not to the *creation* of the earth. Several theological expositors (*Baumgarten, Kurtz, Delitzsch*) adopt this view, and account for the many marks of death and ruin, which Palæontology traces as having taken place before the history of man, by the fall of Satan and his angels, to whom the world had been allotted as their sphere. See Kurtz, *Hist. of the Old Cov.* Vol. I. p. lv. ed. Clark.
—WAS WITHOUT FORM, &c.] The *earth* only is now spoken of, not *the heaven and the earth*, mentioned in the last verse.—WITHOUT FORM, AND VOID] Heb. *thohu va-bhohu*. What is meant to be

expressed by these words becomes apparent on comparing the two other passages where they occur in Scripture. Isa. xxxiv. 11, 'He shall stretch out upon it the line of confusion [thohu], and the stones of emptiness [bhohu];' Jer. iv. 23, 'I beheld the earth, and lo it was *without form, and void* [thohu va-bhobu]; and the heavens, and they had no light.' In the latter passage the prophet evidently takes the state of the world as described in the present verse, as an expressive image of the state of desolation, ruin, and estrangement from God, to which sin was about to reduce Judah.—DARKNESS] We cannot read scripture with any attention, without observing the marked symbolical use made in it of darkness, as if of its own nature it was something hateful to God. Thus it is used to express *sin*, Eph. v. 11, 'Have no fellowship with the works of darkness;' *evil spirits*, Eph. vi. 12, 'The rulers of the darkness of this world;' Col. i. 13, 'who hath delivered us from the power of darkness;' *death*, Job x. 21, 'Before I go whence I shall not return, even to the land of darkness and the shadow of death;' *the abode of evil spirits and the damned*, Matt. viii. 12, 'The children of the kingdom shall be cast out into outer darkness;' Jude 6, 'And the angels who kept not their first estate, but left their own habitation, he hath reserved in everlasting chains under darkness.' On the other side, consider the use made of *light;* 1 John i. 5, 'God is light, and in him is no darkness at all;' 1 Tim. vi. 16, 'Dwelling in the light which no man can approach unto;' and as to the new heaven and the new earth, Rev. xxii. 5, 'There shall be no night there.'—THE DEEP] Heb. *Th'hom, the heaving deep.* From ver. 9 it appears that the earth was covered by the waters of the deep. In the prophetic Scriptures the restless sea is used as a symbol of the heathen as opposed to God and under the direction of Satan: Dan. vii. 3; Rev. xiii. 1. In Rev. xxi. 1, when the new heaven and earth were manifested, it is declared, 'and there was no more sea.' If it were legitimate for us to infer that the Scripture symbolism referred to in these notes was founded on something real in the symbols used, and that they were derived from this passage, we might conclude, with Baumgarten, Kurtz, Delitzsch, that the earth had been reduced to a state of darkness and death, and to be the abode of sin, by some outbreak of Satan or his instruments against God.—THE SPIRIT OF GOD] The third person in the Holy Trinity, 'the Lord and the Giver of Life,' brooded over the waters of the deep which covered the world, to restrain them to their bounds, and to impart life and perfection to God's Creation.—MOVED] This translation is incorrect. The idea of progression is never found in this verb (*Wright*). It expresses the brooding of a bird over her young (*Gesenius*). Milton: 'Thou, dove-like, sat'st brooding on the vast abyss, and mad'st it pregnant.'

ver. 3. AND GOD SAID] There are three persons here visibly spoken of: first, He that spoke, 'Let there be light, and let there be a firmament, &c.;' second, the Word spoken by Him; thirdly, the Spirit of God who is said to have 'moved upon the face of the water.' (Charles Leslie, *Works*, I. 264. Ed. 1721.) From the comparison of such passages as Ps. xxxiii. 6, 'By the word of the Lord were the heavens made, and all the host of them by the breath of His mouth,' and Ps. cxlviii. 5, the ancient Christian writers argued that there is here presented an intimation of the agency of the 'Word of God' in the Creation, 'By whom He made the worlds,' Heb. i. 2, and 'by whom all things were made,' and 'without whom nothing was made,' John i. 3. Comp. Pearson, *On the Creed*, Vol. I. p. 152. ed. Oxf. For the proof of the Church having always held, that The Father, The Son, and The Holy Ghost created the Universe in concert, and that each Person is properly Creator, comp. Pearson, *On the Creed*, I. p. 80; Bull, *Defence of the Nicene Faith*, II. xiii. 10; Waterland, *Moyer Lect. Serm.* II; Wheatley, *Moyer Lect.* p. 129.—LET THERE BE LIGHT] There is doubtless a *difficulty*, but there is no *impossibility*, in the representation of the existence of light independent of the *sun*, which though apparently created when 'the heaven and earth' were created, was not ordained as a source of light until the fourth day. Most astronomers consider the sun to be an opaque solid sphere surrounded by two atmospheres, that nearest the sun non-luminous like our own, and an outer one from which light and heat are radiated. Hence, although created before, the sun may not have been constituted to be the source of the earth's illumination before the fourth day. Kurtz refers to Humboldt's description of the polar light, *Cosmos*, I. p. 188, *Sabine's trans.* as an illustration of the *possibility* of the earth's having other sources of light than that of the sun.—AND

THERE WAS LIGHT] The language in which S. Paul describes the calling forth of light by God should not be passed over when we are attempting to discover the meaning of this revelation of the creation: 2 Cor. iv. 6, 'God, who commanded the light to shine *out of* darkness, hath shined in our hearts.'

ver. 5. AND THE EVENING AND THE MORNING WERE THE FIRST DAY] Lit. *and it became evening, and it became morning, one day.* The common view is, that, as darkness preceded the light, the day is here reckoned from evening to evening, so that the evening is the commencement of the first half, and the morning that of the second half, of the day; a very awkward mode of computing the time, but not sanctioned by the text. For darkness is designated not as *evening* but as night; and evening always presupposes the previous existence of daylight, which retires at the approach of night. The expression, also, *it became*, implies that a period of light had preceded the evening. We are then led to conclude that the natural computation of reckoning from morning to morning is used here, and that the evening denotes the close of the first half, and the morning the close of the second half, of the day and night period. The Hebrew practice of counting the commencement of the day from the evening arose either from the distribution of time being regulated by the changes of the moon (*Delitzsch*); or, as Kurtz more probably suggests, from the social arrangements of the people being based on the institution of the Sabbath. For though the work-day naturally commences with the morning, the day of rest commences with the evening. And therefore since the Sabbath formed the standard for the division of time, and it naturally commenced with the termination of the previous work-day, the arrangement of all other days was made in accordance with it. Comp. Kurtz, Vol. I. p. xx, note; Delitzsch, p. 99.—FIRST DAY] The various attempts to harmonize Scripture with geology make us familiar with the interpretation that the six days of Creation were periods of immense duration figuratively called days. "But it cannot be doubted that the division of time which is here designated as *day* was caused and bounded by the presence of *natural light*. Hence the evening which followed such a day, and the morning which preceded a new day, must similarly be regarded as parts of a *natural* and *ordinary* day; and the latter can only be measured according to the natural and ordinary standard, viz. the occurrence of a natural change of light and darkness (day and night)" (*Kurtz*). How the alternation of darkness and light was effected, before the sun and moon were appointed to rule the day and night, we are not told, and it is useless to conjecture. Any conjectures on the subject, founded on observation of the phenomena of the present state of the universe, are serviceable only as proofs of the *possibility* of the occurrence.

ver. 6. FIRMAMENT] Heb. *rakiah = expanse* (*Gesenius*); the terrestrial atmosphere or sky which divides the waters beneath it from the waters above it, or the sea from the clouds which rise out of it. The language of the text is in such accordance with the language of modern scientific authorities that it is needless waste of ingenuity to have recourse to 'Hebrew conceptions of the universe' for its explanation; *e.g.* "We are thus led to regard the atmosphere of air, with the clouds it supports, as constituting a coating of equable or nearly equable thickness, enveloping our globe on all sides." (Herschel, *Outlines*, § 35.)

ver. 8. HEAVEN] *Sept.* adds, 'and God saw that it was good.' This seems conjectural and erroneous. The reason why this usual expression of complacency over the day's creation is omitted is simply because the second day's work was carried on to the third day and then completed, when the formula occurs. It is only proper with completion. It occurs twice in the third day. (*Blackadder.*)

ver. 9. This verse describes merely the gathering together of the lower waters, and not, as some have inferred, the production of the dry land. On the contrary the land, which is supposed to be already existing, is described as now *appearing* above the receding waters. Comp. Ps. civ. 6—9; 2 Pet. iii. 5.

ver. 11. The productions of the earth are in this verse divided into three classes: (1) *grass*, or the herbage which grows spontaneously without man's care: (2) *the herb yielding seed*, or all herbs which require to be sown or planted: (3) *the tree yielding fruit*, or the trees inclusive of shrubs (*Patrick, Cleric. Rosenmuller*). But Dr Kalisch considers that there are only two classes intimated: (1) herbs of all kinds, and (2) trees. He translates: 'Let the earth bring forth vegetation, the herb yielding seed, and the fruit tree, &c.'—AFTER HIS KIND] so that men do not *gather figs of thorns, nor grapes of the bramble*, S. Luk. vi. 44 (*Ainsworth*). On the subject of distinction and constancy of species, comp. Lyell, *Principles of Geol.* III. p. 82, ed. 1840; Sedgwick, *Discourse on Studies at Cambridge*, p. liv. *Pref.* ed. 1850; H. Miller, *Footprints of the Creator;* Prof. Phillips, *Life on the Earth*, p. 196.

ver. 14. LIGHTS] Heb. *m'oroth* = *light-bearers, luminaries;* not the *light*, Heb. *or*, produced on the first day.—FOR SIGNS, &c.] Different explanations have been given of these words. For *signs* as prognosticating the weather; for *seasons* as appointing certain feasts; and for *days* and *years* as defining the length of the longer and shorter periods of time (*Delitzsch, Knobel*). The sun and moon are destined to be 'the signs of the seasons, days, and years' (*Kalisch*). The simplest and most obvious interpretation is: the *stars* were for *signs* as guiding the mariner or traveller; the *moon* for *seasons*, Ps. civ. 19, 'He appointed the *moon* for seasons;' and the *sun* to regulate the periods of *days* and *years.*

ver. 16. AND GOD MADE TWO GREAT LIGHTS] Lit. *the* two great lights. It is not necessarily implied that the *creation* of the sun, moon, and stars, was the work of the fourth day. The narrative bears on the face of it that it describes creation only in reference to the earth as the abode of men; and therefore when the luminaries are introduced in it, it is to relate that creative influence by which they became what they were destined to be in reference to the earth. When therefore it is said that on the fourth day 'God *made* sun, moon and stars,' the meaning is plain, that He then adapted them for the earth, and that as luminaries in relation to it they then commenced to exist. But this does not imply that they had not been created long before that to exist for themselves, and for the purposes they were to serve independently of the earth. This note is derived from Kurtz, who also infers from Job xxxviii. 4—7, that Scripture declares the existence of the stars before the fourth day of creation. Comp. H. Miller, *Test. of the Rocks*, p. 134; Buckland, *Bridgw. Treat.* I. p. 27.

ver. 17. SET THEM IN THE FIRMAMENT] In representing the stars as set in the firmament, the inspired narrative only uses language in accordance with the conceptions of any ordinary observer of the heavens. An eminent astronomer thus describes the appearance presented by the heavens to any one who views them on a clear evening. "He will perceive, above and around him, as it were a vast concave hemispherical vault, beset with stars of various magnitudes." (Herschel, *Outlines*, § 58.)

ver. 20. AND FOWL THAT MAY FLY] The marginal reading is to be preferred: *and let fowl fly above, &c.* "The original does not oblige us to understand with the Talmud and Rashi, that birds had their origin from the water" (*Blackadder*). The English version in this passage adopted Luther's translation.

ver. 21. WHALES] Lit. *huge fishes*, or *sea-monsters*.

ver. 24. The living creatures of the earth are now divided into three classes: (1) *cattle*, or beasts of burden and animals for domestic use; (2) *beasts of the earth*, or the wild animals; (3) *the creeping thing*, or all reptiles (*Mercer*).

ver. 26. AND GOD SAID, LET US MAKE] There are four explanations of the plural form used here. (a) The later Jewish: that God addresses the angels. But in ver. 27 it is said, 'So God created man in His own image, in the image of God created He him;' thus proving that it was not in the image of angels but of God that man was created. (b) The Socinian: that it is the plural of majesty. But however this mode of speaking may have existed in more modern times, it was unknown in the Bible times. None of the monarchs appearing in the Bible, neither the Pharaohs, nor the kings of Judah and Israel, nor the kings of Assyria, Babylon, and Persia, in the plenitude of their power, used this plural of majesty. It is then an idiom unknown to the Bible, and incapable of application as regards it. (c) 'That it is the plural, usually, though not necessarily, employed in deliberations and self-exhortations' (*Kalisch*). But the only passage alleged to prove this '*usual* employment of the plural' is Gen. xi. 7, which is exactly parallel to the present, and therefore equally requires explanation. (d) The Christian: that the plurality of Persons in the Unity of the Godhead explains naturally the use of the plural. Full and satisfactory proof that the passage was thus understood by the Christian Church from the Apostles' times to the year A.D. 325, will be found in Prof. Burton's two works, *Ante-Nicene Testimonies to the Divinity of Christ,* and *to the Doctrine of the Trinity.*—IN OUR OWN IMAGE AND AFTER OUR LIKENESS] This likeness is not to be sought in the members of the body; for although bodily members are sometimes ascribed to God, yet these expressions are metaphorical; *the right hand* of God being used to signify His *Power*, His *eyes* to signify His *Knowledge*, and His *wings* to signify His *Protection*. Nor was it with reason that some ancient writers taught [who have been lately imitated by Mr Maitland in his *Eruvim;* his view is mentioned with qualified approbation by Mr Barry, *Introd. to O. T.* p. 75] that the Son of God assumed flesh before man was made, and that it was in His likeness that Adam was created. For the words, 'Let us make man in our image,' were the words not of the Son alone, but of the whole Trinity; and moreover, the Son of God did not assume human flesh before man's fall, and hence it is not said that we are made like to Him, but that He was made like to us (Dean Fogg, *Syst. of Theol.* p. 167). The following statement regarding 'the image of God in man' is taken from one of the most accurate writers of our Church: "He [Thomas Aquinas] noteth first, that the image of God consisteth in the eminent perfection which is found in men, expressing the nature of God in an higher degree than any excellency of other creatures doth. Secondly, that this perfection is found principally in the soul. Thirdly, that it is threefold: first, natural; which is the largeness of the natural faculties of understanding and will, not limited to the apprehension or desire of some certain things only, but extending to all the conditions of being and goodness; whose principal object is God; so that they never rest satisfied with any other thing but the seeing and enjoying of Him. The second kind of this perfection is supernatural; when the soul actually, or, at least, habitually, knoweth and loveth God aright, though not so perfectly as he may, and shall be loved hereafter. The third is, when the soul knoweth and loveth God in fulness of happiness. The first is of nature, the second of grace, and the third of glory. The first of these is never lost; no, not by the damned in hell; the second Adam had but lost it, and it is renewed in us by grace; the third we expect in heaven. To think the image of God, considered in the first sort, to be lost is heresy; but Calvin is free from it. To think it lost in the second sort is the Catholic doctrine of the Church, for who knoweth not that man hath lost all right knowledge and love of God by Adam's fall?" (Field, *Of the Church*, Bk. III. ch. 24.)

ver. 28. AND HAVE DOMINION] "At the

creation God made all things for man's use, as He did man for His own service; and as He reserved for Himself His *absolute* sovereignty over man, so He gave unto man a kind of *limited* sovereignty over the creatures, Ps. viii. 6; which dominion over the creatures was one special branch of the glorious image of God in us, after which we were created, and therefore was not, nor could be, absolutely lost by sin, but only *decayed* and *defaced* and *impaired*, as other branches of that image were. So that albeit man by sin lost a great part of his sovereignty, especially so far as concerneth the execution of it; many of the creatures being now rebellious and noisome unto man, and unanswering his commands and expectations; yet the right still remaineth in corrupt nature, and there are still to be found some tracings and characters, as in man of superiority, so in them of subjection. But those dim and confused and scarce legible, as in old marbles and coins, and outworn inscriptions, we have much ado to find out what some of the letters were." (Bp. Sanderson, *Serm.* Vol. I. p. 240.)

Chapter II.

ver. 1. ALL THE HOST OF THEM] All that is contained in heaven and earth; thus called "on account of their vast variety and excellent order" (*Patrick*). The word 'host' is generally applied either to the heavenly bodies, Deut. iv. 19; xvii. 3; Isa. xxxiv. 4; or to the angels, 1 Kin. xxii. 19; Luke ii. 13. Here it is applied also to the creatures of earth, as appears from the parallel passage, Neh. ix. 6. Comp. Bp. Bull, *Engl. Theol. Works*, p. 201, ed. 1844.

ver. 2. HE RESTED] That is, he ceased from works of creation (*Kidder*). But the explanatory addition found in Ex. xxxi. 17, 'He rested and was *refreshed*,' proves that something beyond mere cessation from the work of creation is implied. A *rest* is spoken of in relation to God in other parts of Scripture. David represents the Lord saying of the place where the ark was to be removed, Ps. cxxxii. 14, 'This is my rest for ever: here will I dwell; for I have desired it.'

(*Rest* here is certainly expressed by a different Hebrew word from that which is used in the text, but it is not the *word* but the *idea* which is insisted on in this explanation.) God is therefore said to rest, or to *enjoy rest*, in that place where *He receives the adoration* of His people, comp. ch. viii. 21, *Heb.* Scripture represents God as creating all things that they should render to Him glory. Heaven and earth and all that they contained were intended to reflect their Creator's glory in their order, beauty, and magnificence; comp. Ps. xix, cxlviii.; and man was created to be the High Priest of the visible world, and to interpret the unconscious homage of nature. The song of praise with which the new creation glorifies God is, Rev. iv. 11, 'Thou art worthy to receive glory and honour and power; *for thou hast created* all things, and for thy pleasure they are and were created.' Accordingly, when God ended the six days' work *He rested, and was refreshed,* for His creation was prepared to yield to Him the glory which is His due. And for this reason He sanctified the seventh day to His service, that men should by it be reminded of the great end for which they were created, and on that day appropriately render to their Maker adoration. When the Word of God by His resurrection accomplished the work of the *new creation*, by which He overthrew Satan and restored the creature to its true position of ministering to the Creator's glory, He also is said to have *entered into His rest;* and having done so, it was but suitable that no longer the seventh day, which now had lost its meaning, but the first day, the Lord's Day, should be observed by the new creation to glorify its author. The explanation here given seems to be confirmed from its explaining the inter-connection between the Sabbath rest of creation, the rest of Israel in Canaan, the Redeemer's rest, and the Sabbatism of His people, which are mentioned together in Heb. iv.

ver. 3. BLESSED] Attached a special blessing to it; ordained that they who devoted it to His service should derive a blessing from doing so.—SANCTIFIED] Gave it a distinctive character as a day to be set apart to sacred purposes.

ver. 4. THESE ARE THE GENERATIONS] i. e. this is the account of the generation or origin of the heavens, &c. Throughout Genesis, this, or a similar formula, always refers to what follows it, and points to the introduction of a fresh subject. The sacred writer having given a general account of the six days' creation, proceeds to give a detailed account of the creation of man and the events connected with it, with special reference to the fall.—IN THE DAY] i.e. in the time. The word day is often thus used indefinitely; Numb. iii. 1; Ps. cxxxvii. 7: Isa. xi. 16; Ezek. xvi. 56. Thus Knobel, Davidson, *Introd. to O. T.*—THE LORD GOD] Heb. *Jehovah Elohim.* Hitherto God has been spoken of as acting in his relation towards the creature simply as the Almighty first cause, and therefore the name *Elohim*, which expresses Him in that light, naturally occurs throughout the foregoing narrative. But now when the sacred writer commences to narrate His dealings with man who, as being made in His image, can hold conscious intercourse with God who reveals Himself to him as the Living, Holy, Personal God, he as naturally speaks of Him under the name *Jehovah*, which expresses Him in this character. To it he annexes the name *Elohim*, either because the acts of Him which he is narrating affect not man alone, but also the rest of the creation, the union of the two names expressing the different relations in which the Divine Being stood to man and the remainder of the creation; or, as

Hengstenberg supposes, because he wishes to teach that the God who held converse so humanly with man was identical with the Creator of heaven and earth.

ver. 5. AND EVERY PLANT OF THE FIELD BEFORE, &c.] As God made the earth and the heavens, so He also made every plant of the field and every herb. And that He created the herbs, and that they were not at first the natural productions or growth of the earth, nor yet the effect of man's husbandry, appears from this, that they were made from God's command, on the third day, (1) before God had sent any rain upon the earth, and (2) before man was made to till the ground (*Kidder*).

ver. 6. BUT THERE WENT UP A MIST] That is, after this (1) the ground was watered, ver. 6, and (2) man was formed of the dust of the ground, ver. 7 (*Kidder*). It appears that at that time it had not rained, but that all moisture for the nourishment of plants was supplied by means of dew. The choice of a rainbow as a sign of a covenant with Noah, ch. ix. agrees with this (*v. Gerlach*). However we are relieved from the necessity of making any conjectures about the physical condition of the antediluvian world by adopting the translation of verses 4—6, recommended by Maurer, Tuch, Kalisch, Knobel and Wright: *'These are the generations of the heaven and of the earth when they were created. In the day when the Lord God made earth and heaven, no plant of the field was yet on the earth, and no herb of the field did yet sprout forth: for the Lord God had not caused it to rain upon the earth, nor was there a man to till the ground. And there rose a mist, &c.*

ver. 7. FORMED MAN, &c.] Lit. *formed man* [Heb. *Adam*], dust of the ground [Heb. *adamah= ground* or *earth*, so called from its reddish hue] (*Gesenius*).—MAN] The conclusions arrived at by the majority of the greatest scientific authorities strikingly coincide with this account of the original unity of the human race; comp. Wiseman, *Science and Revealed Religion*, Lect. I—IV; Hardwick, *Christ and other Masters*, Pt. I. ch. II; Somerville, *Physical Geography*, ch. XXXIII. For the proof, that Geology lends no support to any theory of the existence of a Pre-Adamite race of men, comp. Lyell, *Principles*, I. 280; III. 204, ed. 1840; H. Miller, *Test. of the Rocks*, p. 106; Richardson, *Introduct. to Geol.* p. 26; Mantell, *Wonders of Geol.* p. 183.—BREATHED INTO HIS NOS-

TRILS THE BREATH OF LIFE] The fathers laid great stress on God's *breathing* into man's nostrils the 'breath of life;' a privilege peculiar to man above the animal creation: something of God's own infusing and inspiring, something of a purer and diviner substance, spiritual and enduring; the breath of the Almighty, a resemblance, a shadow, an imperfect copy of the Divinity itself (*Waterland*). Comp. on this subject, Bp. Bull, *State of Man before the Fall*.

ver. 8. PLANTED A GARDEN EASTWARD IN EDEN] A tabular view of the many opinions and conjectures respecting the situation of Paradise will be found in Dr Kalisch's *Commentary on Genesis*. As the garden must be sought for in the vicinity of the two well-known rivers Euphrates and Hiddekel, we shall consider only the most plausible of the opinions which place it near them. (*a*) One, which has met with much favour, places Eden on the river Shat-ul-Arab, formed by the junction of the Euphrates and Tigris, and afterwards dividing to enter the Persian Gulf by two principal estuaries. But against this is, (1) that Major Rennell has shown that the two great rivers kept distinct courses to the sea until the time of Alexander (Kitto, *Script. Lands*, p. 3); and (2) that the Hebrew word translated *heads* in ver. 10 denotes only the *branching streams* by which a river flows down from its source, and cannot be taken to express feeding streams running into a common channel, such as the Euphrates and Tigris would be on this hypothesis. (*b*) It is supposed that, though the text speaks of the rivers, as still existing, in the present tense, the convulsion of nature which accompanied the Deluge, may have separated them into four distinct river systems, and that hence the situation of Eden is to be sought in the vicinity of the sources of the Euphrates and Tigris and of two other rivers which satisfy the geographical conditions of the text. The ancient Halys and Araxes seem to correspond to these conditions, and to answer respectively to the Pison and the Gihon. On this supposition Eden was in the neighbourhood of Lakes Urumiyeh and Van, a region which is described by Colonel Chesney as being now beautiful and fertile in the extreme. There is no impossibility in the supposition of the violent separation of the four rivers; see as to the effects of earthquakes in general on the course of rivers, Somerville, *Physical Geography*, p. 165, and with regard to their occurrence and influence in the particular district of Armenia, Kitto, *Scripture Lands*, p. 20.— EDEN] The meaning of the word in Hebrew is *pleasantness, loveliness.* In after ages there was a country which retained this name; 2 Kin. xix. 12; Isa. xxxvii. 12; Ezek. xxvii. 23.

ver. 9. THE TREE OF LIFE] The reference to it in ch. iii. 22 proves that the tree of life was the means provided by God to sustain man's life, "either by the natural virtue of the tree itself continually preserving the decays of nature, or else by the power of God" (Bp. Bull, *State of Man before the Fall*). It appears therefore that this one tree either physically or sacramentally absolutely secured the continued and unimpaired life of the body, but that the fruits of the other trees were only able to keep nature alive for a time, as they do still. Cp. Kurtz, and Fairbairn, *Typol.* I. 216. A tradition of this tree is preserved in the Indian and Persian mythologies.— THE TREE OF KNOWLEDGE] The tree was placed for the trial of man, to prove whether he would decide for the good, or for the evil. If by obeying God's command he decided for the good, he would arrive at the practical knowledge of the good of obedience, and, by contrast, of the evilness of disobedience. His decision for evil would entail the practical knowledge of the misery of sin, and the true good of obedience.

ver. 10. WENT OUT] The Hebrew word expresses the *downward* course of a river from its source.—FROM THENCE] The river flowed through the garden, and, on leaving it, branched out into four streams.—BECAME] was divided into four streams.

ver. 11. PISON] either the Halys or the Phasis.—COMPASSETH] or *passeth along by* (*Ainsworth*).—HAVILAH] On the supposition of the identity of the Pison with either the Halys or the Phasis, this cannot be the Havilah mentioned in the later historical parts of Scripture, which evidently lay to the south of Palestine; see Gen. xxv. 18; 1 Sam. xv. 7. It must be in this case Colchis, a land, according to the ancients, rich in gold. The Egyptian origin of the Colchians may connect their name with the Cushite Havilah.

ver. 12. BDELLIUM] Heb. *b'dolach*, which according to Bochart and Gesenius signifies *pearls;* according to the Septuagint in this passage *the ruby*, but in Numb. xi. 7, *crystal*. The other Greek translators and Josephus take it as denoting *bdellium*, an aromatic gum found in India, Arabia, Babylonia, Media and Bactriana; see Knobel. "It is objected to this view, that bdellium is not so remarkable a product as to render it worthy to be enumerated along with gold and precious stones, and that the land of Havilah should be specially noted for its production" (*Wright*).—ONYX] Heb. *shoham*. It is thus translated in most of the ancient versions.

ver. 13. GIHON] so called from its *bursting forth* from its source (*Wright*). To the present day the Araxes bears this name among the Persians.—ETHIOPIA] Heb. *Cush*. There were settlements of Cushites along the south of Asia from the Red Sea to the Indus; and the name is found in that of the Cossæi at the head of the Persian Gulf; see note on ch. x. 6. Originally the Asiatic Cushites extended far more deeply into the interior. Rawlinson, *Herod.* IV. 220.

ver. 14. HIDDEKEL] the Tigris, Dan. x. 4, by the Syrians called *Digla*, and by the Arabs *Didshlat*, in Old Persian *Tigra*. "That the name of this river signified 'an arrow,' and that it was so called on account of its rapidity, is declared by various authors. The word *tigra, an arrow*, seems to come from the Sanscrit *tig, to sharpen*"

(*Rawlinson*).—TOWARD THE EAST] Kalisch and Knobel translate, *which floweth before Assyria*. As seen from Palestine or any western country, the Tigris flows *before* the old Assyrian empire.

ver. 15. TO DRESS IT AND TO KEEP IT] He had to do a twofold office in respect to the garden, to attend to its cultivation, as far as might then be needful, and to *keep* and preserve it, namely, from the disturbing and desolating influence of evil (Fairbairn, *Typol.* I. 236). Thus after the expulsion of man from Paradise the cherubim were placed, 'to *keep* the way of the tree of life.' There is in this verse, therefore, an intimation given of the existence of evil external to man, which prepares us for the temptation in the next chapter.

ver. 17. THOU SHALT NOT EAT] This precept to Adam was a bridle to the deliciousness of his sense, and a check to the curiosity of his reason, a great experiment of his self-denial in both, and in general a call to the divine life; and so no such slight and easy precept, as some have fancied, either mistaking the first natural constitution of man, or not weighing rightly the nature of the precept itself (Bp. Bull, *State of Man before the Fall*, Eng. Works, p. 455).

ver. 18. The history of the sixth day of creation is resumed in order to narrate the origin of woman.

ver. 19. This verse is appealed to as proof that in this chapter we have an account of the creation contradictory to that given in the first chapter, and therefore composed by a different author. It is said, that here the animals are affirmed to have been made after man, although in the first chapter their creation was placed before that of man. But as Mr Ayre remarks, *Introduct. to O.T.* p. 563, there is no contradiction. The order of particulars in this chapter is not necessarily the order of time; they are named in the order which may best convey all the information which the writer desired to communicate. To maintain that these particulars were disposed in rigorous chronological order, would make the same thing to be done twice. For after the statement, v. 8, that the Lord God 'put the man whom He had formed' into the garden, the growth of trees is mentioned, and then the course of the rivers, and after that it is again said, v. 15, 'the Lord God took the man, and put him into the garden of Eden.' Comp. Keil. *Einl.* p. 71.

ver. 20. GAVE NAMES] It does not follow from his giving names that he knew the *nature* of all these creatures; for the names of them in Scripture are taken from their voice, their colour, their magnitude, and some such external difference, and not from their nature. Therefore this imposing names on them, denotes rather his dominion than his knowledge (*Patrick*).—WAS NOT FOUND AN HELP MEET] The special reason for the proceeding; while all animals were male and female, there was no partner for him (*Blackadder*).

ver. 21. A DEEP SLEEP] By the ancient Christian writers generally understood as an *ecstasy* to prepare him for the receiving of that divine oracle which upon his awaking he uttered; like that *deep sleep* which God sent upon Abraham, ch. xv. 12 (*Bp. Bull*).

ver. 23. WOMAN, BECAUSE SHE WAS TAKEN OUT OF MAN]—*she shall be called woman* [Heb. *Isshah*] *because she was taken out of man* [Heb. *Ish*].

ver. 24. Our Saviour's words, S. Matt. xix. 4—6, prove that Adam spoke this by the inspiration of God.

ver. 25. NOT ASHAMED] So long as man keeps

his body in perfect obedience to the spirit, and is therefore free from all inordinate concupiscence, no lust can arise which makes a hiding of himself necessary, and so no shame (*v. Gerlach*).

Chapter III.

The trial and the fall of man.—On this subject compare Butler, *Analogy*, Pt. I. Ch. v, in which he shows that man, though created good, might, from the constitution of his nature, feel temptation and be liable to yield to it, and also that God might consistently with His Goodness and Justice permit man to be exposed to temptation. The historical reality of the temptation is confirmed by the fact that the myths of heathenism present traces of a tradition of the fall, though in a distorted form, pervading mankind. "*Almost all the nations of Asia* (says Von Bohlen) *assume the serpent to be a wicked being, which has brought evil into the world.* And indeed it is remarkable what a similarity is observable between the traditional tales of Egypt, India, Persia, and even of the northern nations (which we again meet with in the Orphic mysteries of the west), and the old Hebrew narrative." (*Hævernick.*)

ver. 1. THE SERPENT] That it was a real serpent which was engaged in the temptation appears from the plain historical cast of the narrative, and especially from the subtilty of the serpent being particularized. That it was not the sole agent, but only the appropriate instrument which Satan used to tempt man, is also apparent from the different allusions to the fall in Scripture. Thus our Lord, in evident allusion to the falsehood with which Satan plied Adam and Eve and the sad result of their crediting the falsehood, says, Joh. viii. 44, 'He was a *murderer* from the beginning...he is a *liar*, and the father of it.' Comp. 1 Joh. iii. 8: 'The devil sinneth from the beginning;' Rev. xii. 9: 'That old serpent, called the devil and Satan, which deceiveth the whole world;' 2 Cor. xi. 3, 14: 'The serpent beguiled Eve through his subtilty...Satan himself is transformed into an angel of light;' 1 Thess. iii. 5, where the title of *the tempter* is appropriated to Satan. If it be asked why Satan assumed this form, and did not rather address the woman directly, we have a plausible explanation given by Mede: "There is a law in the commerce of spirits and man, that a spirit must present himself under the shape of some visible thing.

Experience with the Scriptures will show that not only evil angels, but good, yea God Himself, converseth in this manner with men. Further, as spirits are to converse with men in some visible shape, so is there a law given them that it must be under the shape of some such thing as may less or more resemble their condition. Hence the devil could not appear in *human* shape whilst man was in his integrity, because he was a spirit fallen from his first glorious perfection, and therefore must appear in such shape which might argue his imperfection and abasement, which was the shape of a beast" (Mede, *Discourse* XL., *Works*, p. 223).—SUBTIL] The word does not necessarily bear a bad sense; it occurs in a good sense in Prov. i. 4; xii. 16, 23: "Because the serpent was more remarkably 'subtil' he was the fittest emblem of Satan's subtilty: and was also the most proper instrument for the tempter to make choice to deceive by; since the apprehension Eve had of his subtilty might make her the less surprised at the hearing him reason and discourse with her" (*Waterland*). Bishop Patrick supposes that the serpent, before the curse pronounced upon it, may have been so beautiful a creature and so like a seraph, that Eve might have mistaken it for an angel. But, as Waterland remarks, she would not have failed to plead this as an excuse afterwards; whereas she had nothing to urge but that 'the serpent beguiled her.'—YEA] In the Hebrew an interrogation expressing surprise and astonishment.—GOD] Heb. *Elohim*. The tempter avoids the use of the name *Jehovah*, inasmuch as it was his interest to lower the woman's conception of God. He therefore uses the name which expresses the unearthly, supernatural nature of the Deity, rather than that which would remind her of her dependence on the living holy God, who had created her in His own likeness. Comp. Hengstenberg, *Pentateuch*, I. 317.—YE SHALL NOT EAT OF EVERY TREE] This would be more correctly translated, with Kalisch, Knobel and Wright, *ye shall eat of no tree of the garden;* comp. Gesen. *Gram.* § 152. 1. The serpent appears to have understood the commandment to include all the trees in the garden.

ver. 3. GOD] Heb. *Elohim*. As Hengstenberg has remarked, the use of this name by the woman shows that already she was yielding. "First there was a depression and obscuration of religious sentiment; then the tree appeared good to eat, and pleasant to the eye—God died in the soul, and sin became alive."

ver. 4. YE SHALL NOT SURELY DIE] By speaking thus he proved himself 'a liar,' as our Saviour says.

ver. 5. FOR GOD DOTH KNOW] He now openly impugns the justice and goodness of God, in order to shake the woman's faith in both. He tells her that God had denied to man the use of the tree of knowledge, only lest man should become equal to Himself. Comp. Luk. xix. 21.— SHALL BE AS GODS, KNOWING GOOD AND EVIL] We have here the real character of the first sin; it was the yielding to the desire to know and to discern for himself what is good and what is evil, instead of leaving that to God's decision. It was the desire to become thus his own master, independent of God, in other words, to be as God. Comp. Mr Barry's *Introduction to the O. T.* pp. 84, 85. Von Gerlach remarks: "The origin of sin lies, not in sense, but in the striving after independence of God, a false self-dependence. But since man's true and eternal self has its existence only in God, this self-seeking caused immediately the fall into the power of sense,— man cares now only for his temporal material *self.* The *form* which man's sin assumes is always belonging to the *flesh* or the *world;* but its *soul,* even in its coarsest form of sensuality, is always *self-exaltation.*"

ver. 6. From the remarks on the foregoing verse it appears that the nature of sin as exemplified in the Temptation is, instead of loving, seeking after, and thinking of the Creator, to love and value only self; that sin is a fall into selfishness. But of selfishness the great exhibitions are, *Pride,* i.e. the inordinate valuing of ourselves; *Covetousness,* the inordinate valuing of created objects; *Self-indulgence,* the inordinate valuing of that which created objects can bring us. Comp. Dean Alford, *Sermons on Divine Love,* IV, XIV. Hence we find the temptations of sin described thus, 1 Joh. ii. 16, 'all that is in the world, the lust of the flesh, and the lust of the eyes, and the pride of life, is not of the Father, but is of the world.'—AND WHEN THE WO-MAN SAW, &c.] The threefold temptation which led the woman to the forbidden act is detailed in accordance with the division pointed out in the last note; the fruit *was good for food,* gratified *the lust of the flesh; pleasant to the eyes,* gratified *the lust of the eyes; to be desired to make one wise,* gratified *the pride of life.*—SHE DID EAT] The successive steps by which the woman was led to her sin illustrate S. James' account of temptation; S. Jas. i. 13—15.—AND HE DID EAT] Comp. 1 Tim. ii. 14.

VER. 7. AND THE EYES OF THEM BOTH WERE OPENED] It actually happened as the seducer promised, though in malice and in an evil sense. *Their eyes were opened,* but they only saw their nakedness, and were ashamed; they knew good and evil, yet only by their sad loss of what was good, and by their disastrous experience of what was evil (*Kurtz*).—AND THEY KNEW THAT THEY WERE NAKED] They found that on departing from God they had lost control over the flesh, and were become servants to sin, hence the feeling of shame.—SEWED] Thus Gesenius and Knobel. Gataker, who is followed by Kidder and Rosenmuller, translates *applied* or *put on.* Ainsworth translates *fastened together* by twisting and plaiting the leaves and twigs.—FIG-LEAVES] Leaves of the *tenah,* the *Ficus Carica,* which is aboriginal in Western Asia, especially in Persia, Syria, and Asia Minor. It is both unnecessary and incorrect to take *tenah* here as the Pisang-tree (*Musa Paradisaica*), the leaves of which certainly attain the length of twelve and the breadth of two feet, but which is nowhere designated by *tenah* (*Kalisch*).

ver. 8. THE VOICE OF THE LORD] This simply means, *the sound of the Lord's footsteps;* comp. 1 Kin. xiv. 6 (*Wright*). It would appear that the Lord in His intercourse with Adam was accustomed to assume a human form; comp. Mede's remark in note on ver. 1.—THE COOL OF THE DAY] Lit. *the wind of the day,* i.e. in the evening when the breeze commences to rise and cools the heat of the tropical day.—HID THEMSELVES AMONGST THE TREES] A very beautiful mystical comment on this is to be found in Franks, *Sermons,* I. 290. ed. Ang.-Cath. Lib.

ver. 10. I WAS AFRAID, BECAUSE I WAS NAKED] Not to be regarded as a mere pretext. He felt himself to be disrobed of original righteousness by the discovery of 'another law in his members, warring against the law of his mind, and bringing him into captivity to the law of sin which was in his members.'

ver. 11. WHO TOLD THEE, &c.] How camest thou to this sense of thy being naked? does not this shame proceed from thy disobedience? (*Kidder.*)

ver. 12. THE MAN SAID, THE WOMAN GAVE ME OF THE TREE] The man first obeys the woman, then complains of her as the author of his fault. Strife between two creatures formed for union, bone of each other's bone, is the consequence of their both forgetting their relation to God, and seeking to please themselves (F. D. Maurice, *Patriarchs and Lawgivers*).—WHOM THOU GAVEST TO BE WITH ME] The first sin not only leads on to strife, but also to further sin against God. He tries to throw the weight of it, not on the woman alone, but even on God who gave the woman.

ver. 14, 15. We have seen that the serpent was the instrument used by Satan in tempting man. Hence, as both were engaged in the transaction, the curse is to be taken as referring to both. But, as the serpent was the ostensible agent behind which the real tempter, Satan, lay hid, while in the literal sense we apply the curse to the serpent, we must take it as chiefly designed to shape out the punishment of the real tempter, Satan. If it be asked, how it was consistent with the justice of God to punish the serpent, which was the irresponsible instrument used by Satan, the answer may be thus given in the language of Mede. All irrational creation was made for the use and service of man. Had man preserved his integrity the rest of creation would have partaken of his happiness; but as he fell, it with him was made subject to vanity. On his account it is that the earth brings forth thorns and thistles, and is laboured with toil, and its creatures become savage and unruly. And similarly on man's account and for man's sake the serpent is punished, in order that, his degradation representing the fate of the real tempter, man might see proof of God's wrath against sin, and also have the comfort of seeing proof of God's merciful determination to overrule the attempts of sin. Comp. Mede, *Discourse* XLI. *Works*, p. 228.—THOU ART CURSED ABOVE ALL CATTLE] This does not necessarily imply that beasts were cursed, any more than the words 'subtil above all the beasts' imply that the beasts were subtil (*Hengstenberg*).—UPON THY BELLY SHALT THOU GO] This shows that in the beginning the serpent had an erect form (*v. Gerlach*). How does this befit the devil? As this grovelling in the serpent signified the abasement of his whole nature from its primitive excellence, so in the devil it signifies his stooping down and falling from his most sublime and glorious condition, lower than the earth itself (*Mede*). 'Extreme contempt,

shame, and abasement shall be thy lot.' Satan imagined that by means of the fall of man he would enlarge his kingdom and extend his power. But to the eye of God the matter appeared in a different light, because with the fall he beheld the redemption (*Hengstenberg*).—
DUST SHALT THOU EAT] Because of its grovelling condition, creeping on the ground, the serpent eats its food soiled and mixed with dust. See Bochart, *Hierozoic.* Lib. I. c. 4. *De Serpente Tentatore*, Vol. I. p. 844. To eat or lick dust betokens extreme abasement and humiliation; see Mic. vii. 17; Isa. xlix. 23; Ps. lxxii. 9. In applying this to Satan, Mede and Patrick take it as signifying that Satan, having lost all relish for heavenly enjoyments in which the life of angels consists, should hunger after nothing but sin and confusion and the misery of God's creatures. Dr W. Berriman interprets it that Satan should be able to devour and destroy "only those among the sons of men who shall be addicted to earthly and sensual satisfactions," and as to the others, should have "power on their body only, which is now made mortal by sin, and as it was composed of dust," so it was to be reduced to dust (*Boyle Lect.* Vol. I. p. 73).

ver. 15. I WILL PUT ENMITY] Experience bears ample testimony to the truth of the divine sentence, in so far as it refers to the instrument of the temptation; for abhorrence of the serpent is natural to man (*Hengstenberg*).— IT SHALL BRUISE] The translation, *she shall bruise*, given in the modern Latin Vulgate, has nothing to support it. All the Hebrew MSS., the Targums, the Samaritan, Syriac, and Septuagint versions, and that of Saadias, and the citations of the passage in many of the ancient Christian writers, oppose it. —IT SHALL BRUISE THY HEAD] Of the result of this enmity there can be no doubt, the woman's seed must trample down the serpent; for, from the degraded, grovelling condition of the one, and the upright condition of the other, while the serpent can only attack man's inferior and less noble parts, man can trample down the serpent's head. —To apply this part of the prophecy to Satan. The parties on the one side are the devil and his seed; on the other, the woman and her seed. By the serpent we are to understand Satan, the prince of darkness and father of devils. The serpent's seed, in the first place, are the whole crew of devils and damned spirits who are fallen from their first estate and condition: see S. Matt.

xxv. 41; Rev. xii. 7, 9. For Satan fell first, and afterwards propagated his apostacy by drawing others after him, over whom therefore he has the chiefdom, and in this respect may be called their *father*, and they his sons, or *seed*, as we know the use of the Scripture is to call princes fathers, and subjects sons. The latter offspring of the devil are the whole company of wicked and reprobate worldlings, as appears from our Saviour's words, S. Joh. viii. 44, 'Ye are of your father the devil.' Again, 1 Joh. iii. 10, the children of God are opposed to the children of the devil. Paul calls Elymas a 'child of the devil,' Acts xiii. 10. Comp. S. Matt. iii. 7; xiii. 25; 1 John iii. 12 (*Mede*). In opposition to this *seed of the serpent* stands the *seed of the woman*, which cannot denote the entire race of mankind, since many of them are included in the *serpent's seed;* and besides it is usual for men considered as fallen to be entitled children of Adam, rather than of Eve (*W. Berriman*). As in Hebrew seed cannot mean an individual, but only a plurality of individuals (*Hengstenberg*), collected into unity and referred to one head or original (*Berriman*), and considered as one organically connected whole (Ellicott *on Gal.* iii. 16), we are necessarily led to take the woman's seed as signifying Christ, who was 'born of a woman,' and hence the seed of the woman only, and along with Him His members who are incorporate with Him into one mystical body. For although Christ's members are naturally the seed of the man as well as of the woman, yet spiritually by this incorporation they are the seed of the woman only, as is their Head with whom they are one. See Gal. iii. 25—29 (*Mede*). —THY HEAD] The serpent's head is the devil's sovereignty, which is called the sovereignty of death, as being a sovereignty under which are those who are liable to death temporal and eternal, and also the power of which consists in bringing to death both body and soul. The sword whereby this sovereignty was obtained, the sceptre whereby it is maintained, or, as S. Paul speaks, the *sting* of this serpent's head, is sin: this is that which got him the kingdom at first, and this is still the right whereby he holds the greatest part thereof (*Mede*). Now, 1 Joh. iii. 8, 'The Son of God was manifested that He might destroy the works of the devil;' and He, Heb. ii. 14, 'took part of flesh and blood, that through death He might destroy him that had the power of death, that is the devil;' and having thus, Col. ii. 15, 'spoiled principalities and powers,' 1 Cor. xv. 25, 'He must reign until He hath put all enemies under His feet. The last enemy that shall be destroyed is death.' And His members, in Him and through Him, share His victory; for, 1 Joh. v. 4, 'whatsoever is born of God overcometh the world;' Rom. viii. 1, 'there is no condemnation to them who are in Christ Jesus, who walk not after the flesh, but after the Spirit;' they, Eph. vi. 11, 'put on the whole armour of God, that they may be able to stand against the wiles of the devil;' they, 1 Cor. xv. 57, 'thank God, who giveth them the victory through the Lord Jesus Christ;' for, Rom. viii. 11, 'if the Spirit of Him who raised up Jesus from the dead dwell in you, He that raised up Christ from the dead shall also quicken your mortal bodies by His Spirit which dwelleth in you.' Nay, so far does their victory go, that, as we are told, S. Jude 6, 'the angels which kept not their first estate He hath reserved unto the judgment of the great day;' so also are we told that Christ's people, 1 Cor. vi. 3, 'shall judge angels.' That Christ's mystical body is thus included in the prediction is confirmed by the reference to it in Rom. xvi. 20.—THOU SHALT BRUISE HIS HEEL] Fulfilled *firstly* and pre-eminently in Christ crucified. Of Judas, who betrayed Him, it is written, S. Joh. xiii. 27, 'Satan entered into him;' of the Jews Jesus declared, S. Joh. viii. 44, 'Ye are of your father the devil, and the lusts of your father ye will do. He was a murderer from the beginning.' When betrayed, He said to them, S. Luk. xxii. 53, 'this is your hour, and the power of darkness.' Thus the sufferings of Jesus were the work of Satan, by the instrumentality of evil men bruising His heel, i.e. the inferior part of His person, "the humanity of our Saviour, as some of the ancients understand it, and not amiss, so it do not point out the similitude too precisely" (Jackson, *Works*, Vol. VIII. 394.) But Satan prevailed only to bruise His heel, for, 2 Cor. xiii. 4, 'though crucified through weakness, yet He liveth by the power of God.' *Secondly*, it is fulfilled in the mystical body of Christ. The servant, says the Saviour, S. Joh. xv. 20, 'is not greater than his Lord; if they have persecuted me, they will also persecute you.' And, accordingly, 2 Tim. iii. 12, 'all who will live godly in Christ Jesus shall suffer persecution.' This is the work of Satan: Rev. xii. 17, 'the dragon was wroth with the woman, and went to make war with the remnant of her seed, which keep the commandments of God, and have the testimony of Jesus.' And thus Christ's people may be said, Col. i. 24, 'to fill up that which is behind of the afflictions of Christ.'

ver. 16. The woman first receives the punishment which was her peculiar share. That which was afterwards adjudged to the man affects her together with him (c. Gerlach). But, even in punishing, the mercy of God appears eminently. Each sentence has its element of blessing to man in his fallen state. If to the woman is announced *the anguish* of child-birth, this announcement is also the promise that she shall bear offspring, and by doing so be the mother of the seed of promise; and thus though she 'was in the transgression, notwithstanding she shall be saved in childbearing,' 1 Tim. ii. 15. The rule of the husband and her desire to him, which were denounced, were to counteract the insubordination and rivalries which man's revolt from dependence on God had introduced into his race.

ver. 17. CURSED IS THE GROUND FOR THY SAKE] The ground is cursed for *man's sake:* thorns and thistles it is to bring forth to him, on purpose that he may not yield to that slavish self-indulgent nature into which he has fallen; on purpose that he may be led to seek help in tilling the earth and subduing it, and in ruling the inferior creatures, from Him who has sent him into the world (Maurice, *Patriarchs and Lawgivers*,.

ver. 19. TO DUST SHALT THOU RETURN. Death itself may be regarded as an act of mercy. "God framed man to His own likeness, a goodly creature, which the envy of the devil presently defaced. And God, perceiving that no skill or power would ever remove from him the bruises and scars that he had received from that envious spirit, resolves to bring him into that dust of death, that so his blemishes might not remain for ever, but that they might be by the furnace of death as it were melted out, and never appear more. Hence you may see that in the judgment of antiquity, sin doth so far deface our nature, that the image of God first impressed upon us, can never be fully repaired, till we be dissolved, and as a statue newly melted' (Bp. Nicholson *On the Creed*, p. 584).

ver. 20. EVE. Heb. *Chavah* = *Life*, or *Living*. She was the *mother of all* living, because He who is the Author of our life and salvation, as well as all who partake of the spiritual life by virtue of their union with Him, were to descend from her; and were reckoned for that seed of the woman mentioned in this promise of Redemption (W. Berriman, *Boyle Lect.* I. p. 90).

ver. 21. COATS OF SKINS] As, in the comparison of Gen. i. 29 with Gen. ix. 3, it appears that at this time the slaying animals for food was not permitted to man, it has been reasonably argued that the Lord now instituted the rite of sacrifice to perpetuate the promise, and that the beasts slain at this time supplied the coats of skin (*W. Berriman, Patrick, Waterland*). These coats were a badge and signal of the divine mercy, as they exhibited a daily emblem of the sacrifice of the death of Christ, and that robe of his righteousness, wherewith his sufferings and merits should clothe them (Wogan, *On Proper Lessons;* Bp. Beveridge, *Serm.* Vol. III. p. 85; Ainsworth). Comp. Magee *On the Atonement, Dis.* LXIV. Fairbairn, *Typol.* I. 259.

ver. 22. AS ONE OF US] These words plainly insinuate a plurality of Persons in the Godhead, and all other explications of them seem forced and unnatural (*Patrick*). The comment of Philo Judæus on the passage is: 'Those words *as one of us* are not put for one, but for more than one.' (Kidder, *Demonst. of the Mess.* III. p. 211). Justin Martyr appeals to the passage in proof of the pre-existence of Christ. Tertullian thus comments on it: "The fact is He used the plural expressions, *Let us make,* and *one,* and *to us,* because the Son, a second person, His Word, was united to Him, and the Spirit, a third person, in the Word" (Burton, *Ante-Nicene Test. to Christ,* p. 47, *to the Trinity,* p. 75).—LEST HE PUT FORTH, &c.] The banishment from the tree of life is the fulfilment of the sentence of death in v. 19. Patrick cites several passages from the early Christian writers in proof that they regarded this as a merciful dispensation, to prevent man being perpetuated in a state of sin.

ver. 24. CHERUBIM] All that we can know of these beings is to be gathered from the passages in Scripture where mention is made of them. From a comparison of Ps. xviii. 10 with Ps. civ. 3, 4, we may infer that they were angels. From the position which they hold in the visions of Ezekiel and S. John (Ezek. i. 10, Rev. iv. 6—8), they are evidently the highest order of angelic beings who dwell in the immediate presence of God. Now, to use the words of Mede, "there is a law in the commerce of spirits and men, that a spirit must present itself under the shape of some visible thing." When therefore it was necessary that these angelic beings should be manifested to man, they were represented in a shape denoting that they were the highest created beings. Man, as created in the image of God, was once the highest, but after the fall he no longer represented the perfection of created life. Hence to the shape of man was added the forms of the eagle, the lion, and the ox—the respective chiefs of the animal creation—in order to express the perfection of created life. When man was banished from Paradise, the tree of life remained conspicuous there, giving hope that man might be restored again to the enjoyment of it. But about it waved the flaming sword, emblem of the consuming fire of the Divine Holiness; and near it were placed the cherubim to show what man must become before he could be readmitted to Paradisaical blessedness. In Rev. xxii. 2 is displayed the fulfilment of the hopes held forth to man in the beginning of Genesis. In the new Jerusalem are seen the river of water and the tree of life. But the cherubims no longer surround the tree of life. Man is restored to the full enjoyment of it. Comp. Kurtz, I. 78; Von Gerlach *on Gen.* iii. 23, and *Ex.* xxv. 20; Hengstenberg, *Pent.* II. 526; Fairbairn, *Typol.* I. 222.

Chapter IV.

It has been objected that this chapter displays ignorance and confusion of history, by representing the earliest inhabitants of the earth as acquainted with agriculture, which supposes an advanced state of civilization, and as engaged in the building of cities and the working of metals, and in other pursuits, which are declared unsuitable to so early an age. This objection is based on the theory of the gradual and progressive self-development of mankind from a savage to a civilized state; a theory quite opposed to *facts* (comp. Archb. Whately, *Polit. Econ.* Lect. v.), and the testimonies of the ancients. According to the Phœnician traditions, the invention of agriculture and the arts, with the discovery of metals, &c., is referred to their early mythic period, and ascribed to the first men. The Egyptian tradition places the origin of music and metallurgy in the time when Osiris reigned. Among the Greeks these events were entirely attributed to the mythic age. Comp. Hævernick, *Introd. to Pent.* p. 104.

ver. 1. CAIN] meaning in Heb. *possession, the acquired one.* She regards her first-born as the fulfilment of the promise of a blessed and victorious seed.—I HAVE GOTTEN] Heb. *Kanithi*, from *Kanah* = *to acquire.*—FROM THE LORD] By the help of the Lord (*Gesenius, Wright, Knobel*).— THE LORD] Heb. *Jehovah*. God had shown by the punishment He inflicted, that He was Jehovah, and now He was also known to be Jehovah by the benefit he conferred (*Hengstenberg*).

ver. 2. ABEL] Heb. *Hebel* = *breath, quickly vanishing vapour*, and hence (comp. Job vii. 16; Jas. iv. 14) *vanity*. She is sensible of her error concerning Cain, and her premature hope vanishes like *breath*.—A KEEPER OF SHEEP,...A TILLER OF THE GROUND] The two most ancient modes of life, which are called in the Arabic language that of the Bedouins and that of the Kabyles, and which to this day in the East are distinguished from each other by their contrary tendencies (*Herder*). The distinction between the two is exemplified in the enmity borne by the agricultural Egyptian to the shepherd race.

ver. 3. IN PROCESS OF TIME] Lit. *at the end*

of days, i.e. after some time had elapsed (*Kalisch, Knobel, Delitzsch*); at the return of some set time of public worship (*Kidder*); at the end of the year (*Ainsworth, Rosenm., v. Bohlen*).—BROUGHT] The word in Hebrew is never used about private sacrifices, but always about public sacrifices, which were brought to the door of the tabernacle to be offered by the priest. And therefore I suppose that they *brought* these offerings to some *fixed* place where they performed sacred offices before God (*Patrick*).—AN OFFERING] Heb. *minchah*, prop. *a gift*, then a gift to God, i.e. *a sacrifice;* always in the law an unbloody sacrifice, opposed to *zebach* (*Wright*). —TO THE LORD] Heb. *Jehovah*. In reference to the use of this name here and throughout the rest of the chapter Hengstenberg remarks: "The offerings were presented not to Elohim, but to Jehovah. The presentation of offerings, like every other religious service, rests on the conviction that God is not secluded in heaven, but reveals Himself as making retribution both in rewards and punishments. Only Jehovah, not Elohim, gives a manifest token of his pleasure or displeasure, and places Himself in a moral relation to men, according to their different conduct.

To Jehovah it belongs to appear as an internal and external avenger. The manifestation of God in conscience is far more vivid and distinct than in external nature."

ver. 4. HAD RESPECT UNTO] was pleased with, as some ancient versions have it. God gave some visible sign of His respect, it being said that 'God testified of Abel's gifts,' Heb. xi. 4 (*Kidder*). As in after-times God declared His acceptance of an offering by sending fire to consume it, comp. Lev. ix. 24; Judg. vi. 21; 1 Kin. xviii. 38; 1 Chron. xxi. 26; 2 Chron. vii. 1, it is supposed that he did so in the present case.— For a laboured argument, derived from this passage, for the divine institution of animal sacrifice, see Magee *On the Atonement*.—ABEL AND HIS OFFERING] To Abel first, and then to his offering. It is the offerer that God principally regards (*Kidder*).

ver. 5. HIS COUNTENANCE FELL] expressing dissatisfaction and jealousy.

ver. 7. SHALT THOU NOT BE ACCEPTED?] Lit. *is there not lifting up* of thy countenance? in reference to the face expressing the elation of the heart conscious of rectitude. Comp. Job x. 15; xi. 15; xxii. 26 (*Maurer, Knobel, Wright,*

Gesenius, Delitzsch).—SIN LIETH AT THE DOOR] i.e. the punishment of thy sin (comp. ch. xix. 15) is not far from befalling thee.—UNTO THEE SHALL BE HIS DESIRE] Thou shalt preserve thy superiority over thy brother (*Kidder*). But the whole verse is by many translated and explained thus: *If thou doest well, is there not lifting up? but if thou doest not well, sin lieth in wait at the door; towards thee is his desire* (i.e. he wishes to make you his prey), *but thou shouldst rule over him* (shouldst withstand his temptations). Sin is represented figuratively as a beast of prey desirous to make a prey of man (*Maurer, Gesenius, Kalisch, Wright*). The interpretation of Lightfoot, *a sin-offering lieth at thy door*, is inadmissible, as sin-offerings were not in use before the Mosaic Law.

ver. 8. TALKED WITH ABEL] Lit. *Cain said to Abel*. What he said is uncertain. Gesenius explains: *Cain said it* (namely, what God had said to him) *to Abel*. A great number of ancient versions read the passage, *Cain said to Abel, Let us go forth into the field*, and although no Hebrew MS. is found containing the added clause, some critics adopt it on the authority of these versions.

ver. 10. CRIETH] calls for vengeance (*Patrick*).

ver. 11. CURSED FROM THE EARTH] Eden was by the presence of God a holy land; like Canaan afterwards it was defiled by bloodshed; comp. Numb. xxxv. 33; Jer. iii. 9. Hence Cain must for his punishment be expelled from it. From the ground itself which had received his brother's blood was to proceed his punishment; when he laboured it, it should not give its increase to repay his toil; and thus he would be compelled to go forth from Eden to wander through the world. There is a distinction in the Hebrew which is not marked in our translation. In v. 11, it should be, *cursed from the ground;* in v. 12, it is correctly given, *a vagabond shalt thou be on the earth;* in v. 14, it should be, *thou hast driven me this day from the face of the ground.*

ver. 13. MY PUNISHMENT IS GREATER THAN I CAN BEAR] From the whole of Cain's remonstrance it is evident that it was the greatness not of his crime, but of his punishment, which distressed him. Hence the translation of the text is preferable to that of the margin.

ver. 14. FROM THE FACE OF THE EARTH] or of the ground or land where he was, and which he had been tilling (*Kidder*); and which is shown to be Eden, where Adam settled, by the next clause, *and from thy face shall I be hid.*—EVERY ONE THAT FINDETH ME SHALL SLAY ME] Whom does Cain expect to meet outside Eden, which is for the time the exclusive dwelling-place of the human race in its infancy? Does the historian forget himself? Certainly not. For as Cain fears to be recognised outside Eden as the notorious murderer, the narrative presupposes that there was in existence but one human family, that of Adam, and no other unconnected with it. It is evidently vengeance for a kinsman's murder that Cain fears when his father's family spreads abroad; for that murder is to be punished by the slaying of the murderer is a law written on every human heart; and in beholding the earth already full of avengers, he displays the characteristic of the murderer, who feels himself on all sides encompassed and tortured by avenging spirits (*Delitzsch*).

ver. 15. SET A MARK ON CAIN] This translation is generally considered incorrect. Almost all the modern interpreters translate, *and the Lord gave a sign to Cain;* just as He did in the case of Noah and Hezekiah. According to Knobel the meaning is, that the Lord ordained a certain sign in reference to Cain, which was to interpose when any attack was made on him. He considers it to have been some heavenly phenomenon, something accompanied with a voice which was to threaten the assailant with sevenfold punishment; comp. Exod. iii. 2, &c.; 1 Kin. xix. 11. By this means, while Jehovah promises protection, He does not ensure perfect security; for the assailant might disregard the sign. The fratricide is not to be relieved of all fear for his life.—LEST ANY FINDING HIM SHOULD KILL HIM] The sacred narrative itself presents intimation of Adam having many children; comp. ch. v. 4. Adam's family would naturally be disposed to take vengeance on Cain for his murder.

ver. 16. THE PRESENCE OF THE LORD] Heb. *of Jehovah*. Jehovah's presence, the Revelation of the living and personal God, was confined to human society, the Church of God. To be driven out of human society and out of communion with God was one and the same thing. Out of Eden there was only Elohim (*Hengstenberg*).—NOD] in Hebrew means *exile*.

ver. 17. BUILDED A CITY] His building a city intimates not only the rapid increase of mankind in his time, but also that a sense of insecurity had arisen amongst men. Hence we may infer that Cain's lawless and violent disposition was inherited by his offspring.

ver. 19. In reference to the marks of civilization and refinement which Cain's family exhibits, Mr Maurice remarks: "All this premature civilization is found in Cain's family. It begins, as so much of the world's so-called civilization has begun, with men breaking loose from family bonds, and forsaking the tillage of the earth, through the desire to sink the consciousness of some crime, in intercourse with their fellows, in the works of their hands, in the delights of sense and sound. Such social progress soon terminates in a deeper barbarism, domestic life having been destroyed to make way for it" (*Patriarchs and Lawgivers*, p. 71). In striking agreement with this is the fact that after the flood we find the highest civilization and refinement exhibited by the race of Ham.—ADAH] The occurrence of female names in a genealogy is peculiar to Cain's race. As these names all refer to attractiveness of appearance, the mention of them seems intended to intimate a development of a sensuous if not sensual character in Cain's race. *Adah = ornament, beauty; Zillah = shade,* in allusion to her thick tresses (*Kurtz*); Naamah = *pleasing*.

ver. 20. THE FATHER] This Biblical form of expression is very common. Any one who should now invent tents, or the custom of living in tents, would be called the father not only of tents, but also of tent-dwelling; indeed the Arabs call a person distinguished for any peculiarity the father of it (Thomson, *The Land and the Book*, p. 307).

ver. 21. JUBAL] Vossius and Bochart have tried to prove that Jubal was afterwards deified and worshipped as Apollo. In agreement with the Biblical account which connects music with the pastoral life, the Greeks and Latins attributed the invention of musical instruments to the gods Pan and Apollo.

ver. 22. TUBAL-CAIN] by Bochart and Vossius similarly identified with Vulcan.—AN INSTRUCTER OF EVERY ARTIFICER] Better translated, *a forger of all kinds of instruments of brass and of iron*.—ARTIFICER] Lit. *a cutting thing*, hence *a weapon* (*Maurer, Wright.*)

ver. 23. AND LAMECH SAID] Among the different intimations given in the foregoing verses of the progressive sinfulness of Cain's race, is the mention of the invention of the art of fabricating implements of metal, and most probably warlike implements, which is ascribed to Lamech's sons. His song is easily interpreted when taken as bearing special reference to his son's invention of weapons of warfare. He exults in the thought that by it he can secure to himself, for any deed of violence he may commit, immunity far greater than even Cain obtained from God. The history of Cain's race thus closing with this sanguinary song of the sword, prepares us for that outbreak of violence in ch. vi. which drew down punishment on the earth. Comp. Herder, *Vom Geist der Heb. Poesie*, I. 344. The translation of this passage in the English version is incorrect. The following translation is taken from Wright: *Surely I will slay a man for wounding me, and a youth for bruising me. If Cain is to be avenged sevenfold, surely Lamech* (shall be avenged) *seventy and sevenfold.* I will slay, says Lamech, whoever offers me violence; but woe to those who try to avenge his death by killing me; my ancestor, Cain, who had no weapons, obtained from God a promise of sevenfold vengeance; my sons have weapons, and can take a far more complete revenge.

ver. 25. SETH] in Heb. means *compensation*. This is no misnomer. Seth is the ancestor of a family, which, continuing in the faith, became heirs of the promise, and whose aims, characters, and tendency, are opposed to those of Cain (*Kurtz*).—FOR GOD, SAID SHE] The defenders of the document hypothesis are perplexed by this occurrence of Elohim. Accordingly they affirm that the verse is interpolated or corrupted; comp. Hævernick, p. 67. Hengstenberg's explanation of the use of the name is, that at this time Eve's religious feelings had grown less lively, and she regarded the event merely as one in the ordinary course of nature, brought about by God's general Providence.

ver. 26. ENOS] *man*, with the notion of weakness, mortality added thereto (*v. Gerlach*).—THEN BEGAN MEN TO CALL UPON THE NAME OF THE LORD] The only correct rendering. A comparison of the parallel passages where the phrase occurs, shows that it does not denote prayer in general, which must have been contemporaneous with the very beginnings of the human race, but the solemn calling on God in a consecrated place, in church-fellowship, so that it implies the existence of a church. Comp. Gen. xii. 8; xiii. 4;

xxi. 33; xxvi. 25 (*Hengstenberg*). The gathering of men into religious communities seems to have been an attempt to counteract the progress of irreligion.

Chapter V.

The Hebrew text, the Septuagint or Alexandrian Greek version, and the Samaritan version of the Pentateuch, differ materially in the Chronology of the Antediluvian period. On the subject of the respective claims for preference of the different systems, see Prof. Davidson's *Introd. to the O. T.* p. 345. Subjoined is a Table, taken from Kurtz, of the three systems; H. denotes the Hebrew Text, A. the Septuagint or Alexandrian, and S. the Samaritan.

With regard to the strange phenomenon of the great longevity of the Antediluvians, the remark of F. Schlegel deserves to be considered: "We should ever bear in mind what a mighty wall of separation, what an impassable abyss, divides us from that remote world both of nature and of man. With respect to human life we have completely lost every criterion by which to estimate its original duration; and it would be no slight problem for a profound physiological sci-

PREFATORY.

		Year of Paternity.	Remainder of Life.	Duration of Life.
Adam	H.	130	800	930
	A.	230	700	930
	S.	130	800	930
Seth...............	H.	105	807	912
	A.	205	707	912
	S.	105	807	912
Enos	H.	90	815	905
	A.	190	715	905
	S.	90	815	905
Cainan...........	H.	70	840	910
	A.	170	740	910
	S.	70	840	910
Mahalaleel	H.	65	830	895
	A.	165	730	895
	S.	65	830	895
Jared	H.	162	800	962
	A.	162	800	962
	S.	62	785	847
Enoch	H.	65	300	365
	A.	165	200	365
	S.	65	300	365
Methuselah	H.	187	782	969
	A.	$\binom{167}{187^1}$	$\binom{802}{782^1}$	969
	S.	67	653	720
Lamech	H.	182	595	777
	A.	188	565	753
	S.	53	600	653
Noah	H.	500		(950)
	A.	500		(950)
	S.	500		(950)

[1] The lower numbers are those of the Codex Alexandrinus.

ence to discern and explain, from a deeper investigation of the internal constitution of the earth, or of astronomical influences, which are often susceptible of very minute applications, the primary cause of human longevity" (*Philos. of Hist.*). With regard to the support which the Biblical representation receives from *Physiology*, comp. Hævernick, *Introd. Pent.* p. 107, and for that from *History*, Hamilton, *Pentateuch and its Assailants*, p. 181.

ver. 1. THE BOOK] The catalogue of the posterity of Adam, yet not of all, but only of those through whom Noah was descended from him. The Heb. *sepher*, here translated 'book,' often expresses any short writing or document; cf. Josh. xviii. 9; Neh. vii. 5.—GOD] Heb. *Elohim*. Hengstenberg thus accounts for the use of this name in this connexion. God is here represented as standing at the head of the genealogy. But in this respect He cannot be spoken of as Jehovah. Even the angels are never described as sons of Jehovah. Only the indefinite notion of a participation in the divine nature suits creatures.

ver. 3. IN HIS OWN LIKENESS, AFTER HIS IMAGE] Words which seem to mark the difference from the image and likeness of God, wherein

Adam was made, and which though not quite lost, was lamentably defaced (*Patrick*). But there seems no reference intended to the effects of the Fall. The clause seems simply designed to teach that Adam's descendants by their birth stood in the same relation to God as Adam did.

ver. 24. ENOCH] Comp. Jude, 14, 15.—WALKED WITH GOD] Lived in close communion with God. It is said of Enoch and Noah that they walked with *God*, not that they walked with *the Lord*. To walk with the Lord would seem to express an intense consciousness of the living personal God on the part of man, and a manifestation of Himself to man on the part of God, for which fallen man is at present not capable. In the next clause the use of the name is easily explained. Enoch walked with God, and in recompense God translated him.—HE WAS NOT; FOR GOD TOOK HIM] He was taken out of this world to the bliss of Paradise, without tasting of death, like Elijah. Comp. Heb. xi. 5. Von Bohlen and others think that no more is intimated than that he died a sudden death. But, as Mr Wright remarks, a different Hebrew word is used to express the death of every other person in this chapter, and hence we may gather from the text itself, independently of the authoritative explanation in Heb. xi. 5, that there was some remarkable difference between his case and theirs. The Targums of Onkelos and Pseud. Jonathan agree with our interpretation.

ver. 29. NOAH] in Heb. means *rest*.—SAYING, THIS SAME SHALL COMFORT US, &c.] Cain, by his deed of blood-shedding, had drawn down on the earth God's holy wrath; Gen. iv. 10. His descendants went on filling up the measure of their father's iniquity, and even drew the family of Seth on to participate in their wickedness. Hence the Lord was obliged to visit the whole earth with punishment. Now it is particularly said that the offence for which the flood was brought on was that 'the earth was filled with *violence*,' ch. vi. 11; and thus the judgment of the flood is put in marked connexion with Cain's sin, which introduced the curse on the earth. This curse was kept suspended until men by multiplying their father's sin drew it down, when they might have averted it by avoiding their father's example; comp. S. Matt. xxiii. 34, 35. The *comfort* which Lamech expected was in reference to this threatened infliction on the earth, the speedy approach of which he inferred from the spread of wickedness over *all* mankind. Through the prophetic spirit he foresaw that Noah should preserve the race of man from total destruction when punishment should be inflicted on the earth, and that he should receive the promise, 'I will not again curse the ground for man's sake,' ch. viii. 21. For a different interpretation, see Sherlock, *On Proph.* Disc. IV.; Davison, *On Proph.* p. 78.—THE LORD] This name is used, because an act of the living, personal, holy God is spoken of (*Hengstenberg*).

ver. 31. Bishop Kidder, after Ainsworth, remarks that, when the years of these pious patriarchs are computed, it will be found that all of them must have died before the flood was brought 'on the world of the ungodly;' and that to show this may have been one reason for the particularity in recording their chronology.

Chapter VI.

In the fourth chapter we found recorded the first open outbreak of wickedness, and God's sentence denounced on this wickedness. Intimations were found also in it of a sinful development characterizing Cain's family, according to which they were imitating and filling up the measure of their father's iniquity. In the present chapter we find the reason given of the punishment or curse not being restricted to that family. In time even the family of Seth became infected with the corruption of the Cainites. Seduced by the beauty of their women they made alliances with them, and thus were entangled in the wickedness of that race; so that at last, not merely the Cainites, but 'all flesh had corrupted his way upon the earth,' and 'the earth was filled with violence.' All were involved in Cain's sin; therefore all were punished.

ver. 1. MEN] The offspring of Cain, or the wicked portion of mankind, seems to be here denoted (*Rosenmuller*).

ver. 2. THE SONS OF GOD] Passing by the Jewish interpretation *sons of Princes*, there are two opinions regarding the meaning of this passage to be considered. (a) *The angels.* But (1) the angels 'neither marry, nor are given in marriage,' Luk. xx. 35. (2) Men would then be punished for sin which was introduced by angels, and not by men. (3) To use the language of St Chrysostom: "If the saints who had been partakers of the Holy Ghost could not bear the sight of the angels, and Daniel himself lay lifeless by reason of such visitation, who would be so irrational as to suppose that the immaterial and spiritual natures could ally themselves with the fleshly?" (4) This interpretation destroys the connexion according to which the passage teaches the way in which corruption had spread over the whole race of Adam. (b) *The descendants of Seth*, who called on the Lord, as opposed to the descendants of Cain, who dwelt away from the presence of the Lord. Pious worshippers of God are thus called in Scripture; comp. Hos. i. 10; Rom. viii. 14. On the other hand, idolaters are said to be *children* of their false Gods, Mal. ii. 11.—The question, why are pious worshippers of God called sons of Elohim, and not sons of Jehovah? is thus answered by Hengstenberg. Sons of Jehovah would have expressed too much. This dignity was first bestowed on those among whom the character of Jehovah had been fully unfolded; Deut. xiv. 1. Comp. notes on ch. v. 1, 24.—SAW THE DAUGHTERS OF MEN THAT THEY WERE FAIR] The words present an additional proof that the sons of God were not angels. It is here intimated that they could have formed alliances on better grounds, and that their criminality consisted in regarding beauty instead of goodness.—DAUGHTERS OF MEN] the women of the race of Cain.—FAIR] This was already intimated in the names Naamah, Adah, Zillah.

ver. 3—8. The name Jehovah occurs naturally throughout these verses, which represents God as personally interesting Himself in the doings of men, and dealing forth just retribution. Comp. Maurice, *Patriarchs*, &c. p. 62.

ver. 3. MY SPIRIT, &c.] i.e. *My spirit*, either speaking by preachers of righteousness and prophets, such as Noah and Enoch, or working inwardly in men's hearts, *shall not always strive with*, or chide and reprove *men* to bring them to repentance, *for that he also is flesh*, entirely abandoned to fleshly inclinations; *yet* he shall have an *hundred and twenty years* to repent in before the coming of the flood. Thus *Ainsworth*,

Patrick and *Kidder*. The passage is involved in much difficulty. The English translation of it, and the preceding explanation, seem to have at least as much to recommend them as any others. Delitzsch's last interpretation is: *My spirit*, i. e. the Divine breath in men, *shall not always prevail*, i.e. it shall be taken from *man, since he is indeed flesh*, i.e. yields to his animal nature. The passage has been also translated: *My spirit shall not always rule* (*Maurer, Knobel*), or *be humbled* (*Gesenius, Tuch*) *in man; because of transgression he is flesh*, a transitory mortal being (cp. Ps. lxxviii. 39; Job x. 4), *yet his days shall be a hundred and twenty years;* his life for the future shall be limited to that number of years. *Spirit* in this case is taken as denoting the divine breath which God breathed into man at his creation. Raphall's translation, which was supported by Delitzsch in his first edition, gives a better meaning: *My spirit prevails not always in man; in the phrenzy of lust he is flesh*, i.e. his animal nature obtains the upper hand over the better principle within him, viz. My spirit; *therefore his days shall be one hundred and twenty years*, a respite for repentance of one hundred and twenty years shall be afforded him.

ver. 4. The corruption of the age is proved, first, from the apostasy of the pious race; secondly, from the violence of those whose bodily strength corresponded with their pride and success (*Hævernick*).—GIANTS] Heb. *nephilim*, derived by Gesenius from the Heb. *naphal = to fall*, so as to mean *those who fall on others, assailants*, men of violence. In this sense it is translated by the Greek translators Aquila and Symmachus. By Tuch it is derived so as to signify *men of distinction*, men distinguished by their size and strength from ordinary men. As the word is used in Numb. xiii. 33 to denote giants, we are obliged to take that meaning of it here. It is to be observed that the present passage does not derive the race of giants from the mixed marriages between the sons of God and the daughters of men. It only declares that the gigantic race which already existed was rapidly augmented by these unions.

ver. 5. GOD] This should be *the Lord*. The Hebrew printed copies have *Jehovah;* and thus it is in Ainsworth's translation.—SAW THE WICKEDNESS OF MAN] They were not cherishing their foul conceptions, pursuing their mad calculations, uncared for. There was an eye looking down upon their most inward secrets, penetrating the intents of their hearts. And that was the eye of one who desired to make them right within; who had determined that His earth should be purged of its corruptions,—should fulfil all the ends of His creation (Maurice, *Patriarchs*, &c. p. 63).

ver. 6. IT REPENTED THE LORD] As for these phrases of *repenting, grieving*, &c., God frameth His language to our dulness, and teacheth us by our own phrases what He would have us learn. But what is so spoken by God after *the manner of men*, must yet be understood so as befitteth the *majesty* and perfection of His *Divine nature*. When He *repenteth*, then we are not so to conceive it, as if God changed His mind, or altered any thing of His everlasting counsel and purpose, either in substance or circumstances: it only importeth that He now doeth not that which so far as we could reasonably conjecture by His *words*, or *works*, or our *deserts*, or otherwise, seemed to us His purpose to have done. Thus for the phrases: but yet the main doubt for the thing itself standeth uncleared. Abimelech and Hezekiah shall die, and yet Abimelech and Hezekiah shall not die; Nineveh shall be destroyed, and yet Nineveh shall not be destroyed. How is there not here a plain change of God's mind? The answer is briefly this. All God's promises, how absolutely soever expressed, are made on continuing in obedience; and all His threatenings, how absolutely soever expressed, conditionally on continuing in impenitency. This is plain from Jer. xviii. 7, 8; Ezek. xxxiii. 7—20. The examples make it plain. Abimelech *shall die* for taking Sarah: understand *unless he restore her*. *Forty days and Nineveh shall be destroyed:* understand it with this reservation, *unless they repent*. And so of all the rest (Bp. Sanderson, *Serm.* ii. on 1 Kin. xxi. 29, condensed). On this subject useful remarks will be found in Jackson, *Works*, Vol. VI. 96; VIII. 300; Waterland, *Works*, Vol. IV. p. 180.

ver. 9. THESE ARE THE GENERATIONS OF NOAH] The formula intimates the introduction of a fresh subject; see note on ch. ii. 4.—The whole mass of mankind had become forgetful of their relationship to God, and had reduced themselves to a level with the brute creation. It is now no longer the Lord interesting Himself in the state of the race of which He is the Head, who is spoken of in vv. 9—22, but the Creator bringing destruction on the earth of His creation, and by His Providence providing for the safety of those portions of it which He chooses to save. Hence we naturally meet throughout this passage only the name *Elohim.*—PERFECT IN HIS GENERATIONS] i.e. among the men of the ages in which he lived. So in Matt. xi. 16; xii. 42, *generation* is expounded by the *men of this generation* in Luk. vii. 31; xi. 31 (*Ainsworth*).

ver. 10. SHEM, HAM, AND JAPHETH] In Hebrew the names respectively signify, *Name* or *Glory; Heat; Enlargement.*

ver. 12. ALL FLESH] Mankind, and also all the inferior animals.—IS COME BEFORE ME] Has been determined on by me (*Maurer*).—WITH THE EARTH] i.e. the surface of the earth which bears and nourishes man (*Maurer*).

ver. 14. AN ARK] Heb. *tebah,* a word used only in the case of Noah's ark and in Exod. ii. 3, 5, to denote the *ark* of bulrushes in which Moses was placed. It is probably an original Egyptian word. In the Egyptian a boat is called *tept,* and in the Coptic a chest or box is called *taibe, taibi, taebe, thaebi, thebi;* see Bunsen, *Egypt's Place,* I. 589 (*Knobel*). According to Mr Thomson (*The Land and the Book,* p. 224) *taboth* is the Arabic for a *coffin.*—The ark was neither intended nor suited for nautical purposes. It was meant for *carrying freight*, for which it was much more suited than if it had been constructed according to the principles of ship-building. The vessel, after the model of the ark, which F. Jansen built at Hoorn in 1609, was capable of carrying one-third more than ordinary vessels of the same tonnage, but was unfit for navigation. N. Tiele shows in his Comment, that the ark was sufficiently large to receive all the animals which were to be preserved (*Kurtz*). Computations on the dimensions of the ark, and its relative capacity, may be found in H. Miller, *Test. of the Rocks.*—GOPHER WOOD] Probably the cypress, which abounded in Babylonia.

ver. 15. CUBIT] Thenius makes the old Hebrew Mosaic cubit equal to 19·05 of our inches. The dimensions of the ark were, according to this, in round numbers, 477 English feet long, 79 broad, and 47 high (*Blackadder*).

ver. 16. A WINDOW] Heb. *light*, collectively for *windows* (*Gesenius*, *Wright*); *a window*, in the singular, as there was only one; comp. ch. viii. 6 (*Maurer*, *Knobel*, *Delitzsch*). Rosenmuller renders the word, *roof*.—IN A CUBIT SHALT

THOU FINISH IT] viz. *the ark*. The top of the ark was to be raised with a slope of one cubit, to carry off the falling waters (*Kidder, Dathe, Rosenmuller*). Or, taking *it* to refer to *window, to a cubit from the top shalt thou make it;* there was to be a cubit space between the top of the window and the top of the ark, and thus the projecting roof would not impede the light (*Knobel*). Or, the window was to be a cubit square (*Delitzsch*).

ver. 17. FLOOD] Heb. *mabbul*, used only in the history of the Deluge, and once by the Psalmist, xxix. 10, when describing the omnipotence of God (*Raphall*).

ver. 18. COVENANT] which relates to Noah merely as part of the whole creation which was embraced in it. Hence it is *Elohim* who makes it.

ver. 29. CREEPING THINGS OF THE EARTH] as distinguished from aquatic animals, which are also called creeping things; Gen. i. 21.—SHALL COME] I see no incongruity in affirming that God, by the ministry of his angels, brought them to the ark (*Patrick*).

Chapter VII.

The Scriptural narrative of the Deluge is remarkably confirmed by the legends of almost every nation on the earth. The Chaldeans had their tradition of a flood, from which Xisuthrus and his family were saved in a vessel built by command of the God Belus, and which was stored with provisions and with fowls and four-footed beasts. The Hindoos preserved the tradition of a flood from which were saved Satyavrata, and seven holy men, and their respective wives, together with pairs of all animals, in a capacious vessel miraculously prepared by Vishnu. The Apamean medal shows it to have been preserved in Phrygia. Traces of it are found among the Chinese. The memory of the Deluge is traced in the ancient legends of the Greeks and Scandinavians in Europe; among the Egyptians in Africa; in North America, among the Crees, the Choctaws, and the tribes of the lakes; in Central America, among the Mexicans; in South America, among the primitive tribes of the Orinoco, of Brazil, and of Peru. The legends of the people of Tahiti and the Sandwich Isles prove that it still lingers among the islands scattered over the Pacific (Stanley Faber, *Hor. Mos.* c. IV; Hamilton, *Pent. and its Assailants*, Lect. IX; H. Miller, *Test. of the Rocks*, c. VII; Rawlinson, *Bampt. Lect.* pp. 55—66; Humboldt, *Views of Nature*, p. 147; Prescott, *Hist. of Mexico, Appendix;* Davis, *Chinese*, p. 84; Ellis, *Polynesian Researches*, I. 62). It is found among the legends of the Scandinavians. That must have been an historical event to which the traditions of the human race all over the globe thus give testimony; and the freedom of the Scriptural account from the mythological and legendary details which are found in all these traditions, is a weighty evidence of the inspired nature of that account.

Although traces of the event may not be brought to light by geological investigations, a very late writer of a popular treatise on geology affirms decidedly that it is perfectly consistent with the conclusions of that science. "After all that has been explained of the series of convulsions which terminated the succession of periods in the history of the earth, it will be evident that the Mosaic narrative of the Deluge contains nothing incompatible with that course of events, which may be said without exaggeration to have been of habitual occurrence on our planet" (Lardner, *Pop. Geol.* § 564).

Whether the Deluge was of universal prevalence over the earth, or confined to that immediate area which was occupied by the human race, has been disputed. The universality of it has been warmly argued for by Hamilton, *Pent. and its Assailants*. The late Mr H. Miller, in his *Testimony of the Rocks*, maintains that it was merely local. It is, however, hardly safe to bring the still necessarily imperfect conclusions of Geology to decide imperatively on a subject like this.

ver. 1. THE LORD] The directions which are now given in reference to the beasts go beyond the general care of the Creator for their preservation. He is now providing that His preserved people should be able to offer sacrifice to Him; and the direction to this effect of itself was a promise to man of being permitted again to regard God as the God of grace.

ver. 2. The candid mind will discern no discrepancy between the directions of this chapter regarding the number of animals to be taken into the ark, and those of ch. vi. In ch. vi. when Noah was desired to build the ark, he was told in general that pairs of animals were to be preserved. In this chapter, when the time to enter the ark had arrived, the special direction to preserve of the clean animals seven pairs was given. See Ayre's *Introd. to the O. T.* p. 451. —CLEAN BEAST] i.e. allowed for sacrifice; comp. viii. 20. Many things established afterwards in the Law of Moses, obtained before that Law, and were generally practised by the worshippers of God; e.g. sacrifices, Gen. iv. 3, 4; viii. 20; xiii. 18; paying of tithes, xiv. 20; xxviii. 22; circumcision, xvii. 11; the right of primogeniture, xxv. 33; making vows, xxviii. 20; xxxi. 13; marrying deceased brother's wife, xxxviii 8. And those things which Moses forbade were some of them forbidden before the Law; as the eating of blood, and murder, which was a capital crime before the Law, ix. 4—6. And there is no doubt that the difference of clean and unclean beasts with respect to sacrifices, was known and observed before the Law of Moses and before the Flood (*Kidder*). In the works of Jones of Nayland there is an interesting essay, in which he argues that the classification of certain animals as unclean and unfit for sacrifice was based on the fact, that these animals from their habits and propensities were fit emblems of the vices and passions unpleasing to God.—BY SEVENS] Seven couples (*Knobel, Wright*). Thus of the clean beasts there were enough for sacrifice, enough for food, and enough to maintain the breed (*Patrick*).

ver. 11. SECOND MONTH] of the year; i.e. October. The year began in Tisri, which corresponded to our September.—FOUNTAINS OF THE DEEP...WINDOWS OF HEAVEN] What the *fountains* are to the lower, the *apertures* [windows] are to the upper waters. The first indicate volcanic eruptions, which opened subterranean fountains, and caused the seas to rise; and the second, the atmospheric process connected with these phenomena, and which caused the clouds to discharge a torrent of water (*Raphall*).

ver. 16. THE LORD SHUT HIM IN] Notice the difference in the use of the names of God. "*God* takes care for His creation to preserve it; but when the *Lord* provides, it is only for His true servant who has found favour in His sight" (*v. Gerlach*).

ver. 17. THE FLOOD WAS FORTY DAYS] There is no real discrepancy between this and the statement of ver. 12, that 'the rain was upon the earth forty days.' One place only states generally what the other specifies more exactly. In one place the cause, the descending rain, in the other the effect, the flood, is specified. Comp. Davidson, *Introd. to O. T.* p. 510; Ayre, *Introd.* p. 452.

Chapter VIII.

ver. 1. REMEMBERED] Spoken of God after the manner of men. We are said to remember what we take care of. God is said to remember when He relieves and shows mercy, Heb. vi. 10; Ps. cxxxvi. 23 (*Kidder*). Here the word alludes to Noah's temptations while God still hid Himself from him. "It shows that from the day that Noah entered the ark, no word, no revelation from God, was granted him. He was permitted to behold no ray of the Divine grace, but was confined to the promises he had received; and so while the water raged about him, it was as though God had forgotten him." Luther (*v. Gerlach*).

ver. 3. WERE ABATED] *decreased* (*Kalisch*). There is no discrepancy between this statement and ch. vii. 24. After 'the rain from heaven was restrained,' and 'the fountains of the deep were stopped,' the waters began to abate; but they prevailed or were strong for 150 days; so that it was not till the end of that time that any considerable abatement could be observed (*Ayre*, p. 452). Similarly, *Davidson*, p. 510.

ver. 4. SEVENTH MONTH] i. e. of the year.—ARARAT] A name always in Scripture denoting a *district*, namely a portion of Armenia which lay between the two lakes Van and Urumia; 2 Kin. xix. 37; Isai. xxxvii. 38. In Jer. li. 27, it stands for the whole of Armenia (*Gesenius*). The mountain of Ararat, which is regarded as the resting-place of the ark, is by the Armenians called Massis. Correctly speaking, it consists of two mountains, the Great and the Less Ararat, the summits of which are distant one from the other about seven miles. The Great Ararat is about 17,210 feet, and the Less Ararat about 13,000 feet, above the level of the sea. The mountain lies in the centre of a number of large rivers radiating from it, and which formed the natural channels for the human race to spread itself over the earth.

ver. 7. A RAVEN] to discover if the earth was yet dry. The raven feeds on carrion, see Prov. xxx. 17; if the earth had been dry the smell of the dead carcases would have allured it from the ark (*Patrick*).—WENT FORTH TO AND FRO] Lit.

going and returning; i.e. it often went from the ark, and as often returned. Finding nothing but water, it still betook itself to the ark (*Patrick*).

ver. 10. OTHER SEVEN DAYS] This computation of time by periods of seven days is the strongest of the usual arguments for the observance of the Sabbath prior to the Mosaic Law.

ver. 11. The connexion of the dove with the olive is quite natural. The olive-groves are their favourite resort; there they build their nests and rear their young. The olive-tree, which is an evergreen, and thrives even in water (Plin. *H. N.* XIII. 50; Theophrast. *H. P.* IV. 8), is found in Armenia, not indeed on the heights of Mount Ararat, for even in Syria it does not flourish more than 3000 feet above the sea (Thomson, *Land and the Book*, p. 52), but in the valleys to the south of it. As the dove did not return till the evening, it is intimated in the narrative that she had to make a considerable flight to reach the plains in which the olive-tree appeared when the flood subsided.—PLUCKT OFF] and not found floating, or washed on the mountain by the waves of the flood. This translation is supported by the Targum of Onkelos, the Arabic version of Saadias, and by Knobel and Delitzsch.

The translation of the Latin Vulg. *the fresh leaf of an olive*, is preferred by Gesenius, Davidson, and Kalisch.

ver. 15. GOD] Heb. *Elohim*, who as such is caring for the whole creation, and provides for the multiplication of the living creatures in the world.

ver. 20. AN ALTAR] The first express mention of an altar, though it be supposed in ch. iv. 3, 4 (*Kidder*).—UNTO THE LORD] The name of Jehovah is here suitable, since this act of worship implies the greatest activity of the religious principle, and belongs not to a vanishing but a personal God (*Hengstenberg*).—BURNT-OFFERINGS] The most ancient kind of sacrifice, called *Kalil, whole*, from the *entire* victim being consumed by fire, or *olah, ascension*, from the whole sacrifice *ascending* in flame to the Lord. From Lev. i. 4, 'He shall put his hand on the head of the burnt-offering, and it shall be accepted for him,' it appears that the burnt-offering was of a *propitiatory* as well as of an *eucharistic* nature. For the offerer, by placing his hands on the victim's head, professed to transfer his own sins to the head of the sacrifice, and to look to God to accept that life instead of his own. The signification of the burnt-offering in the case of Noah, was the solemn confession that he and his had been saved, not by reason of their own righteousness, but of God's grace, and that their guilt required expiation before God; the expression of a belief that God will, of His grace, forgive their sin; and the thanksgiving for their preservation founded on this confession and this belief (*v. Gerlach*).

ver. 21. SMELLED A SWEET SAVOUR] i.e. God was pleased with the sacrifice, which showed the humble and contrite spirit of Noah.—SAID IN HIS HEART] resolved in Himself (*Patrick*).—I WILL NOT AGAIN, &c.] The meaning is, that God delights so much more in the offerings of righteousness than in the inflictions of judgment, that He would now direct His providence, so as more effectually to secure the former—would not allow the imaginations of man's evil heart to get such scope as they had done before, but perceiving and remembering their native existence in the heart, would bring such remedial influences to work that the extremity of the past should not again return (Fairbairn, *Typol.* I. p. 293).

Chapter IX.

In reference to the covenant conveyed to Noah, Mr Davison remarks: "It is a charter of natural mercies and blessings, comprehending a second grant to man of dominion over the creatures, and over the earth; the promised multiplication of his species; and the pledge of an orderly succession and return of the seasons; with one specific stipulation added of God's mercy, that He would visit the earth with a deluge no more......Its promises were adapted and with a peculiar fitness to the occasion: for to the relics of the human race newly escaped from the terrors of the great deep, the wreck of the world, and the general extirpation of their kind, what other engagements of the divine favour could there have been more seasonable, or more instructive at this time, than that God had recalled His wrath with the flood, and restored the earth to them again, secured to their peaceful use and dominion?" (Davison, *Discourses on Pro-*

phecy, p. 76). From these remarks it may be inferred how appropriately God is mentioned throughout the chapter, except in v. 26, under the name which represents Him especially as the Great First Cause. Comp. Hævernick, p. 71.

ver. 2. DELIVERED] The words are stronger than ch. i. 26, to which they point, and clearly show that nature generally, and the animals in particular, had become estranged from man. At the first creation man had dominion over the brutes by means of the bond by which he was more nearly united to nature, and by his own spirit which was in closer communion with God: now he ruled through fear and dread (*v. Gerlach*).

ver. 3. MEAT FOR YOU] The grant made originally to man concerning food is now enlarged. Man is now for the first time permitted the use of *animals* for food. "This is the general sense of the Jews, and of the Christian fathers, and of the first reformers" (*Patrick*).

ver. 5. YOUR BLOOD OF YOUR LIVES] A circumlocution for *your blood* (*Rosenmuller, Maurer, Wright*); or, *your blood for your lives*, i.e. to preserve your lives I shall require your blood (*Gesenius, Tuch, Schumann, Knobel*); or, *I shall demand back your blood, for your lives* of which you have been deprived by your murderers, i.e. the murder of a human being shall be avenged by the blood of the murderer (*Kalisch*).—I WILL REQUIRE] i.e. bring to account and punishment. —AT THE HAND OF EVERY BEAST] So that the ox, for instance, which slew a man had to die, Ex. xxi. 28 (*Knobel*).—AT THE HAND OF MAN; AT THE HAND OF EVERY MAN'S BROTHER] The clause, *at the hand of every man's brother*, is added to remind men of the relationship they bore one to the other as members of the one human family, and thus to impress the unnatural and fratricidal character of murder.

ver. 6. BY MAN, &c.] God had kept the punishment of murder in His own hand till now; as we may gather from the story of Cain, whom He banished, but suffered no one to kill him. He here gives authority to judges to call every one to account for it, and to put them to death (*Patrick*). Comp. Hammond, *Pract. Catechism*, Part II. § 5.—IMAGE OF GOD] And so the injury is not only to man, but to God Himself.

ver. 11. MY COVENANT] In the O. T. reference is more than once made to this covenant with Noah; Ps. lxv; Jer. xxxiii. 20, 21, 25; Isai. liv. 9. In the last passage it is taken as an illustration of God's redeeming mercy through Christ. In the vision of Ezekiel, i. 28, and that of S. John, Rev. iv. 3, the rainbow, the token of the covenant with Noah, is used to represent God as ready to deal forth mercy.

ver. 13. I DO SET MY BOW IN THE CLOUDS] There is great difference as to the sense in which these words are to be understood. Some, as Kurtz, Knobel, Delitzsch, Fairbairn, *Typol.* I. 293, think that the passage represents the rainbow to have appeared now for the first time, and accordingly infer that some remarkable change was made in the physical relation of the earth by which the phenomenon of the rainbow was produced; see especially Fairbairn, *as above*, and Kurtz, I. p. 105. But an explanation which necessarily involves hypotheses concerning the physical condition of our globe, which are quite out of the reach of our experience, is to be avoided, if any other natural interpretation which is free from this objection presents itself. Hence we are inclined to prefer that adopted by Waterland, and well expressed by Nachmanides. "After mentioning the bow which he had set in the cloud, He proceeds to say, *that shall be for a sign of the covenant*, as if He had said,

'Henceforth this my bow, which heretofore I have set in the cloud, shall be held and considered a sign of the covenant between me and you.' For whereas every agreement between two parties is called a *covenant*, so any object which, when seen, may recall to their minds the nature and obligation of the covenant, is called *a sign* or *a witness;* comp. ch. xvii. 11; xxxi. 52. Thus the *bow* is the *visible sign* of the covenant established with Noah. Whether the rainbow had been visible ever since the days of creation, or only became visible after the establishing of the covenant, the reason why a token was appointed remains the same" (*Raphall*).

ver. 18. CANAAN] *Low*. The name probably bore reference to the situation of the maritime country colonized by Canaan, which appeared low in comparison with the high table-land east of Jordan. Hengstenberg gives a less probable reason of the name: "Canaan, *the submissive one*. Ham gave this name to his son from the obedience he demanded, but did not himself yield." Ham had other sons, but Canaan only is here mentioned, on account of his being concerned in the prophetic curse soon to be narrated.

ver. 20. PLANTED A VINEYARD] These words

are sometimes taken as if meaning that he was the first to cultivate the vine. But they do not necessarily imply this, any more than the words *began to be an husbandman*, imply that he was the first to till the ground.

ver. 21. WAS DRUNKEN] "By trying to excuse the patriarch in this, some put from them the consolation which the Holy Ghost has deemed it needful to give to the Church, namely, that even the greatest saints may at times stumble and fall." Luther (*v. Gerlach*).

ver. 22. AND HAM...SAW] Ham rejoiced to find a nakedness in him whose reproving earnestness had often been a burden to his sinful soul. Luther remarks: "There is no doubt that Noah must have done much that was offensive to his proud, highminded, and presumptuous son. For this reason we must not regard this deed of Ham's as an action destitute of significance, but as the result of the hatred of Satan, by which he excites his members against the true Church, and especially against those in the ministry" (*Hengstenberg*).

ver. 23. SHEM AND JAPHETH TOOK A GARMENT] Hengstenberg remarks that the Hebrew for *took* is in the singular. He argues from this that Shem was chiefly in the writer's mind, as the first proposer and chief agent in this act of reverence, and that Japheth only joined in readily with the pious deed when it was proposed by Shem. Hence we may account for Shem's holding the chief place in his father's blessing.

ver. 25—27. The series of Messianic predictions which has its commencement in Gen. iii., is here advanced a stage. Jehovah, the God of salvation, is the God of Shem; Shem is the chosen of Jehovah; and from the tents of Shem is to come the promised salvation. Japheth, though not the primary channel of blessing to man, is to have an important part. He is to be received into intimate communion with Shem, and, as God will mightily enlarge him and cause him to spread abroad, he will thus be the means of extending the blessing of Shem. But although evil would, as they saw already from Ham's sin, display itself against Jehovah's people, every enemy of the Lord would be overcome by those who dwelt in communion with Him. Only one of Ham's offspring is singled out to represent the God-hating world, in order to show that it was only Ham's *spiritual children* who were denounced,—those who walked in the ways of Ham. And Canaan is selected, because Noah through the prophetic spirit saw the sinful spirit of Ham concentrated in Canaan beyond his other children, and so foresaw (dimly and partially it may have been) that in time the Lord would relieve the overburdened land of Canaan of its impious inhabitants, and make it the theatre on which He should carry out that series of transactions with which Israel was so closely connected, and which were preparatory to the whole world being redeemed from the power of the evil one, and made the fitting abode of His new and perfected creation.

ver. 25. CURSED BE CANAAN] Why is Canaan cursed and not Ham? Ham is punished in this son because he followed most decidedly the example of his father's impiety and wickedness. To this view we are led: (1) By the whole doctrine of Scripture concerning the visitation of the guilt of the fathers on the children. (2) By Gen. xv. 16, 'In the fourth generation they shall come hither again: for the iniquity of the Amorites is not yet full.' According to this the curse on Canaan can only be realized on him when his own iniquity has been fully matured. (3) By what is reported in Genesis concerning the moral depravity of Sodom and Gomorrah, which in the development of the sinful germ inherent in the race had outrun all others, and were therefore before all others overtaken by punishment. (4) By Levit. xviii. and the parallel passages, where the Canaanites appear as a nation of abominations which the land rejects; and by what ancient writers report regarding the deep corruption of the Phœnicians and Carthaginians (*Hengstenberg*).—A SERVANT OF SERVANTS] i.e. the lowest of servants; thus Eccles. i. 2: 'vanity of vanities.'—TO HIS BRETHREN] In a manner fulfilled in the conquest of Canaan and the possession of the land afterwards by Israel, and by those of Gentile origin who were admitted into the number of the chosen seed, and who thus dwelt in the tents of Shem. But this outward and partial fulfilment, and indeed every instance of the Lord's providential arrangements by which He makes in general virtue even in this life to overcome vice (see Butler, *Anal.* Pt. I. c. iii.), is but introductory to the perfect fulfilment in Christ when the woman's seed shall bruise Satan's head; Heb. ii. 8, 9, 'Now we see not all things put under him, but we see Jesus,' &c. Comp. Rev. ii. 27; iii. 21.

ver. 26. BLESSED BE THE LORD GOD OF SHEM] The manner in which God is here spoken of indicates *indirectly* in what the blessing consists. First, He is called by the name Jehovah, which has reference to His manifested Personality, to His revelations, and to His institutions for salvation. Secondly, Jehovah is called the God of Shem—the first passage in Scripture in which God is called the God of some person. Both these circumstances indicate that God is to enter into quite a peculiar relation to the descendants of Shem, that He will reveal Himself to them, establish His kingdom among them, and make them partakers of His earthly and heavenly blessings. The thought when fully developed is: 'Blessed be God, who will in future reveal Himself as Jehovah and as the God of Shem' (*Hengstenberg*).

ver. 27. GOD SHALL ENLARGE JAPHETH] Thus early was announced that great extension of Japheth by which his race has spread over the north of western Asia and the entire of Europe, and is rapidly occupying the Americas and the islands of the Pacific. We should remark that it is *God*, not *Jehovah*, who is mentioned as the cause of this. It is a work of His Omnipotence, not of

Grace.—AND HE SHALL DWELL IN THE TENTS OF SHEM] *Japheth* shall dwell in the tents of Shem. Though the promised salvation is not to come from the race of Japheth, still he is to partake of it by being admitted into the holy family which was to proceed from Shem; Rom. xi. 17; Gal. iii. 14. "Japheth shall dwell in the (*spiritual*) tents of Shem, i.e. he shall be received into the fellowship of that salvation which is to proceed from the race of Shem" (*Kurtz*).

Chapter X.

ver. 1. THESE ARE THE GENERATIONS] The importance of this register of nations has been especially of late years recognized, on account of the continual fresh proofs of its accuracy which have been afforded by modern investigation and discovery. In many points it has been found to tally exactly with the conclusions which Ethnography has arrived at. In reducing all mankind to three great families, it differs certainly from the classifications of late eminent ethnographers; Blumenbach making five varieties, and Prichard seven. Nor is this strange. For it is, as Kurtz remarks, inconceivable that the three kindred original types should have at once separated into individual races; and the continual efforts on the part of ethnographers to reduce still more the number of varieties show the necessary imperfection of their classifications.

In considering the Table of Nations we must keep in mind, (1) that it brings down the development and spread of nations only to the time of Moses, and (2) that the names in it are not to be taken as applying only to individuals. They chiefly refer to groups of nations, the latter name of a nation being transferred to its ancestor. Thus the names Mizraim, Aram, were first transferred from the country to the nation, and then from the latter to the founder. When the personal name of a founder of a tribe was not preserved by the remembrance of events connected with him, it gradually sank into oblivion, and the name of the nation took the place of that of its founder. Comp. *Kurtz*, I. p. 113.

ver. 2. THE SONS OF JAPHETH] In the mythical traditions of Greece we find all the Grecian races traced up to a common ancestor Japetus.— GOMER] The name is traced in the *Cimmerians* of Homer (*Od.* XI. 14), *Cimmeria* of Æschylus (*Prom. Vinct.* 748—750), and of Herodotus, the *Gimiri* of the Babylonian inscriptions, the *Cimbri* who invaded and overran Europe from the east, the *Cymry*, as the Celtic inhabitants of Wales called themselves, and in the modern names of *Crimea, Cambria, Cumberland, Cambray*. Gomer therefore almost certainly represents the *Cimmerians* who inhabited the tract between the Danube and the Don, and who under the pressure of hostile invasion poured into Europe and spread over most of it. From them originated the Celtic races of Ireland, Scotland, Wales, Isle of Man, Brittany. Dr Prichard (*Eastern Origin of the Celtic Nations*) has put beyond doubt the affinity of the Celtic to the Indo-European language; and Arndt, Rask, and Bunsen, consider the Celtic to have been the earliest of the three great streams from the Indo-European source which peopled Europe from the East. Comp. Wiseman, *Science and Rev. Rel.* I. 54; Winning, *Comp. Phil.* II. c. 4.—MAGOG] generally considered to represent the Scythians, who according to their own legends originally occupied the country between the Wolga and the Don as far as the Caucasus. Knobel, who with Wright derives the name from the Persian *makoh, mountain-land*, thinks that they were thus named from occupying that locality. They spread into Europe, and dispossessing the Cimmerians, occupied the country from the Don to Thrace. They seem to have originated the great Sclavonian family which overspread the north-east of Europe and north of Asia, and which embraces the ancient races of the Sauromatæ or Sarmatæ, of mixed Mede and Scythian origin, the Venedi or Wends, the modern Russians, Poles, Czechs, Servians, Slowaks, Croats, &c. The affinity of the Russians with Magog is confirmed by the notice in Ezek. xxxviii. 2, of Gog of the land of Magog, 'The Prince of Rosh, Meshech and Tubal.' The Indo-European origin of the Sclavonian family is acknowledged. Comp. Knobel, *Erkl.*, Winning, II. c. 1.—MADAI] the Medes, in old Persian called *Mada*, the primitive colonists of Iran, "in which were spoken three distinct but cognate languages, Sanskrit in the north-east, Median in the north-west, and Persian in the south. Of these Iranian dialects, the Sanskrit had no direct communication with Europe, but proceeded into India; the old Median or Zend, and old Persian or Parsi, extended westward, and are the elder sisters of all our European idioms" (Winning, p. 22).—JAVAN] the Ionians, as the Greeks were generally termed by their eastern neighbours; an application of the name arising from the fact, that the Ionians occupied the eastern parts of Greece, and thus were best known to Asiatics.—TUBAL AND MESHECH] mentioned several times by Ezekiel, and always connected together as here; hence inferred to be two nations occupying adjacent territories. Generally identified with the *Tibareni* and *Moschi* of Herodotus, and the *Tuplai* and *Muskai* of the Assyrian inscriptions, who are always found similarly coupled together. "The Moschi adjoined Colchis. In the flourishing period of Assyrian history they were the principal people of northern Syria, Taurus and Cappadocia. In the last place, their name long continued in the appellation of the city *Mazaca*. Driven northward across the Caucasus, they ultimately found a refuge in the steppe country, where they became known as *Muskors*" (Rawlinson, *Her*. Vol. IV. p. 222). Hengstenberg identifies Meshech and the Moschi with the Mashoash of the Egyptian inscriptions. The Muscovites have been recognized as belonging to the Tchud or Finnish race, which was conquered by the Sclavonic Russians (*Id*. I. 652). Mr Rawlinson assumes the Turanian origin of the Tchud family; but Mr Winning, p. 92, asserts its affinity with the Celtic.—TIRAS] from whom came the Thracians and, as Knobel thinks, the Agathyrsi. His opinion is confirmed by statements of Herodotus, who affirms that the customs of the Agathyrsi resembled those of the Thracians, and also speaks of the river *Tyras*, now Dniester, as running through the country of the Agathyrsi. We have here probably the Lithuanian family, which also is of Indo-European descent; comp. Winning, II. c. 2.

ver. 3. The comparison of the cases of Javan, Cush, and Aram, leads to the conclusion, that the three sons of Gomer mentioned in this verse denote three races derived from him in addition to that race, which peculiarly bore his name.— ASHKENAZ] according to Knobel meaning the *race of As*. The name is traced in the *Pontus Axenus*, as the Black Sea originally was called; in the name *Ascanius*, given to a gulf, lake, and river in Bithynia; in *Scandinavia*, the settlement of the Goths; in *Aschan* or *Aschanes*, the legendary name of the first Saxon king. The legends of the Scandinavian and German races testify to their Eastern origin, and the affinity of the Teutonic languages with the Iranian has been long recognized. Ashkenaz of Jer. li. 27 appears to have been a portion of the nation which remained in Asia; possibly the *Bithynians*, whose Indo-European origin is asserted by Mr Rawlinson, *Herod.* I. 676.—RIPHATH] according to Josephus the Paphlagonians, an Indo-European family; Rawlinson, *Her.* Vol. I. p. 676. The name seems to appear in that of the *Ripæan* or Carpathian mountains; hence Knobel regards Riphath to be a Celtish race, who, according to Plutarch, having crossed the Ripæan mountains, separated into two bodies, the one of which marched to the northern extremities of Europe, and the other to Gaul, between the Alps and Pyrenees. This conjecture seems confirmed by the connexion which Mr Winning points out, between the British Celtic and the language of the Finnish or Tchud race who occupied the north of Europe. —TOGARMAH] mentioned in Ezek. xxxviii. 6 in connexion with the Scyths and Cimmerians, and in Ezek. xxvii. 14 as a people rich in horses and mules. This suits the Armenians and Phrygians, who were famous for horses, and are by Josephus represented under Togarmah. The Armenians, who derive themselves from Thorgom, and the Phrygians were, according to ancient authorities, originally the one people who possessed Armenia, and at first the greatest part of Asia Minor (*Knobel*). The Indo-European character of the Phrygians is apparent from the remnants of their language (Rawlinson, *Her.* Vol. I. p. 666). The Armenian is also of the same family.

ver. 4. ELISHAH] hence *Elis* in the Peloponnesus. In Ezek. xxvii. 7 the isles of Elishah are said to produce the purple and scarlet which covered the Tyrians. "We possess the testimony of ancient writers that on the coasts of Peloponnesus the shell-fish, the juice of which yields the much-valued purple, were abundantly found. Phœnician inscriptions at Athens prove an early commercial intercourse between the Greek and Tyrian coasts" (*Kalisch*). Elishah therefore probably denotes the Æolian race, one of the settlements of which was Elis.—TARSHISH] The name is afterwards in Scripture applied to a place represented in Ezek. xxvii. 12 as a great commercial emporium, from which silver, iron, tin, and lead were exported to Tyre; and in Jon. i. 3, Isai. xxiii. as a city at a great distance from Palestine, to be reached only by sea. In these respects it answers to Tartessus in Spain, not far from the modern Cadiz. The present passage would make Tartessus a Greek colony; and this is corroborated by the representation given by Herodotus, I. 163, IV. 152, of the friendly feeling it displayed towards the Phocæans, who were Ionians. Subsequently it fell under the power of the Phœnicians; and thus Isaiah, ch. xxiii. 10, speaks of its being held by the girdle of the

Tyrians. We may identify therefore Tarshish with the *Tyrseni* or *Tyrrheni*, who are found in the earliest times spread over portions of Italy (Tusci, Etrusci), and Spain. The name is traced in *Tar*ragonensis, *Tur*ditania, *Tar*tessus.—KITTIM] the inhabitants of Cyprus, whose chief city was *Citium*. Their Greek origin was asserted by the Cyprians themselves (*Herod.* VII. 90). The island was subdued by the Phœnicians before the age of Solomon. From the use of the name in other parts of the Bible and in the Apocrypha, the Cittim seem to have spread over Macedonia, and portions of Greece and Italy.—DODANIM] According to Knobel, the Dardani belonged to them. Some trace the name in *Dodona*.

ver. 5. ISLES] The Hebrew denotes not merely an island, but also a maritime region (*Wright*). At the conclusion of this enumeration of nations descended from Japheth, we may notice the striking confirmation presented to its accuracy by the results of the investigations in Comparative Philology. It is now proved that the Sanskrit, Median or Zend, and Old Persian, the Celtic, Teutonic, Sclavonian and Lithuanian, the Armenian, the Greek and Latin languages, are all intimately connected.

ver. 6. CUSH] in the O. T. denotes not only African Ethiopia, but also the country on the Arabic side, if not on both sides, of the Persian Gulf. See Numb. xii. 2, compared with Ex. ii. 16, and Hab. iii. 7; 2 Chron. xxi. 16; Ezek. xxix. 10. In strict agreement with this Scriptural representation of the race of Cush as occupying Asia as well as Africa, are the notices of the heathen authors, and the discoveries of Ethnography. Manetho (Rawlins. *Her.* Vol. II. pp. 176, 364) speaks of Ethiopians who came from the Indus and settled in Egypt at the close of the eighteenth dynasty; according to Strabo, the ancient opinion was that the Ethiopians occupied the entire seacoast from the Indus to Abyssinia. The name is preserved in that of the Cossæi of Susiana. Mr Rawlinson informs us "that recent linguistic discovery tends to show that a Cushite race did, in the earliest times, extend along the shores of the southern ocean, from Abyssinia to India. The cities on the northern shores of the Persian Gulf are shown by the brick inscriptions to have belonged to this race. It can be traced by dialect and tradition throughout the whole south coast of the Arabian peninsula; and it still exists in Abyssinia, where the language of the principal tribe, the Galla, furnishes, it is thought, a clue to the cuneiform inscriptions of Susiana and Elymais, which date from a period probably a thousand years before our era" (*Her.* Vol. I. p. 650). —MIZRAIM] A dual form expressing the division of Egypt into Upper and Lower Egypt—*the two Mazors.* On the ancient monuments the name for Egypt is *Chemi*, *Khem*, or *Khemo*, corresponding to the Scriptural expression 'the land of Ham' (Wilkinson, *Her.* Vol. II. p. 146). Knobel rejects this explanation of the dual form on account of the not unfrequent application of the name to Lower Egypt as distinct from Upper Egypt. He derives the word from the root preserved in the Chaldee *mezar, boundary, limit,* and considers the dual to express the position of Egypt, *hemmed in on both sides* by the two ranges of mountains which enclose the valley of the Nile.—PHUT] Libya. The land of the nine bows was a term applied to Libya, which was also called *Phit, the bow* (Sir G. Wilkinson, in Rawl. *Herod.* Vol. II. p. 175).—CANAAN] The Hamite origin of the Canaanites or Phœnicians has been questioned (Winer, *Reallex.* I. p. 244; Bunsen, *Phil. of Univ. Hist.* I. 190, 244), chiefly on account of the affinity of their language to the Hebrew; see Davidson, *Introd.* p. 7. However, history witnesses clearly for the Hamite origin of the Phœnicians. Herod. I. 1; VII. 89; Strabo, I. 42; XVI. 766; Just. XVIII. 3, all testify to the tradition that the Phœnicians migrated into the land of Canaan from the shores of the Persian Gulf, which, as we have seen, were colonised by descendants of Ham. On two islands in the Gulf, whose names are reproduced in the Sidonian colonies of Tyrus and Aradus, there were Phœnician temples, and the inhabitants of them claimed the Phœnicians as their colonies. The mythical tradition of Agenor, king of the Phœnicians, being son of Poseidon and Libya, and brother of Belus, represents Phœnicia to be ethnically connected with Libya, Egypt, and Babylon, all confessedly of Hamite origin. The difficulty arising from the Shemitic character of the language may be removed by the hypothesis of Knobel and Kurtz. On the dispersion of nations the Shemitic families moved up the Euphrates and westward. The family of Aram colonised the country touching Canaan on the north and north-east. It is only natural to suppose that some other Shemitic family moved on with it (*Lud*, according to Knobel), and peopled the land of Canaan with those inhabitants whom we find occupying it before the Canaanites; see Gen. xiv. 5; Deut. ii. 23. The Hamite Canaan, who appears from his place among the sons of Ham to have been the latest of that race to spread abroad, probably did not enter the land until it was occupied by Shemites, and when he did, as the first settlement was Sidon, it appears to have been for the purpose of commerce. The commercial character of the people (evidenced in Gen. xxxiv. 20, 21) makes it not improbable that they settled amongst the primitive Shemite inhabitants as peaceful colonists, and not as a conquering race. If this was so, it was natural for them to adopt the language of the people who received them; and this supposition is made more probable by our finding that Abraham, in like manner, adopted the language of Canaan; for ch. xxxi. 47 proves that his immediate descendants spoke a different dialect from that of his family in Haran. The gradual character of the Phœnician occupation of Canaan is also intimated in the book of Genesis. (a) In this chapter, ver. 18, it is said, and 'afterward were the families of the Canaanites spread abroad.' (b) When Abram entered the land, he wandered about without hindrance. In the next generation, the contention between Isaac and Abimelech shows the pressure of an increasing and encroaching population. (c) Abraham found it necessary to purchase only a place of burial for his family; Jacob had to purchase a place of abode. (d) The change of the names of cities evidences a change of their occupants; e.g. the change from Hebron to Mamre, and again to Kirjath-Arba. It must not be passed over that the hypothesis defended here has against it the authority of Sir H. Rawlinson and the Rev. G. Rawlinson. They make the Hamites to have been the primitive colonists of Canaan; and the Phœnician emigrants from the Persian Gulf they consider to be of Shemitic origin, and also not to have migrated to Canaan until the time of the Judges, when they seized upon the sea-board of Canaan. Comp. *Herod.* Book VII. *Append. Essay* ii.

ver. 7. THE SONS OF CUSH] The localities occupied by these are to be looked for both in Africa and the part of Asia which was occupied by Cush. On referring to vv. 26—29 we find a Sheba and Havilah mentioned among the sons of the Shemitic Joktan, as well as among the sons of Cush. In accordance with this is the remark of

Sir H. Rawlinson, that "ethnologers are now agreed that in Arabia there have been three distinct phases of colonisation; first, the Cushite occupation; secondly, the settlement of the Joktanides [a Shemitic race], and thirdly, the entrance of the Ishmaelites" (Rawlinson, *Herod.* Vol. I. p. 447).
—SEBA] From Isa. xlv. 14' we may infer it to be in Africa, and that hence Josephus was correct in identifying it with Meroë, in the farthest south of Egypt, and the native name of which is Suba (Kitto, *Scripture Lands*, p. 30).—HAVILAH] the *Avalitæ* inhabiting the shore of the Sinus Avalites, now called Zeila, to the south of the straits of Bab-el-Mandeb (*Gesenius*); or *Chaulan* in Arabia Felix.—SABTAH] placed by Josephus near Meroë. Gesenius identifies the name with the Ethiopian city *Sabat* (Strabo, XVI. p. 770), on the shore of the Arabian Gulf, where Arkiko now is.
—RAAMAH] probably *Rhegma*, on the Arabian side of the Persian Gulf.—SABTECHAH] The obvious resemblance of the Ethiopian name *Subatok*, found on the monuments, renders the position in Arabia improbable. The Targum Jonathan seems to identify it with the African district Nigritia or Zanguebar, which is not inappropriate (*Kalisch*).
—SHEBA] *Saba*, the principal city of *Yemen* in

Arabia Felix. The land of Sheba was bordered on the west by the Arabian Gulf, reached in the south to the Indian Ocean, and to the north nearly to the territory of the Idumeans. It yields frankincense and aromatics, with which it supplied Egypt by way of caravan-trade; it has rich copper-mines, which are still worked, and most likely formerly possessed the precious metals also (*Kalisch*). Comp. 1 Kin. x. 10; Jer. vi. 20; Job vi. 19; Ezek. xxxviii. 13; Ps. lxxii. 15; Isa. lx. 6; Ezek. xxvii. 22.—DEDAN] Sufficiently defined by the Biblical allusions both with regard to geographical and social condition. It was a commercial nation of Arabia, which traversed the deserts with their goods, Isa. xxi. 13; their exports consisted especially of ivory and ebony, which they carried to Tyre, Ezek. xxvii. 15. They are sometimes described as immediate neighbours of the Idumeans, Jer. xlix. 8, whose territory is said to have extended between Teman and Dedan, Ezek. xxv. 13; but in other passages they are called the inhabitants of an island, Jer. xxv. 23. It is therefore evident that the tribes of Dedan settled in two different regions; partly on the north-western coast of the Arabian Gulf, and partly nearer the mother-land Raamah, perhaps on the island *Daden* in the Persian Gulf (*Kalisch*).

ver. 8. NIMROD] The name signifies 'we shall rebel' (*Hengstenberg*). Sir H. Rawlinson is of opinion that we have the founder of the Babylonish empire deified in the Babylonian God *Bilu-Nipru, Bel-Nimrod*. He derives *Nipru* from a root signifying *to pursue* or *make flee;* and the name thus derived agrees with the Scriptural description of Nimrod being a mighty hunter (Rawlinson, *Herod.* Vol. I. 594). The Septuagint translator writes the name *Nebrod*, and Josephus *Nebrodes*.

ver. 9. A MIGHTY HUNTER BEFORE THE LORD] He led his wild oppressive life *in defiance of* and *in contempt of* the Lord.

ver. 10. AND THE BEGINNING OF HIS KINGDOM WAS BABEL] The Babylonian empire is here asserted to have been founded by a Cushite or Ethiopian. This statement of Scripture is proved to be in strict accordance with the results of modern investigation. The language of the primitive Babylonians is proved to "belong to that stock of tongues...of which we have probably the purest modern specimens in the *Mahra* of Southern Arabia and the *Galla* of Abyssinia"

(Sir H. Rawlinson, *Herod.* Vol. I. p. 442). And with this agree the early traditions. "Diodorus relates that Belus, the son of Poseidon and Libya, led colonists to Babylon, and that the Chaldeans were descendants of the Egyptians" (Hævernick, p. 127).—BABEL] Babylon; the ruins of which exist near Hillah.—ERECH] Probably *Warka*, on the left bank of the Euphrates, eighty miles south and forty-three east of Babylon.—ACCAD] Which seems to have been named from the race of *Akkad*, as the Babylonians are called in the early inscriptions. Mr Rawlinson identifies it with the *Kinzi-Accad* of the inscriptions (*Bampton Lect.* p. 370). "But the ruins near *Akker-Kuf* to the north of Babel give a probable site for it, and also account for the various readings of *Archad* and *Accur* given by Greek and Syrian translators" (*Kalisch*).—CALNEH] Probably *Nipur*, the modern Niffer. The monumental inscriptions prove that *Warka* (Erech), *Kinzi-Accad* (Accad), *Nipur* (Calneh), and *Mugheir*, were founded by Urukh and Ilgi, the two earliest kings whose names are given on the monuments, and who were of the race of Ham. See *Dissert. on Ancient Babyl. Hist.* in Rawlinson's *Herodot.* Vol. I.—IN THE LAND OF SHINAR] Shinar is not only in this passage, but in Isaiah xi. 11, distinguished from Assyria; it is further different from Mesopotamia, Gen. xiv. 1; but yet it had its defined boundaries, and was governed by kings, Gen. xi. 2, xiv. 1; Zech. v. 11; it is not only in the O. T. clearly used for Babylon, but the Septuagint renders it so in several passages; Dan. i. 2; Zech. v. 11; Isa. xi. 11. Shinar is, therefore, the southern district of Mesopotamia, from the Persian Gulf to the so-called Median Wall, which separated it from Mesopotamia Proper, and which ran from the Tigris, a little north of Sittace, across the plain to the Euphrates; in the west and south-west it extended across the Euphrates to the tracts of Arabia. On the celebrated black obelisk, found in the central palace of Nimroud, there is a passage, according to Rawlinson's reading, which shows the limited extent of Shinar even at the time of that monument, probably the ninth century. The king of Assyria is stated to have first marched down to the land of Shinar, where he founded temples in the cities of "Shinar, of Borsippa, and Ketika," after which he went on "to the land of the Chaldees, occupied their cities, and marched on as far even as the tribes who dwelt on the sea-coast," and he then received, "in the city of Shinar, the tribute of the kings of the Chaldees." It is obvious from these words: 1. That the town of Babylon was not unusually called Shinar; 2. That Shinar comprised, at that time, only the district round that town; 3. That it was in the south bounded by the territory of the Chaldees; 4. That even the latter did not occupy the tracts on the shores of the Persian Gulf; but, 5. That, though the Babylonians and Chaldeans had each their own king, both were sometimes comprised under the name of Chaldees (*Kalisch*).

ver. 11. OUT OF THAT LAND WENT FORTH ASSHUR] In opposition to the translation of the text, it is argued with apparent justice that the mention of the Shemite founder of the kingdom of Asshur is quite out of place in the list of the descendants of Ham. It breaks the order so strictly observed through the whole chapter. Hence the majority of modern authorities adopt the translation of the margin: *out of that land he* [*Nimrod*] *went forth to Assyria*. As this translation is not contradicted, as asserted by Mr Rawlinson, *Bampt. Lect.* p. 69, by the monumental evidence, which merely proves that the kingdom of Babylon existed long before that of Assyria, and that the latter kingdom borrowed its civilization from the former, just as the conquerors of China adopted the civilization of their subjects; so is it supported by the legendary tradition, and apparently by the authority of another passage of Scripture. In Micah v. 6 Assyria *appears* to be called 'the land of Nimrod.' Babylon *might* be meant in this passage; therefore it is not decisive. Hence we may allege in proof the tradition which makes Ninus, the mythical founder of Nineveh, to be the son of the Babylonian Belus (*Herod.* I. 7).—NINEVEH] Its ruins have lately been discovered near Mosul. The very great antiquity of the present portion of the Bible appears in the manner in which these Assyrian cities are spoken of. Nineveh whose importance, though of later date, eclipsed all the other cities in after times, is here passed over with brief notice in order to dwell on the greatness of Resen!—REHOBOTH] Extensive ruins bearing this name are existing at present on the right bank of the Euphrates about three miles and a half S.W. of Mayadin (*Chesney*).—CALAH] by Sir H. Rawlinson considered identical with *Nimroud.*

ver. 12. RESEN] On the map of Western Asia in Mr Rawlinson's Herodotus, Resen is identified with *Asshur.* But this places Resen far to the south of both Nineveh and Calah, instead of between them. In fact, Sir H. Rawlinson's views as to the sites of these Assyrian cities are involved in great difficulties, if we attempt to reconcile them with the Scriptural statements. Mr Layard places *Nimroud* within the circuit of ancient Nineveh. Sir H. Rawlinson removes the site of Nineveh to the ruins, five miles in circuit, at *Nebi Yunas;* while *Nimroud* he identifies with *Calah*. A glance at a map will demonstrate the impossibility of a *great city* existing between two cities at Nebi Yunas and Nimroud. Assuming therefore Nimroud to be within the site of ancient Nineveh, and, in accordance with a former view of Sir H. Rawlinson, Calah to have been on the site of *Holwan*, situated near the Dialah, about 130 miles north-east of Bagdad, we have a site for Resen, corresponding with the statement of Scripture, at *Kalah Sherghat*, thirty miles south of Nimroud, where there are extensive mounds of ruins. See Kitto, *Scripture Lands*, pp. 46—50.

ver. 13. LUDIM] mentioned in Jer. xlvi. 9 and Ezek. xxx. 5 among the confederates of Egypt, and connected with other nations known to be African; hence not to be confounded with the Lydians of Asia Minor, an Indo-European nation.

The name may possibly be traced in that of the river *Laud* in Tingitania, Plin. *H. N.* v. 2; and may therefore denote the dwellers of Mauretania.—ANAMIM] The similarity between this name and *sanemhit, tsanemhit,* the Egyptian name of Northern Egypt, leads Knobel to place this people in the Delta.—LEHABIM] Probably the *Lubim* of 2 Chron. xii. 3, Nahum. iii. 9; a people apparently living to the west of the Delta.—NAPHTUHIM] The people of middle Egypt. In their capital Memphis they worshipped the God *Phthah*, and hence in Coptic would be named *na-phthah,* those (the worshippers) *of Phthah (Knobel).*

ver. 14. PATHRUSIM] the people of Upper Egypt. The meaning of the name in Coptic is *the region of the south (Wright).*—CASLUHIM] The inhabitants of the sandy and parched district lying between the Delta and Palestine. In it was a mount Casius, and the district was called Cassiotis. The name is derived from the Coptic *ghäs* or *cas (a mountain),* and *lokh* or *rokh (to be burnt, parched) (Knobel).* This hypothesis is rejected by Mr Poole in the article *Casluhim,* in Smith's *Dictionary,* on the ground that the country from its nature was unfit to support a tribe. But up to the time of the Crusades a city existed in this region named by Roman geographers Casium. Its site is called Gatieh. And the striking connexion between the name of the Philistine offshoot of the Casluhim, and the name of the fortress Pelusium in the vicinity of Cassiotis, seems to confirm Knobel's conjecture.—PHILISTIM] The Philistines are here said to be descendants of the Casluhim. In the book of Genesis they are represented as dwelling about Gerar, to the south of that portion of Canaan which they possessed afterwards. In the period between Isaac's time and the exodus they seem to have been increased by a second band, who coming forth from the kindred tribe of the Caphtorim, invaded the south of Palestine, and drove out the Avim, who occupied that portion of the land from Gaza, or Azza, to the part afterwards occupied by Benjamin; see Deut. ii. 23; Josh. xiii. 3; xviii. 23. It is to this tribe of Philistines that the name Cherethites, or Cherethim, which seems to connect them with Crete, properly belongs. In the Prophets the Philistines are spoken of as having been removed forth from the power of their enemies in Caphtor, just as the Israelites had been delivered out of Egypt; see Jer. xlvii. 4=Amos ix. 7. The word, according to a derivation from an Ethiopic root, means *strangers* or *emigrants*.—CAPHTORIM] This name is traced, by Sir G. Wilkinson and Mr Poole, in the ancient Egyptian name of *Coptos*, or, as written in hieroglyphics, *Kebt-Hor*. Mr Poole is inclined to place the Caphtorim in the Coptite Nome of Upper Egypt. From their juxtaposition with the Casluhim, and also from the notice of them as a maritime race in Jer. xlvii. 4, we should probably look for their original habitation on the sea-board of the Delta.

ver. 15. SIDON] Heb. *Tsidon*, derived from a word signifying in Hebrew *to fish*. The mention of Sidon, and the omission of Tyre, is another evidence of the great antiquity of this table of nations. Tyre, which was in existence in the time of Joshua, Josh. xix. 29, rose to such splendour as to cast Sidon, the mother-city, quite into the shade; and hence, in later writers, when the two cities are mentioned, they are spoken of as Tyre and Sidon; the daughter-city being placed first. But here Tyre is unnoticed, as either not yet in existence, or of comparative unimportance. —HETH] Heb. *Kheth*, from whom sprung the race in our translation called Hittites. The name Hittite is sometimes used as a name common to all the Canaanitish nations; either because all, except the Sidonians, were derived from Heth, or because he was the progenitor of the most powerful and famous tribe. From Gen. xxiii. it is inferred that they dwelt in the neighbourhood of Hebron in the time of Abraham; and from Numb. xiii. 29, that they occupied the mountain-country of that part of Judah. No distinct mention of them, beyond their regular enumeration in the list of the Canaanitish nations, is found in Joshua and Judges. In 1 Kin. x. 29, the kings of the Hittites are mentioned in connexion with the kings of Syria; and in 2 Kin. vii. 6, the Syrian besiegers of Samaria suppose that they are attacked by 'the kings of the Hittites, and the kings of the Egyptians,' hired by the king of Israel. These notices lead to the conclusion that the Hittites occupied, after the conquest of Canaan by Israel, some of the country beyond Jordan, in the neighbourhood of the Syrians. This is confirmed by the historical notices derived from the Egyptian and Assyrian monuments, which speak of a people under the name of *Khita*, *Shita*, or *Khatta*, as dwelling in the valley of the Orontes. On the Egyptian monuments, the Khita or Shita are placed next to Naharany

(Mesopotamia) in the list of nations conquered by Rameses II. (Wilkinson, *Herod.* Vol. II. 184).

ver. 16. THE JEBUSITE] the inhabitants of Jebus, afterwards Jerusalem.—AMORITE] a name according to the Heb. deriv. signifying *mountaineer*. In Abraham's time they are found in Hebron, Gen. xiv. 13; the spies of the children of Israel speak of 'the Hittites and the Jebusites and the Amorites' who 'dwell in the mountains,' Numb. xiii. 29; Moses speaks of 'the Mount of the Amorites,' as bordered by the wilderness through which the Israelites travelled, Deut. i. 7, 19, 20; some of the nation crossed the Jordan and invaded part of the territory of the Ammonites, Jud. xi. 12—18, from which they and their king Sihon were driven by Moses, Numb. xxi. The name is sometimes used for all the Canaanites in general, Gen. xv. 16; Josh. xxiv. 18; Jud. xi. 23.—GIRGASITE] From Josh. xxiv. 11, it is proved that the Girgasites dwelt on the west of the Jordan; and as they are never mentioned in the list of Canaanite nations after the destruction of Jericho, we may infer that they dwelt in and about that city.

ver. 17. HIVITE] according to the Heb. deriv. signifying *a dweller in villages;* in Jacob's time the Hivites inhabited Shechem; at the time of the Israelitish conquest they possessed the powerful city of Gibeon, Josh. ix. 7, and also occupied the country 'under Hermon in the land of Mizpeh,' Josh. xi. 3; in the time of the Judges they were still in existence, dwelling 'in Mount Lebanon, from Baal-Hermon unto the entering in of Hamath,' Jud. iii. 3.—THE ARKITE] inhabitant of Arca; the ruins of which are found near the modern Arka, which lies a little to the north of Tripolis, not far from the sea-shore. Its fortunes in the times of the Romans, the Crusaders, and the Mohammedans, are detailed by Dr Robinson, who visited it in 1852 (*Bib. Res.* Vol. III. p. 578).—SINITE] Strabo, XVI. 2. § 18, mentions the mountain-fortress of *Sinna* near Libanus; Jerome, *Quæst. Heb. in Gen.* mentions *Sinen* (*Gesenius*).

ver. 18. THE ARVADITE] inhabiting Arvad or Aradus, a Phœnician city built on the island Aradus, opposite the modern Tartus, by Sidonian colonists. The name probably signifies *exile, the place of the exiles* (*Gesenius*).—THE ZEMARITE] whose name is traced in the ancient *Simyra* (Strab. XVI. p. 518) and in the ruins of the city called Sumra, lying at the foot of the western slope of Libanus (*Gesenius*). Dr Thomson states

that he had visited a place named *Zimri* in the far north of Palestine; *Land and Book*, p. 164.
—THE HAMATHITE] Hamath (not to be confounded with Hammath in Naphtali, Josh. xix. 35), signifying, according to its Heb. deriv., *a fortress*, and called by Amos, vi. 2, 'the great,' was a city of great importance on the Orontes, and the capital of a country bordering on Palestine, Josh. xiii. 5. Its king sent tributary gifts to David. It was conquered by Solomon, 2 Chron. viii. 3, but, taking advantage of the intestine troubles of Palestine after his death, it revolted. It combined with Benhadad of Damascus, and the Hittites and Phœnicians, against the Assyrian king Shalmanubar. It was reconquered by Jeroboam II. and annexed to the kingdom of Samaria, 2 Kin. xiv. 28. In the reign of Hezekiah it was conquered by the Assyrians, Isa. x. 9, under Sargon (Rawl. *Her.* Vol. I. p. 473), and some of its inhabitants were transplanted to Samaria, 2 Kin. xvii. 24. The city survived all its calamities, and was known to the Greeks and Romans under the name Epiphania. It exists at the present day under the name Hamah, with a population of 30,000 (Gesen. *Lex.;* Rawlins. *Herod.* Vol. I. *Es.* vii.; Robinson, *Bib. Res.* III. 551).

ver. 19. GERAR] Mr Rowlands found traces of an old city, called *Khirbet el Gerar, the ruins of Gerar,* near the Joorf el Gerar, three hours S.S.E. from Gaza. Comp. Robinson, *Bib. Res.* II. 43; Thomson, *Land and Book,* p. 558.—GAZA] Still existing under the name Ghuzzeh. It is about an hour's distance from the sea-coast, and is the southernmost city of Palestine on its western border. The Canaanites are described as extending from Sidon southward to Gaza, and from Gaza eastward to Sodom, and the other cities of the plain of Jordan.—SODOM, &c.] See note on xix. 28. —LASHA] Its position is most uncertain. Gesenius derives the name so as to make it signify a *cleft* or *fissure.* This would agree with Jerome's view (*Quæst. in Gen.*), that it was *Callirhoe,* on the east of the Dead Sea, famed for its warm springs.

ver. 21. CHILDREN OF EBER] i.e. the Hebrews. *Eber* signifies *beyond,* and the children of Israel were so called by other nations on account of having come from *the country beyond the Euphrates.* In the O.T. the name is used for the Israelites "only by strangers, or by Israelites when speaking of themselves to others, or when they are contrasted with others" (*Gesenius*); an evidence that the name was not assumed by Israel, but conferred by the nations about them. The Septuagint translates the word *Hebrew* in Gen. xiv. 13, *Abraham from the other side.* The common derivation of the name is that which makes it a patronymic from *Eber;* but the children of Israel, though descended from Eber, were but *one* nation of the many which sprang from him, and could not be properly called *all the children of Eber* (*Hengstenb., Kurtz, Gesenius*).—THE BROTHER OF JAPHETH THE ELDER] According to the idiom of the Hebrew this may also mean *the elder brother of Japheth.* But as subsequently we are informed, that 'Shem was one hundred years old, and begat Arphaxad two years after the flood' (xi. 10), it follows that Japheth was the elder; for Noah was five hundred years old when he began to have children, and the deluge took place in the six hundredth year of his age. His eldest son must consequently have been one hundred years old at the time of the deluge; whereas we are expressly informed that Shem did not arrive at that age till two years after the deluge (*Rashi*). The translation of the text is supported by the versions of the Sept. and Symmachus, and by the later critics, Michaelis, Dathe, Delitzsch. The translation, *Shem the elder brother of Japheth*, is supported by Knobel, Kalisch, Wright.

ver. 22. ELAM] The district in the Bible called Elam, and known on maps as Elymais. It is not to be confounded with Persia. It rose early to importance, and in Abraham's time, Gen. xiv. 1, had a king of its own, who appears superior to the king of Shinar or Babylon. Though made subject by the Assyrians and Medes, it retained its distinct existence as a nation. It was the only nation which, far from being subdued by the Parthians, imposed a tribute on them (Strabo XI. 524, cited by Kalisch). Mr Rawlinson, both in his *Herodotus* and the *Dict. of the Bib.*, limits the district to the territory called by Greek geographers Susiana, but by Herodotus Cissia; and as the *Cissians* or *Cossæans* are a Cushite race, this theory obliges him to invent a Cushite invasion of the Shemite Elam. But Susiana or Cissia appears to have been but a portion of the Elymais of Scripture, as "it is historically established that Elymais was often in violent hostilities with Susiana" (*Kalisch*).—ASSHUR] from whom was derived the powerful nation of Assyria, occupying the country chiefly on the eastern side of the Tigris. From vv. 11, 12 we may infer that the Babylonians in the earliest times invaded Assyria and built strongholds there. It is not until about B.C. 1273 that the Assyrian kingdom had its rise (Rawlinson, *Herod.* I. p. 454).—AR-PHAXAD] The name (when spelt in Hebrew it is *Arpach'sad*) is by Ewald derived so as to mean *the stronghold of the Chaldees*, or *Chasdim*. According to Knobel, it signifies *highland of the Chasdim*. He was the progenitor of the Chaldees, and the name is preserved in *Arrhapachitis*, the northern part of Assyria, bordering on Armenia. —LUD] Knobel derives from Lud the Arabic tribe *Laud* or *Lud*, to which he ascribes the Shemitic colonisation of Palestine. This conjecture receives some confirmation from Rosellini's opinion concerning the *Ludim*, a nation represented on the Egyptian monuments. From the manner in which they are represented he has inferred that they dwelt in the neighbourhood of Canaan and Mesopotamia (Hengstenberg, *Egypt.* 198). *Lud* is generally identified with the Lydians of Asia Minor (*Josephus, Gesenius, Kalisch*); but Mr Rawlinson pronounces the Lydians to belong to the Indo-European family.—ARAM] *Highland;* the country of the Syrians, who occupied the upper part of Mesopotamia and extended on to the north-east of Palestine. When used alone, Aram *generally* denotes the western part of Syria about Damascus.

ver. 23. UZ] *The sandy land;* hence *Ausitis* in the north of Arabia Deserta, between Palestine, Idumea and the Euphrates (*Gesenius*).—HUL] Mr Stanley seems inclined to trace a connexion between *Hul* and Lake Huleh, the uppermost lake of the river Jordan (*Sinai and Palestine*, p. 387, note).—GETHER] It, may be identical with the kingdom of Geshur, to which Absalom fled, which is expressly stated to have belonged to Aramæa, and was situated on the banks of the Orontes (*Kalisch*).—MASH] The name is traced in the mountain-chain of *Masius* to the north of Mesopotamia. By some identified with Mysia.

ver. 25. PELEG] *Division.*—FOR IN HIS DAYS WAS THE EARTH DIVIDED] Reference is here made to the dispersion of nations consequent on the attempt to build the tower of Babel. It has been supposed (*Cambridge Essays*, 1858, p. 137) that the *division* here referred to was the cutting of the canals which are found in such numbers between the Tigris and the Euphrates. It would, however, be strange for the sacred writer to interrupt the important and very brief statement contained in this chapter for the purpose of interweaving a notice of so purely local and unimportant an event.—JOKTAN] About three days' journey north of Nedsheran are a province and a town of *Kachtan*, which is the ancient Arabic name for Joktan (*Kalisch*).

ver. 26—29. Of these Arab tribes it is needless to spend time in conjecturing their localities. *Sheba*, of v. 28, denotes probably a Shemitic element in the tribe of the Sabæans; see note on v. 7. The Joktanian *Havilah* is by Gesenius distinguished from the *Cushite*, see note on v. 7, and placed in the region of the *Chaulotæi*, on the shore of the Persian Gulf, where Niebuhr mentions a city and region of *Chawila*.

ver. 30. AND THEIR DWELLING WAS, &c.] Gesenius translates: '*And their dwellings were from Mesha to Sephar, and on to the Arabian mountains.*'—*Mesha* is *Mesene*, a region once of some importance at the head of the Persian Gulf. The ruins of *Sephar*, once the seat of Himyaritic kings and boasting primeval antiquity, are found between the Port of Mirbat and Cape Sadjar (*Kalisch*).—A MOUNT OF THE EAST] The chain of mountains in the middle of Arabia running from the neighbourhood of Mecca and Medina almost to the Persian Gulf (*Gesenius*).

ver. 32. BY THESE WERE THE NATIONS DIVIDED] Bryant (*Ancient Mythology*) considers that the outspreading of the descendants of Noah, which is the subject of this chapter, was quite a different event from the scattering narrated in ch. xi. The first was universal, regulated, orderly, quiet, and progressive; the second local, embracing only a part of mankind, sudden, turbulent, and attended with marks of the divine displeasure. He considers that the first was a formal *migration* of families to the several regions appointed for them by the Almighty; and that the second was a dissipation of others, who would not acquiesce in the Divine Dispensation.

Chapter XI.

ver. 1. OF ONE LANGUAGE, AND OF ONE SPEECH] The original unity of languages is maintained by the most eminent modern ethnographers; see the testimonies of A. von Humboldt, Merian, Klaproth, F. Schlegel, in Wiseman, *Science and Revealed Religion*, Lect. II. Comp. Davidson, *Introd.* p. 9; Delitzsch, pp. 314—320. In his paper on the "Possibility of a Common Origin of Language," in Bunsen's *Phil. of Universal History*, Prof. Max Müller states that "the two following points have been gained by comparative philology: 1. Nothing necessitates the admission of different independent beginnings for the material elements of the Turanian, Semitic, and Arian branches of speech,—nay, it is possible even now to point out radicals, which, under various changes and disguises, have been current in these three branches ever since their first separation. 2. Nothing necessitates the admission of different independent beginnings for the formal elements of the Turanian, Semitic, and Arian branches of speech;...we can perfectly understand how, either through individual influences, or by the wear and tear of grammar in its own continuous working, the different systems of grammar of Asia and Europe may have been produced." Whilst thus Comparative Philology reveals the possibility of a common origin of man, Physiology, on the other hand, by showing the infinite assemblage of causes which may be assigned for producing the varieties of the human race, teaches how the offspring of one parent, Noah, might have divaricated into the variety of widely differing races which the world presents. Comp. Wiseman, *Science and Rev. Rel.* Lect. III; Somerville, *Physical Geog.* ch. XXXIII. pp. 483—487. What the *one original language* was, has been, and is, much questioned. Hævernick, Scholz, and Baumgarten defend the old opinion that it was Hebrew. But the principal argument for this view—viz. the fact that the Scriptural names occurring before the flood are of Hebrew derivation—proves only that the Hebrews preserved in their own language the recollections of primeval persons and facts. A more prevalent opinion among ethnologers is, that the primeval language was of the class called Turanian, of which the modern Chinese is the best type. Comp. Rawlinson, *Herod.* Vol. IV. p. 222, note.

ver. 2. AS THEY JOURNEYED] from the neighbourhood of Mount Ararat. "While all the types of animals and of plants go on decreasing in perfection from the equatorial to the polar regions, in proportion to the temperature, man presents his purest and most perfect type at the very centre of the temperate regions, almost in the middle of the great north-eastern continent, in the regions of Iran, of Armenia, and of the Caucasus; and departing from this geographical centre, in the three grand directions of the lands, the types gradually lose the beauty of their forms in proportion to their distances...Does not this surprising coincidence seem to designate the Caucasian regions as the cradle of man, the original point of departure for the tribes of the earth?" (Guyot, *The Earth and Man*, pp. 137—139).—FROM THE EAST] To come from the region in Armenia, in which the Tigris and Euphrates have their source, to Babylonia, it is necessary to keep along on the east side of the Median mountains, and then to issue at once *from the east* into the plain. Such is now the daily route of caravans going from Tabreez (on the borders of Armenia) to Baghdad. They go south as far as Kermanshah, and then, making an almost right angle, take a western direction to Baghdad (Kitto, *Script. Lands*, p. 5). By this natural explanation, given by a traveller in the country, we are relieved from any necessity of adopting the translations: *in the east* (*Kalisch, Wright*), in their journeying to the country which lay *on the east* (*Knobel, Delitzsch*).—LAND OF SHINAR] Comp. note on ch. x. 10.

ver. 3. BRICK FOR STONE, AND SLIME FOR MORTER] The Babylonian ruins, uncovered in our own days, are found to be composed of *bricks* both sun-dried and kiln-dried. The *slime* is the *bitumen* which is found in great abundance near Babylon. Mr Layard remarks, in reference to the ruins of Birs-Nimroud, that "the cement by which the bricks were united is of so tenacious a quality, that it is almost impossible to detach one from the mass entire."

ver. 4. LET US BUILD US A CITY AND A TOWER] It is difficult to discern the *intention* of the builders of Babel, and the nature of the sin which called down the visitation of God. The common view is that of Josephus, namely, that it was to secure themselves against another flood, and thus to set the vengeance of God at defiance. But no intimation is given of this in the sacred narrative, and *the plain* of Shinar would have been an unlikely place to attempt such a design. Perizonius (*Orig. Babylon.* ch. 10—12) maintains that the tower was meant to be a land-beacon, to prevent the people wandering and being dispersed on that great plain. In a Latin tractate, ascribed to Archbishop Whately, it is maintained that the intention was to institute the worship of the Heaven, and as in the plain there was no mountain, they built this high place, "whose top should be *dedicated* to Heaven." The following explanation, founded on the text, is suggested. We find *two* acts proposed, and *two* reasons assigned for carrying out these acts. It is proposed to build *a city* and *a tower*, and the reasons assigned are *to make them a name*, and *to prevent their being scattered over the earth*. We find also in ch. x. particular mention made of Nimrod as a God-defying tyrant, and of Babel being *the commencement* of his kingdom. We find also the prophet Noah declaring that, though God had ordered men to replenish the earth, Japheth's race was to be absorbed into the community of Shem; and that therefore indirectly the predominance was to be given to Shem. To contravene both these decrees of God, Nimrod commenced the city and the tower. By compelling all to concentrate themselves about his city instead of spreading abroad, he would thus effect that all the families of the earth should dwell within the tents of Ham. *The tower* was built to be the sign of that *name* (= *glory, honour, fame*) of universal sway which the race of Ham sought. The Pyramids of Egypt, the palace of Nebuchadnezzar (Dan. iv. 30), the edifices connected with the names of the Roman Cæsars, prove how natural it was to connect with the *name* of universal sway the striking sign of a gigantic edifice. The city was to be the means of arriving at it; hence the interposition of the Almighty. He saw that unless restrained at once, all the evil imaginations of men's hearts would have the former ill effect, and the earth would be filled with violence and impiety. By the confusion of tongues the race of Ham was broken up into discordant sections; and so, though Nimrod was enabled to extend his kingdom and build his strongholds and invade his Shemitic neighbour (ch. x. 10, 11), the race of Ham was broken up and scattered. That with the design of conquest was associated that of a false worship of the Heaven is not improbable, especially as we find the Hamite nations, even in the earliest stages of their history, immersed in the grossest forms of idolatry. Rom. i. 21—23.—TO HEAVEN] Expressive of great height; Deut. ix. 1 (*Kidder*).— A NAME] *Fame and renown;* comp. Gen. vi. 4; 1 Chron. xvii. 8; 2 Sam. vii. 9 (*Kidder*).—LEST WE BE SCATTERED] While they consult to defeat God's purpose, they do that which was the occasion of bringing it to pass (*Kidder*).

ver. 5. CAME DOWN] God is said to descend when he reveals Himself by word or deed to us who live in the lower world (*Kidder*). Jehovah, not Elohim, is said to come down. "God here came forth in his most essential, personal character" (*Hengstenberg*).— THE CHILDREN OF MEN] See note on ch. vi. 2. This expression, therefore, confirms the view that it was an act of defiance against God on the part of the irreligious descendants of Noah.

ver. 6. IMAGINED TO DO] God sees it necessary to interpose miraculously to check the sinful development of men,'who if left to give effect to their 'sinful imaginations' would have multiplied iniquity as before the flood. There seems an allusion to the promise of ch. viii. 21.

ver. 7. LET US GO DOWN] See note on Gen. i. 26.—AND THERE CONFOUND THEIR LANGUAGE] The differences of languages have been sometimes accounted for by the necessary uniform action of natural causes. But, "as another proof how little the history of languages suggests to the philosophical glossologist the persuasion of a uniform action of the causes of change, I may refer to the conjecture of Dr Prichard, that the varieties of language, produced by the separation of one stock into several, have been greater and greater as we go backwards in history:—that the formation of sister dialects from a common language, (as the Scandinavian, German, Saxon dialects from the Teutonic, or the Gaelic, Erse, and Welsh from the Celtic,) belongs to the first millennium before the Christian era; while the formation of cognate languages of the same family, as the Sanskrit, Latin, Greek and Gothic, must be placed at least two thousand years before that era; and at a still earlier period took place the separation of the great families themselves, the Indo-European, Semitic, and others, in which it is now difficult to trace the features of a common origin...Thus in the earliest stages of man's career, the revolutions of language must have been, even by the evidence of the theoretical history of language itself, of an order altogether different from any which have taken place within the recent history of man" (Whewell, *Indications of the Creator*, p. 164). That the separation of the one original language into many was effected by some violent and sudden force, is the conclusion arrived at by Herder, Turner, Abel-Rémusat, Niebuhr and Balbi; see Wiseman, *Science and Rev. Rel.* Lect. II. p. 106.

ver. 9. BABEL] according to its Hebrew derivation meaning *confusion*. The tower is here represented to have been left unfinished. The ruins of Birs-Nimroud are supposed to present the remains of it. Jewish tradition declares it to have been levelled to the ground miraculously. There is no sufficient evidence to lead us to identify it with any ruins found in Chaldæa.

ver. 10. Here, as in the chronology of the Antediluvian period, differences of numbers occur in the Hebrew text, and in the Septuagint or Alexandrian, and Samaritan versions. The subjoined table of the numbers of the three

IN THE CHRONOLOGY.

		Year of Paternity.	Remainder of Life.	Duration of Life.
Shem	H.	100	500	600
	A.	100	500	600
	S.	100	500	600
Arphaxad	H.	35	403	438
	A.	135	$\binom{400}{^1430}$	$\binom{535}{^1565}$
	S.	135	303	438
Cainan............	H.			
	A.	130	300	460
	S.			
Shelah............	H.	30	403	433
	A.	130	330	460
	S.	130	303	433
Eber	H.	34	430	464
	A.	134	$\binom{270}{^1370}$	$\binom{404}{^1504}$
	S.	134	270	404
Peleg	H.	30	209	239
	A.	130	209	339
	S.	130	109	239
Reu	H.	32	207	239
	A.	132	207	339
	S.	132	107	239
Serug	H.	30	200	230
	A.	130	200	330
	S.	130	100	230
Nahor	H.	29	119	148
	A.	$\binom{179}{^179}$	$\binom{125}{^1129}$	$\binom{304}{^1208}$
	S.	79	69	148
Terah	H.	70	(135)	205
	A.	70	(135)	205
	S.	70	(75)	145

[1] The lower numbers are those of the Codex Alexandrinus.

texts, is taken from Kurtz. H denotes the *Hebrew* text, A the Septuagint, S the Samaritan.

ver. 25. TERAH] In his days idolatry had pervaded even the family of Shem, Josh. xxiv. 2, 'Your fathers dwelt on the other side of the flood in old time, even Terah, the father of Abraham, and the father of Nachor: and *they served other gods.*'

ver. 28. UR OF THE CHALDEES] Now proved to be "at Mugheir, on the right bank of the Euphrates, not very far above its junction with the Shat-el-Hie," says Mr Rawlinson, *Bampt. Lect.* p. 370. I have found no other proof of this than the high antiquity of Mugheir, and the fact of the name *Hur* being supposed to be deciphered on certain commemorative cylinders found there. The objections to this identification are: (1) It places Ur too far south and at an immense distance from Haran. (2) According to it the Chaldees or Chasdim would be represented as occupying the country about the southern portion of the Euphrates at this early period, contrary to the plain intimations of historic documents. For, (*a*) as is admitted by Sir H. Rawlinson (*Herod.* Vol. I. p. 449, note), the name *Kaldai* for the ruling tribes on the lower Euphrates does not occur on the Assyrian inscriptions before the ninth century: they are termed *Akkad*. (*b*) Greek authorities place the original seat of the Chaldees in the mountains of Armenia and the land of the Carduchi, and near the Black sea; Xenoph. *Cyr.* III. 1. 34; *Anab.* IV. 3. 4; VII. 8. 25; Strab. XII. 545, 549. This testimony requires more to overthrow it than the assertion of its being merely 'a Greek fiction,' Rawlinson, *B. L.* p. 370. (*c*) In Isa. xxiii. 13, the Chaldeans are declared to have been brought into Babylon by the Assyrians. (*d*) The late introduction of the Chaldees into Babylon is intimated by the name Chaldee never being applied to the predicted oppressors of Judah before the time of Isaiah. Putting these proofs together, we infer that the Babylonian Empire was originally founded by a Hamite tribe, apparently the Akkad; that the Chaldeans were a Shemitic tribe, connected with Arphaxad, inhabiting either Arrhapachitis, or the country still farther north; that they were introduced into Babylonia about the ninth century before Christ, and at length became the dominant power in that kingdom, the true Chaldean dynasty seeming to commence with Nabopolassar, B. C. 750. Hence

Ur of the Chaldees is to be sought for in Arrhapachitis, or even farther to the north. Its form (compare *Galilee of the Gentiles*) leads us to regard it not as a city but as a region; and this is the view adopted by the Septuagint translators, who translate it *the country of the Chaldees;* and with this agrees Ewald, who takes *Ur=place of residence.* Bertheau derives *Ur* from the Zend root *vare=country*. According to Knobel it means *mountain of the Chaldees*.

ver. 29. SARAI] The daughter of Abram's father, but not of his mother; ch. xx. 12.

ver. 31. AND THEY WENT FORTH WITH THEM] i.e. others of the same race or family joined with Terah's family in their emigration (*Saadias, Michaelis, Schumann, Tuch, Delitzsch, Wright*). But Knobel and Kalisch insist on translating: *they went with each other.*—HARAN] *Carræ* of the classical writers, in the north-west of Mesopotamia, a day's journey from Edessa (*Knobel*).

ver. 32. AND THE DAYS OF TERAH WERE TWO HUNDRED AND FIVE YEARS] As he died before (Acts vii. 4) Abram, at the age of seventy-five years (ch. xii. 4), left Haran, on the supposition that Abram was his eldest son, born to him when he was aged seventy, he could not have been more than 145 years old. It is not, however, necessary to suppose that Abram was the eldest son because in v. 26 he is the first mentioned; comp. 1 Chron. i. 28. We may, therefore, adopt Ussher's opinion, that Abram was not born until sixty years after the birth of Terah's eldest son. Comp. Lee, *Inspiration of Holy Script.* p. 531, ed. 2; Ayre, *Introd. to O. T.* p. 452.

Chapter XII.

ver. 1. LORD] Abram is chosen from the family of Shem, as the father of that family to whom God was to reveal Himself. "God comes forth from His generality, lays aside His Elohim nature, to come into relation to man, before man can come into relation with Him" (*Hengstenberg*). —HAD SAID] when Abram was in Ur, which he left in obedience to the Lord, Acts vii. 2—4; Nch. ix. 7.— GET THEE OUT OF THY COUNTRY, AND FROM THY KINDRED] That the special thing here demanded is only the result of the general duty of renunciation and self-denial, appears from the circumstance that the promise was renewed at a subsequent period, when, with a willing heart, he had offered up his son Isaac as a spiritual sacrifice to his God (Hengstenberg, *Christol.* I. p. 37). We may observe, that on each occasion on which the promise was renewed to Abram, some act of self-renunciation and self-denial on his part had been mentioned immediately before: we may then regard each renewal of the promise as a reward to him from God, and an encouragement for the future.—WHICH I WILL SHEW THEE] At first it was hidden from Abram whither he was to go; Heb. xi. 8, 'By *faith* Abraham, when he was called to go out into a place which he should after receive for an inheritance, obeyed; and he went out, *not knowing whither he went.*'

ver. 2. I WILL MAKE OF THEE A GREAT NATION] This is often taken by commentators as relating to the nation of Israel, and as fulfilled in the greatness of that nation. S. Paul certainly understood it differently, and as meant of those who being 'baptized into Christ' should 'put on Christ,' and thus being 'Christ's,' should become 'Abraham's seed' (Gal. iii. 27—29). In Rom. iv. 16, 17, he thus appeals to the passage, Gen. xvii. 4, which is parallel to this: 'To the end the promise might be sure to all the seed, *not to that only which is of the law,* but to that also which is of the faith of Abraham; who is *the father of us all, as it is written, I have made thee a father of many nations,*—AND MAKE THY NAME GREAT] Thus Abram by the obedience of faith obtained the promise of that honour, which the builders of Babel attempted in vain to obtain by defiance of God.

ver. 3. AND I WILL BLESS THEM, &c.] Abram is here not viewed as an individual, but as the representative of the chosen race, and as the medium by which the great salvation was to be developed. Hence those who cursed him were not his personal enemies, but those who opposed the Divine plan; in Abram and his seed they hated not the person, but the calling, and the place which God had assigned to it in reference to other nations. The whole history of Israel shows the literal fulfilment of the curse. One after the other, the Egyptians, the Amalekites, the Edomites, the Moabites, the Ammonites, the Syrians, the Assyrians, the Chaldeans, the Persians, the Greeks, and the Romans, have fallen under this curse (*Kurtz*).—AND IN THEE SHALL ALL FAMILIES OF THE EARTH BE BLESSED] Repeated afterwards to Abram twice, ch. xviii. 18; xxii. 18; to Isaac, xxvi. 4; to Jacob, xxviii. 14. Referred to, Ps. xxii. 27, lxxii. 17; Zech. xiv. 16, 17. Explained by S. Paul as meant of Christ, Gal. iii. 14—16.

ver. 5. THE SOULS THAT THEY HAD GOTTEN] The slaves whom they had become possessed of.

ver. 6. THE PLACE OF SICHEM] "From the hills through which the main route of Palestine must always have run, the traveller descends into a wide plain; the wildest and the most beautiful of the plains of the Ephraimite mountains; one mass of corn, unbroken by boundary or hedge; from the midst of which start up olive-trees, themselves unenclosed as the fields in which they stand. Its western side is bounded by the abutments of two mountain-ranges, running from west to east. These ranges are Gerizim and Ebal; and up the opening between them, not seen from the plain, lies the modern town of ¦Nablous,— 'Nablous' being the corruption of 'Neapolis,' the 'New Town,' founded by Vespasian after the ruin of the older Shechem, which probably lay further eastward, and therefore nearer to the opening of the valley. A valley, green with grass, gray with olives, gardens sloping down on each side, fresh springs rushing down in all directions; at the end, a white town embosomed in all this verdure, lodged between the two high mountains which extend on each side of the valley—that on the south, Gerizim, that on the north, Ebal—this is the aspect of Nablous, the most beautiful, perhaps it might be said, the only very beautiful, spot in central Palestine" (Stanley, *Sinai and Pal.* p. 231). Dr Robinson also gives a glowing description of the beauty and richness of this the first abode of Abram in Canaan; *Bib. Res.* II. p. 302. It is here called only the *place of Sichem*, whence we infer that the city was not yet built. The importance which Sichem held in the minds of Abram's descendants, on account of its being the first place where he settled and worshipped the Lord in the midst of the idolatrous inhabitants, is evident from their history. Here Jacob purified his family before he went to fulfil his vow at Bethel, ch. xxxv. 4, and perhaps it was under the very oak under whose shade Abram worshipped, that he deposited the idols and amulets of his family. Here, at the oak, Joshua assembled Israel to pledge them against idolatry; Josh. xxiv. 1, 26, 27. Here Abimelech was crowned; Jud. ix. 6. Here Rehoboam assembled Israel to accept him as their king; 1 Kin. xii. 1.—THE PLAIN OF MOREH] Rather, *the oak* of Moreh.—THE CANAANITE WAS THEN IN THE LAND] The pre-occupation of the promised land by the Canaanite is mentioned apparently for the purpose of pointing out the great trial of Abram's faith, in being called to resign his own country for the promise of another which he beheld occupied by strangers.

ver. 7. TO THY SEED WILL I GIVE THIS LAND]

A promise repeated to Abram on two other occasions, ch. xiii. 15; xv. 18. The possession of the land of Canaan by Israel was certainly a fulfilment of it, Deut. i. 8; Josh. xxi. 43; but the reference made to this promise by S. Paul, Rom. iv. 13, proves that we are to look for the perfect fulfilment of it to the time when the new heavens and new earth shall appear, and the inheritance of the saints in light will not be limited to the bounds of Canaan; consider in connexion with this, Heb. xi. 13—16.

ver. 8. BETHEL] Thus named by Jacob, ch. xxviii. 19; called by the Canaanite inhabitants *Luz;* captured by the Ephraimites, who restored to it the patriarchal name of Bethel; famous in after times as one of the sites of Jeroboam's calf-worship. It has lately been discovered by Dr Robinson under the modern name *Beitin*, the site of which agrees with the position assigned by Jerome and Eusebius to Bethel, viz. twelve Roman miles from Jerusalem, on the east of the road leading to Sichem.—HAI] or *Ai*, captured by Joshua, Josh. viii. Dr Robinson considers that he discovered it in some ruins, one hour's distance from Bethel, and to the south of Deir Duwân; *Bib. Res.* I. 575.

ver. 10. AND THERE WAS A FAMINE] A new trial awaits Abram. The country assigned to him in place of that which he had surrendered is visited by famine. To avoid the impending danger, without waiting for direction he leaves the land of Canaan, and journeys into fertile Egypt. Thus he escapes indeed the trial which God had prepared for him, but he rushes into an ordeal much more trying and severe (*Kurtz*).—EGYPT] Enriched by the periodical overflowing of the Nile, this country was often the resort of neighbouring nations in a time of famine.

ver. 12—13. With regard to the deception practised by Abram, see some valuable remarks in Hengstenberg's Essay, *The Unholiness of Sacred Persons*, in *Genuineness of the Pentateuch*, Vol. II. p. 432. The Jewish Rabbis, some of the Christian Fathers, e. g. Chrysostom and Augustine, and even later Christian writers, e. g. Luther, and still later, Waterland, *Works*, IV. 186, have tried to justify Abram's conduct in this instance. But in doing so they not only lower the standard of morality, but they also by their treatment of the passage, cast away the teaching which it was meant to convey. "Here is a man, not picked out as a model of excellence; not invested with some rare qualities of heart and intellect; one apt to fear; apt to lie; certain to fear, certain to lie, if once he began to speculate according to his own sagacity on the best way of preserving himself.... What he is apart from his Teacher, we see in his journey to Egypt; a very poor paltry earth-worm indeed; one not to be despised by us, because we are earth-worms also; but assuredly worthy of no reverence for any qualities which were his by birth, or which became his merely in virtue of his call. What he was when he was walking in the light, when *that* transfigured him from an earthworm into a man, his after story will help us to understand" (Maurice, *Patriarchs and Lawgivers*, p. 84).

ver. 15. PHARAOH] Rosellini, Lepsius, and Sir G. Wilkinson suppose that Pharaoh is the ancient Egyptian word *Ph-rah,* i.e. *the sun,* used to express the royal dignity; but Gesenius defends the derivation given by Josephus, *Antiq.* 8. 6. § 2, from the Coptic *ouro,* or with the masculine article *pouro, the king.* In the present uncertainty of Egyptian history and chronology, it is impossible to fix with any approach to accuracy the period in Egyptian history corresponding to the time of Abram's visit. From the circumstance mentioned regarding *horses* in the note on v. 16, and from the reception which the shepherd Abram met at the Egyptian court, it is most probable that it took place in the reign of one of the Hycsos or shepherd-kings.

ver. 16. AND HE HAD SHEEP, &c.] On the ancient Egyptian monuments are found represented all the animals mentioned here with the exception of the camel, no representation of which has been found, excepting one of late time. (Sir G. Wilkinson, Rawlinson's *Herod.* Vol. IV. p. 77.) The camel could properly have been of little service to an agricultural people like the Egyptians. It is of use especially to Arabs and nomadic races. The fact, then, of this Pharaoh possessing camels leads to the suspicion that he was of that shepherd or nomad race who held Egypt in subjection before the 18th dynasty. This suspicion is in a measure corroborated by the *omission* of *horses* among the presents made to Abram. Famous as Egypt was from the time of the Exodus for horses, see Deut. xvii. 16, it is now generally concluded that the horse was unknown to Egypt before the 18th dynasty, i.e. that which succeeded the Hycsos or shepherd-kings. See Rawlinson's *Herod.* Vol. II. pp. 178, 354.

ver. 17. AND THE LORD PLAGUED PHARAOH] The main design of the narrative is to manifest God's watchful care of his chosen servant, how he delivered him from a perplexity that was humanly inextricable, in which he had been involved by his own fault; how while Abram by his carnal policy did his utmost to make the promise of no effect, Jehovah took care that the chastity of the mother of the chosen race should be preserved inviolate; how the most powerful monarch of the day was made to bow before the defenceless Abram, and render back his prey (*Hengstenberg*).

Chapter XIII.

ver. 1. THE SOUTH] The southern part of Canaan; this part of the land is called the south, Josh. x. 40 (*Kidder*).

ver. 3. ON HIS JOURNEYS] Lit. *by stations* (*Gesenius*).—AT THE BEGINNING] "The tent and altar were not strictly speaking at Bethel, but 'in the mountain east of Bethel, having Bethel on the west, and Ai on the east.' This is a precision the more to be noticed, because it makes the whole difference in the truth and vividness of the remarkable scene which follows. Immediately east of the low grey hills, on which the Canaanitish Luz, and the Jewish Bethel afterwards stood, rises —as the highest of a succession of eminences, each now marked by some vestige of ancient edifices—a conspicuous hill, its topmost summit resting, as it were, on the rocky slopes below, and distinguished from them by the olive-grove which clusters over its broad surface above. From this height, thus offering a natural base for the patriarchal altar, and a fitting shade for the patriarchal tent, Abraham and Lot must be conceived as taking the wide survey of the country 'on the right hand and on the left,' such as can be enjoyed from no other point in the neighbourhood" (Stanley, *Sin. and Pal.* p. 215).

ver. 6. THE LAND WAS NOT ABLE TO BEAR THEM] As it was already inhabited by the Canaanite and Perizzite, there was not room in it for both Abram and Lot.

ver. 7. CANAANITE AND PERIZZITE] This notice is thrown in to account for the land not affording room to both Abram and Lot. The Perizzites—the word means *inhabitants of unwalled towns or villages*—were the Canaanite inhabitants of the open flat country who were devoted to husbandry, as distinguished from the other Canaanites, who probably were devoted to commerce (*Hengstenberg, Kurtz*).

ver. 10. ALL THE PLAIN OF JORDAN ... AS THOU COMEST UNTO ZOAR] The two clauses are to be thus connected; the intermediate words are a parenthetic description of the country.—IT WAS WELL WATERED EVERY WHERE] "No crust of salt, no volcanic convulsions had as yet blasted its verdure." "Then, as now, it must have received in some form or other the fresh streams of the Jordan, of the Arnon, of Engedi, of Callirrhoe; and at the southern end, as Dr Robinson has observed, more living brooks than are to be found in all the rest of Palestine" (Stanley, *Sin. and Pal.* pp. 216, 285.)—AS THE GARDEN OF THE LORD] The garden of Eden. The beauty and richness of the country induces Lot to make it his abode, notwithstanding the notorious wickedness of the people. His selection of it brings on him many evils: (1) 'In seeing and hearing he vexed his righteous soul from day to day with their unlawful deeds,' 2 Pet. ii. 8; (2) he is taken captive when the land is overrun by the four kings, ch. xiv.; (3) he barely escapes with life from the destruction brought on the land by its wickedness, and sees all his family perish in it but two daughters, ch. xix.; (4) he is betrayed into incest by these two daughters, who were contaminated by the sensuality of their associates.

ver. 13. BEFORE THE LORD] The phrase denotes the open and avowed manner of their sinning. Comp. ch. x. 9.

ver. 14. LIFT UP THINE EYES] "Those bleak hills were indeed to be the site of cities whose names would be held in honour after the very ruins of the seats of a corrupt civilisation in the garden of Jordan had been swept away; that dreary view, unfolded then in its primeval desolation before the eyes of the now solitary Patriarch, would be indeed peopled with a mighty nation through many generations" (Stanley, *Sin. and Pal.* p. 217).

ver. 15. FOR EVER] The land of Canaan is the pledge and type of the new world, which the faithful, who are the children of Abraham, shall receive for an everlasting possession; and therefore did his seed after the flesh possess it, in order to make ready for the kingdom of God on the whole earth; comp. Rom. iv. 13 (*v. Gerlach*).

ver. 18. IN THE PLAIN OF MAMRE] Rather, *by the oaks of Mamre*. At one hour's distance from Hebron, a little off the road to Jerusalem, Dr Robinson came upon some remains of great antiquity, called by the natives Râmet el-Khulil, which he conjectures to mark the position of Abram's abode *by the oaks of Mamre* (*Bib. Res.* I. 215). Both he and Mr Stanley notice a magnificent oak of great antiquity close to Hebron. —HEBRON] "The earliest seat of civilised life, not only of Judah, but of Palestine. Its very name indicates 'community' or 'society'" (Stanley, *Sin.*

and Pal. p. 162). It was built (Numb. xiii. 22) 'seven years before Zoan in Egypt.' From Mamre, a contemporary of Abram, it derived the name *Mamre* (Gen. xxiii. 19), which was again exchanged for *Kirjath-arba, the city of Arba,* who was the progenitor of a race of giants; Josh. xiv. 15. Its earliest name, Hebron, so intimately connected with the history of the Father of the nation, was restored to it by the Israelites on their conquest of Canaan, according to their custom in similar cases.

CHAPTER XIV.

TUCH, in an elaborate article, translated in the *Journal of Sacred Literature*, Vol. I., contends that this expedition of the four kings was with the particular political object of securing the commercial route to the Gulf of Akaba.

ver. 1. AMRAPHEL] derived by Von Bohlen from the Sanscrit *amarapâla = worshipper of the Gods.—*SHINAR] Babylonia; see note on ch. x. 10.—ARIOCH] According to Von Bohlen is the Sanscrit *âryaka=venerable.—*ELLASAR] According to Knobel, *Artemita*, to the north of Babylonia; according to Sir H. Rawlinson, *Senkereh*, on the east bank of the Euphrates, between Mugheir and Warka, which on the inscriptions is named *Larsa*. —NATIONS] Heb. *Goim*, by Aquila translated *Pontus*, by Symmachus, *the Scythians.—*CHEDORLAOMER] Among the names of the earliest kings of Babylon recorded in the inscriptions, Sir H. Rawlinson found that of *Kudur-mapula*, with the additional title of *Apda-Martu*, which he interprets *ravager of the west*. He has thrown out the conjecture of the identity of Chedorlaomer of the Bible with this Kudur-mapula of the inscriptions. However, not only is Chedorlaomer called here king of *Elam*, but he is also distinguished from the king of Babylon or Shinar, and thus the hypothesis is overthrown that he was a king of Elam, who ruled by conquest over Babylon. But still the discovery of a Babylonian monarch bearing the significant title of 'ravager of the west' is of great service in corroborating the Scripture narrative, as it proves that even in those early times predatory expeditions were made by the trans-Euphratian nations into the regions on their west.

ver. 3. VALE OF SIDDIM, WHICH IS THE SALT SEA] The vale of Siddim, at the destruction of the cities of the plain, became the southernmost portion of the present Dead Sea.—VALE OF SIDDIM] Lit. *the vale of the fields* (Aquila, Onk., Saadias), *of the plains* (Knobel), *of the low stony ground* (Gesenius, Wright, Kalisch).

ver. 4—8. A parenthetic explanation of the fact mentioned in v. 3, that all these kings met in battle in the vale of Siddim.

ver. 5. REPHAIMS] translated by the Septuagint, *giants*. It appears to denote a race of tall stature, who occupied Canaan previously to its colonisation by the Canaanites. Og, King of Bashan, on the far side of Jordan, was of this race; and the *valley of Rephaim* near to Jerusalem, Josh. xv. 8, xviii. 16 (in the E. V. it is *the valley of the giants*), and *the country of the Rephaims* or giants in the lot of Ephraim, Josh. xvii. 15, afford proof that they were spread over the country to the west of Jordan. From 2 Sam. xxi. 15—22, we may plausibly conclude that they occupied the country also which the Philistines possessed after them.—ASHTEROTH KARNAIM] i.e. 'Ashteroth between the two mountains;' *Karnaim* signifies two horns or high places (*Kidder*); or ' Ashteroth (*Astarte*) with the two horns,' on account of this Goddess being worshipped there; now *Tel Asherah*, five miles north by west from Mezarcib on the eastern side of Jordan (Kitto, *Script. Lands*, p. 212).—ZUZIMS] The name signifies *the prominent*. We gather from the position assigned to them here that they were a giant tribe inhabiting the district between the Jabbok and the Arnon. They are, therefore, the same as the race of giants whom the Ammonites, who expelled them, called the Zamzummim; Deut. ii. 20; Jud. xi. 13; Josh.

xii. 2 (*Kurtz*).—HAM] Nothing is known of it.—
—THE EMIMS] The name signifies *the terrible*
(*Kurtz*); they dwelt between the Arnon and the
Sared. They were expelled afterwards by the
Moabites; Deut. ii. 9—11.—SHAVEH] Lit. *the plain
of Kiriathaim.*—KIRIATHAIM] *The double city*,
a town of Moab on the east of Jordan, afterwards
in the possession of Reuben.

ver. 6. HORITES] The name signifies *dwellers
in caves, Troglodytes.* They were descended from
the Canaanite Heth, and were driven from Mount
Seir by Esau; Deut. ii. 12.—MOUNT SEIR] A mountainous tract extending from the Dead Sea to
the northern end of the Gulf of Elath on the Red
Sea. It seems to have derived its name *Seir,
rugged*, from the nature of the country.—EL-
PARAN] Rather, *the oak of Paran.* The whole
desert region south of Palestine was designated
as the wilderness of Paran, extending down to
the mountainous regions of Sinai (Kitto, *Script.
Lands*, p. 74). Tuch considers *El-Paran* to be
Elath on the Red Sea, which seems to have derived its name from the palm *trees*, groves of
which are still found there (Stanley, *Sin. and Pal.*
p. 82). His view of the march of the kings receives
some confirmation from its being along the route

by which the Israelites (travelling in the opposite direction) passed from Kadesh through Elath to Moab. Mr Stanley remarks against Tuch's supposition of the identity of El-Paran and Elath, that the word *midbar* (*wilderness*) is used in connexion with El-Paran instead of *arabah*.

ver. 7. EN-MISHPAT] Lit. *The fountain of judgment;* comp. Numb. xx. 12.—KADESH] placed by Dr Robinson at *Ain el Weibeh*, two good days' journey to the north of Mount Hor, on the border of Edom (*Bib. Res.* Vol. II. pp. 174, 194). But see against this view, Stanley, *Sin. and Pal.* p. 92. Placed with greater probability by Mr Rowlands at *Ain Kades*, twelve miles to the east-south-east of Moilahhi (Kitto, *Script. Lands*, p. 81).—THE COUNTRY OF THE AMALEKITES] The country afterwards occupied by the Amalekites, the powerful tribe descended from Esau (ch. xxxvi. 12).—HAZEZON-TAMAR] Lit. *the falling of the palm*, afterwards called Engedi, *spring of wild goats*, a city of Judah near the Dead Sea; 2 Chron. xx. 2. The ruins of it close to the fountain '*Ain Jidy* were discovered by Scetzen, and visited by Dr Robinson. They were found about midway on the western coast of the Dead Sea. Robinson, *Bib. Res.* I. 504—509; Stanley, *Sin. and Pal.* p. 293.

ver. 10. SLIMEPITS] *wells of bitumen;* the Heb. word for slime is that used in describing the building of the walls of Babel, ch. xi. 3, which are known to have been cemented with bitumen. An account of the working of bitumen-wells sunk from remote ages near Ijon is given by Dr Robinson, *Bib. Res.* III. 379, and by Mr Thomson, *The Land and the Book*, p. 223. It is true that bitumen-wells are no longer to be found in the vicinity of the Dead Sea; but there is every reason to believe that the vale of Siddim in which they existed was submerged at the time of the catastrophe of the cities of the plain, and that it now forms the southern portion of the Lake. The fact of bitumen being found only in this portion of the lake renders this supposition still more probable, and agrees with the mention in the text of bitumen-wells. Mr Stanley, *Sin. and Pal.* p. 287, thinks that *quicksands* are meant, which might then, as now, abound at the northern and southern extremities of the Lake.

ver. 13. THE HEBREW] See note on ch. x. 21.

ver. 14. HE ARMED HIS TRAINED SERVANTS] Better translated, *he led forth his tried,* or *experienced,* or *faithful men* (*Gesen., Knob., Kalisch, Wright, Delitzsch*).—DAN] Situated near the source of the Jordan, at Tell-el-Kâdy, seven miles distant from Banias, the ancient Paneas, with which it is not to be confounded. Robinson, *Bib. Res.* III. 392. "It may be necessary to notice the position advanced by Hævernick (*Pentateuch*, p. 148), that 'Dan,' the Danite settlement and the northern boundary, was different from 'Dan' in Gen. xiv. 14, and was situated not in the sources of Jordan, but in the plain of Cœle-Syria. The only argument in favour of this position is the mention, in Jud. xviii. 28, of Beth-Rehob, which, in Num. xiii. 21, appears on the way to Hamath. But this (in the total uncertainty of the site of Rehob) can hardly stand against the precise identification of the northern Dan with the sources of the Jordan, in Josephus, *Ant.* VIII. 8. 4, its connexion with Bashan, in Deut. xxxiii. 22, and the use of the word 'Emek' for valley, in Jud. xviii. 28, instead of 'Bikah,' the word uniformly applied to the district of Cœle-Syria" (Stanley, *Sin. and Pal.* p. 396). We are, therefore, left to suppose that Dan, having lost its name for Laish under its Phœnician possessors, had its primitive name restored to it by its Danite conquerors in remembrance of the achievement of their ancestor

Abram. Compare the changes of the names of Hebron and Bethel. As regards the direction taken by Abram in the pursuit of the kings, Hævernick observes: "He pursues the kings as far as the sources of the river Jordan, and drives them back thence into the district of Damascus (a military road went from Paneas to Damascus, Joseph. *Bell. Jud.* III. 18); precisely as in the contrary case, the Damascene king Benhadad immediately took possession of this territory, 1 Kin. xv. 20."

ver. 15. HOBAH] At the distance of two miles [to the north] outside the walls of Damascus is the village of Hobah, said to be that to which Abram pursued the kings (Stanley, *Sin. and Pal.* p. 408).—THE LEFT HAND] Both the Chaldee paraphrasts say, *north of Damascus*, and that rightly; for the East is counted the foremost part of the world, and the West [called in Heb. *the sea*] the hindermost, and the South is called the right side, opposed to the north, Isa. ix. 12 (*Ainsworth*).

ver. 17—20. On his return, the king of Sodom went to meet Abram as far as the *king's valley*, to the north of Salem, where the roads leading from Hebron and Sodom to Jerusalem met. Melchizedec, king of Salem, and a priest of the most High God, also came to salute the victor.

ver. 17. THE VALLEY OF SHAVEH, WHICH IS THE KING'S DALE] In 2 Sam. xviii. 18, we read that Absalom erected 'for himself a pillar, which is in the king's dale.' It is not likely that he would have erected this memorial of himself out of his own tribe, and away from the immediate vicinity of the capital. Hence it is probable that the king's dale and the valley of Jehoshaphat, traversed by the brook Kidron, were the same. Although there is no historical ground for connecting this valley of Kidron with the valley of Shaveh, the former answers in all respects to what is said in Genesis of the latter valley. The valley of Jehoshaphat compasses Jerusalem on the north and east, and then is continued in the modern Wady-en-Nâr, which leads to the Dead Sea, and would be the natural route for the king of Sodom to traverse when proceeding to meet Abram in his march southwards to Hebron. In the near vicinity of Jerusalem (Salem) we find a part of the valley in like manner corresponding to the details of the history. "Before reaching the city, and also opposite its northern part, the valley spreads out into a basin of some breadth, which is tilled, and contains plantations of olive and other fruit-trees. In this part it is crossed obliquely by a road leading from the north-east corner of Jerusalem" (Robinson, *Bib. Res.* I. 270).

ver. 18. MELCHIZEDEK] Heb. vii. 2, 'Being by interpretation King of righteousness.' He was probably king of one of the Shemitic pre-Canaanitish tribes which settled at Jerusalem, whence it was expelled by the Jebusites. Hævernick remarks: "His God is 'the most High God, possessor of heaven and earth;' and these designations of the Deity we find again in the Phœnician religions, from which it is clear that we have here in a purer state the original element of a religion and worship that afterwards became more corrupt" (*Introd.* p. 150).—SALEM] Heb. vii. 2, 'which signifies peace.' In Psal. lxxvi. 2, Jerusalem is called Salem. The Targums and Josephus take Salem to be Jerusalem. Abram's course from Damascus to Hebron would almost of necessity lead him by Jerusalem; and the king of Sodom's route, as he proceeded to meet Abram, would naturally lead him into the valley of Kidron. A large proportion of the best German critics consider that Jerusalem is here intended; viz. Gesenius, Winer, Hævernick, Hengstenberg, Kurtz, Hofman, and Delitzsch. Mr Stanley (*Sin. and Pal.* p. 235) defends the Samaritan opinion that *Gerizim* was the place where Melchizedek met Abram. His argument is not clear. He seems to identify Salem with the insignificant village of Shalim, which Dr Robinson discovered near Nablous; and he represents Abram to have marched southwards from Damascus, and the king of Sodom northwards from Sodom, on the *east* side of Jordan, until they met in some valley on that side of Jordan, where they were also joined by Melchizedek. How they all got to Gerizim he does not say. However, the judgment of one familiar with the country by long residence in it, is most material on a question like this. Dr Thomson decidedly negatives Mr Stanley's view in every point. "Abraham would naturally return on the *western* sides of the lakes Huleh and Tiberias. I have been round the eastern side of both, and affirm that he could not have selected that road, encumbered as he was with a large company of rescued prisoners, and their baggage. Nor could he have followed the valley of the Jordan. No one who has ever travelled that impracticable

Ghor will believe that this great company took that path; and, after wandering over these regions in all directions, I am quite sure that the way by which Abraham led back the people of Sodom was along the ordinary road from Galilee to Jerusalem....This route would bring Abraham to Jerusalem, where the king of Sodom would most naturally meet him. Mr Stanley supposes that the king of Sodom went round the *eastern* shore of the Dead Sea; but that is quite impracticable, unless one makes a long *détour* through the interior" (*The Land and the Book*, p. 474). This reasoning also disposes of the opinion that Salem was identical with the place of that name where John baptized, and which is by Jerome placed on the Jordan, eight miles (Roman) south of Scythopolis. To have brought him near this Salem, the Patriarch's line of march must have been along the impracticable *Ghor* of the Jordan.—BROUGHT FORTH BREAD AND WINE] "The old learned fathers say not, Melchisedek offered the same [bread and wine] in sacrifice to God; but he brought it forth as a present, as the manner was to refresh them after the pursuit and chase of their enemies. And S. Hierome, in his translation, turneth it not *obtulit*, 'he sacrificed,' but *protulit*, 'he brought it forth.' Josephus reporteth the matter thus: 'Melchisedek feasted Abraham's soldiers, and suffered them to want nothing that was necessary for their provision. And likewise he received Abraham himself to his table.' In like manner Philo Judæus says that the bread and wine were offered not to God, but to Abraham. Chrysostom and Epiphanius say thus: 'He brought forth to them bread and wine.' Tertullian saith: 'Melchizedek offered bread and wine (not unto God, but) unto Abraham returning from the fight.' So S. Ambrose: 'Melchizedek came forth to meet, and offered (not to God, but) unto Abraham, bread and wine.' [Cyril Alex., also, in his comment on this passage, says, 'The blessing Abraham and presenting *him* bread and wine.'] By these few it may appear that Melchizedek brought forth bread and wine and other provision, not as a sacrifice unto God, but as a relief and sustenance for Abraham and his company" (Bp. Jewel, Vol. I. p. 731. Ed. P. S.). The ancient Christian writers who connected this incident with the Eucharist were far from regarding it as a sacrifice. They viewed it thus: In Abraham they saw the figure of all Christ's faithful people; in

Melchizedek, refreshing Abraham on his return from the slaughter of the kings, they saw an image of Christ refreshing the souls of his believing people with the spiritual food of his Body and Blood exhibited in the Lord's Supper. On this subject may be consulted, Jackson, *Works*, Vol. VIII. 236, &c.; Waterland, *Appendix to Christian Sacrifice Explained;* Brevint, *Depth and Mystery of Romish Mass*, ch. XI.; Patrick's *Treatise* in Gibson's *Preserv.* However, besides the *typical* meaning of this act of the priest of God in refreshing Abram, thoughtful writers have seen that even to Abram the presentation of the bread and wine was intended to convey more than mere bodily refreshment. Thus Jackson writes: "These elements of bread and wine being considered with the solemnity of the blessing, have, besides the literal sense, a symbolical or mystical importance, and are thus far at least sacramental, that *they served for earnests to secure Abraham* that his posterity should quietly enjoy and eat the good things of that pleasant land wherein he was now a sojourner. Briefly, Abraham, in sacred banquet which the king of Salem exhibited to him, did, as we say, take *livery de seisin* of the promised land" (*Works*, Vol. VIII.

237). Similarly Kurtz.—THE PRIEST] More correctly, *a priest;* see Gesen. *Gram.* § 115. 2, *a*.

ver. 19. HE BLESSED HIM] i. e. Melchizedek blessed Abram.

ver. 20. BLESSED BE THE MOST HIGH GOD] When God blesses man, He bestows benefits on him, Deut. xxviii. 1, 2; man blesses God when he *praises* Him for His benefits, Matt. xxvi. 26 compared with Luk. xxii. 19 (*Kidder*).— HE GAVE HIM TITHES OF ALL] Heb. vii. 4, 'Consider how great this man was, unto whom even the patriarch Abraham gave the tenth of the spoils.' This presentation of the tithe of the spoils was made by Abram *before* the king of Sodom had offered them all to him as a gift, and therefore when they were strictly the property of the king of Sodom. The king of Salem, therefore, appears to have stood in some acknowledged relation of superiority to the Sodomites, because Abram gives him as a matter of course an offering from the property of the latter people. See a series of interesting papers on *The Rephaim* in *The Journal of Sacred Literature,* Vol. I. He appears to have been the recognised head of the Shemitic race, which occupied Palestine previous to the

Phœnician immigration. Entering the land as traders, the Phœnicians would of course at first pay allegiance to the chiefs of the country, and for some time after, even when their rising power might enable them to resist the exaction.— THE MOST HIGH GOD] Here and in the conversation with Abram the names of God are used most appropriately. Melchizedek worshipped the true God, and that not merely as one out of many gods, but as the Most High, whose dominion was over the whole universe. He knew Him not however as Jehovah. In the earlier history, Jehovah both in name and fact was the common property of the whole human race; but the recollections of God as such gradually grew dim, until they were lost in heathenism. The religion of Melchizedek was just at the stage when the knowledge of Jehovah was merged into the knowledge of the one highest and infinite Being, and before this true though partial conception of the Divine Being gave way to Polytheism. Abram, by repeating the designation used by Melchizedek, acknowledged that he possessed that conception of God which is the basis of true religion; by adding the name Jehovah, he declares that to himself the Most High God was something more. See Hengstenberg, *Pent.* I. 337.

ver. 22. I HAVE LIFT UP MINE HAND] i. e. *I have sworn;* Exod. vi. 8; Numb. xiv. 30.

ver. 23. FROM A THREAD EVEN TO A SHOE-LATCHET] i. e. *neither a thread nor a shoe-latchet.* He would not take from him the most worthless thing of his, much less anything of consequence.—LEST THOU SHOULDEST SAY, I HAVE MADE ABRAM RICH] He had taken valuable gifts not very long before from Pharaoh. His refusal therefore in the present instance must have been dictated by the desire to avoid any intercourse or communion with a people of such abandoned wickedness as the Sodomites.

Chapter XV.

ver. 1. THE WORD OF THE LORD] Throughout this and the next chapter we naturally meet with the name Jehovah.—IN A VISION] in the night-time, see vv. 5—11.—AFTER THESE THINGS] This seems to intimate that the following promise of the Lord was meant to reward Abram for having spurned the valuable offer of the king of Sodom.—FEAR NOT] Though exposed to such dangers as he had just incurred, and having to dwell amidst strangers and sinners like the Amorites, he should have no real reason for fear. "Humanly speaking, his expedition against the powerful king of the East had been a most dangerous undertaking. It was reasonable to suppose that the vengeance of this powerful conqueror would overtake him" (*Kurtz*).—THY EXCEEDING GREAT REWARD] Lit. *thy reward* [shall be] *very great;* thus translated by Sept., Ainsworth, Kalisch, Delitzsch, and Wright. Knobel retains the translation of our version.

ver. 2. THE STEWARD OF MY HOUSE IS THIS

ELIEZER OF DAMASCUS] This clause is involved in much difficulty. It seems best to translate it with Simonis, Gesenius, Maurer and Knobel: *the possessor* or *heir of my substance will be this Eliezer of Damascus.*—THE STEWARD] Lit. *the son of the possession* of my house, i.e. *my heir.*—IS THIS ELIEZER OF DAMASCUS] Thus translated by Onkelos, Syr., Gesen., Maurer, Knobel. But Sept., Latin Vulg., Jerome, and Kalisch, taking Dammesek as a proper name, render the clause, *he is Dammesek Eliezer.*

ver. 3. BORN IN MY HOUSE] Lit. *son of my house*, which may mean merely *one belonging to his household*, and not that Eliezer was born in Abram's house.

ver. 5. TELL THE STARS, IF THOU BE ABLE TO NUMBER THEM] Neh. ix. 23, 'Their children also multipliedst thou as the stars of heaven, and brought them into the land, concerning which thou hadst promised to their fathers, that they should go in to possess it.' But the complete realization (Rom. iv. 16—18) was seen by John when in spirit he 'beheld, and lo, a great multitude, which no man could number, of all nations ......stood before the throne, and before the Lamb,' Rev. vii. 9.

ver. 6. HE BELIEVED IN THE LORD] 'Being not weak in faith, he considered not his own body now dead, when he was about an hundred years old, nor yet the deadness of Sarah's womb; and being fully persuaded that, what He had promised, He was able also to perform,' Rom. iv. 19—21.—HE COUNTED IT TO HIM FOR RIGHTEOUSNESS] Faith was reckoned to Abram as righteousness, or sinless perfection; not that it strictly or literally was so, but it was so accepted in God's account (Waterland, *Works*, IV. p. 575).

ver. 8. WHEREBY SHALL I KNOW?] That Abram seeks a sign is not displeasing to God, more than in the case of Gideon or Hezekiah (Jud. vi. 36, 2 Kin. xx. 8). Nay, the contrary may be displeasing to Him, as we find in the instance of Ahaz (Isa. vii. 12). It depends on the mind which prompts the request or refusal, whether the request is prompted by belief, which desires confirmation, or by unbelief, which is concealed under the pretence of the uncertainty of the revelation (*v. Gerlach*). Similarly Patrick. .

ver. 9, 10. The Lord now enters into covenant with Abram. As God only passes between the parts of the sacrifice, the covenant for the present is on God's side only; afterwards, by the right of circumcision, Abram on his side ratifies the covenant and undertakes its obligations. The covenant is made by *sacrifice*. For God is holy, and He can therefore only enter into covenant with man, when sin, which had separated between God and man, had been removed. The division of the sacrificed animals into two portions represents the two parties to the covenant. As these portions constitute in reality only one animal, so are the two parties to the covenant joined into one. The passing through the portions of the sacrifice represents, as it were, the means by which they who had been separated were to be united (*Kurtz*). That the rite was of the nature of *a covenant* appears from Jer. xxxiv. 18—20. The explanation generally adopted of the symbolical purport of this rite, viz. that it signified "that so should they be cut asunder who broke the covenant" (*Patrick*), is very revolting when we remember that the Lord was one party to the covenant. And as Kurtz remarks, "it militates against the institution of sacrifices, as in this case the killing and shedding of blood would not represent the atonement, on the basis of which the covenant was to be made, but only and exclusively an idea wholly foreign to that of sacrifice."—TAKE AN HEIFER, &c.] The animals which the Levitical Law afterwards authorized. This is one of the proofs we find that the Levitical constitution was not a code of perfectly new institutions.—THREE YEARS OLD] Because then in their prime (*Kidder, Patrick, and interpreters generally*). But why then did the Levitical Law consider animals one year old to be sufficient to be offered to God? The view therefore adopted by Delitzsch is better: "The animals were three years old, and Jehovah accepted them when in their *fourth* year, because the seed of Abraham was only to enter the land of promise in their *fourth* generation." Similarly Fairbairn, *Typol.* I. 317.

ver. 11. FOWLS] Literally in the Heb. *ravenous birds which feed on flesh, birds of prey*.— The birds signify the Egyptians, who persecute Abram's descendants, but Abram drives them away, that is, God redeems them for His promise made to Abram (*Luther*).

ver. 12. HORROR OF GREAT DARKNESS] A token of the affliction of his seed, predicted in the next verse. Comp. Esther viii. 16; Ps. lxxxviii. 6; cvii. 14 (*Kidder*); similarly Fairbairn, *Typol.* I. 318.

ver. 13. FOUR HUNDRED YEARS] From the juxtaposition of the four hundred years and the fourth generation in the words to Abraham, the one must be understood as nearly equivalent to the other, and the period must consequently be regarded as that of the actual residence of the children of Israel in Egypt from the descent of Jacob—not, as many after the Septuagint, from the time of Abraham. For the shortest genealogies exhibit four generations between that period and the exodus. Looking at the genealogical table of Levi (Exod. vi. 16), one hundred and twenty years might not unfairly be taken as an average lifetime or generation; so that three of these complete, and a part of a fourth, would easily make four hundred and thirty (Exod. xii. 40, 41). In Gal. iii. 17, the law is spoken of as only four hundred and thirty years after the covenant with Abraham; but the Apostle merely refers to the known historical period, and regards the first formation of the covenant with Abraham as all one with its final ratification with Jacob (Fairbairn, *Typol.* I. 318). Similarly *Delitzsch*.

ver. 14. JUDGE] Punish.—WITH GREAT SUBSTANCE] Fulfilled in the gifts which the departing Israelites obtained from the Egyptians.

ver. 15. THOU SHALT GO TO THY FATHERS] i.e. *thou shalt die.* This phrase (found also Gen. xxv. 8; xxxv. 29; xlix. 29, 33; Deut. xxxii. 50) proves the belief in a future state to have existed among the pious of the earliest ages. As Abram was buried far from the sepulchres of his fathers, its force cannot be explained as a periphrasis for being buried in the same place with one's fathers.

ver. 16. THE INIQUITY OF THE AMORITES IS NOT YET FULL] Hence we see that the extirpation of the Canaanites was the just punishment of their sin, delayed until they had abused all opportunities for repentance. When the Lord saw that the time was come to redeem this portion of the world from the evil which oppressed it, He used Israel as the instrument of His judgments. For proof of the iniquity of the Canaanites, see Lev. xviii. 27.

ver. 17. A SMOKING FURNACE] Such as is common in the East, shaped like a cylinder, at the upper opening of which fire enveloped in smoke bursts forth. It was a symbol of the gracious presence of God. The devouring fire of His

Holiness, before which the sinner cannot stand, is in grace enveloped (*Kurtz*).

Ver. 18. FROM THE RIVER OF EGYPT, &c.] It was not necessary on the present occasion to define the exact geographical bounds of the promised land. Just as the length of the Egyptian captivity was given in round numbers, so here the position of Canaan is described generally as being between the two great empires of Egypt and Mesopotamia, which, as in other places, are represented and denoted by the two rivers, the Nile and the Euphrates, which flowed through them. In Numb. xxxiv. 3, when the occasion required it, the boundaries of the promised land are accurately defined. Thus, Hengstenberg, Hævernick, Kurtz, Keil.—THE RIVER OF EGYPT] The Nile, and not the brook Rhinocorura, or Wady-el-Arish, which is never termed, as here, *nahar* (*a river*), but always *nahal* (*a brook*).

Ver. 19. THE KENITES, AND THE KENIZZITES, AND THE KADMONITES] Tribes supposed to have been original inhabitants of the land, descended from Shem. *Kenites* mean those who carry lances; *Kenizzites* mean hunters (*Kurtz*). The Kadmonites are supposed to have resided about the head-waters of the Jordan. This name is still preserved among the Nusairîyeh, north of Tripoli, and they have a tradition that their ancestors were expelled from Palestine by Joshua. A fragment of this strange people still cling to their original home near the foot of Hermon. I have repeatedly travelled among them in their own mountains, and many things in their physiognomy and manners gave me the idea that they were a remnant of the most ancient inhabitants of this country (Thomson, *The Land and the Book*, p. 164).

vers. 20, 21. See notes on ch. x. 15, 16; and ch. xiv. 5.

CHAPTER XVI.

ver. 1. Sarai's name has never yet been mentioned in the promises as that of the mother of Abram's seed. In her impatience she considers herself excluded, and tries by indirect means to bring about a fulfilment of the promise. Abram yields to her suggestion, and by so doing is involved in domestic troubles and sorrows.

ver. 2. MAY OBTAIN CHILDREN] Lit. *may be builded* by her. In illustration of the expression, comp. Ruth iv. 11; Ex. i. 21.

ver. 5. MY WRONG BE UPON THEE] *My wrong is through thee; thou art to blame for the wrong which I suffer.* Abram would seem to have borne with Hagar's unbecoming conduct, on account of her being likely to have children (*Maurer, De Sola*). Or, *may you suffer for the injury done to me* (*Knobel, Wright*).—JUDGE BETWEEN ME AND THEE] *Decide our difference,* by punishing thee for thine unthankfulness, and assisting me to get my due (*Knobel*).

ver. 7. THE ANGEL OF THE LORD] Throughout the whole of the O. T. there runs the distinction between the hidden God and the Revealer of God, Himself equal with God, who most frequently is called 'the Messenger,' 'the Angel of the Lord,' 'Malachi Jehovah,'—one with Him, and yet distinct from Him. This Messenger of the Lord is the Guide of the patriarchs, ch. xlviii. 16; the Caller of Moses, Ex. iii. 2; the Leader of the people through the wilderness, Ex. xiv. 19; xxiii. 20; comp. xxxiii. 14; Isa. lxiii. 9; the Champion of the Israelites in Canaan, Josh. v. 13; and also the Guide and Ruler of the people of the Covenant, Jud. ii. 1; vi. 11; xiii. 3; or, as He is called, Isa. lxiii. 9, 'the Angel of His Presence.' In Zechariah He measures the new building of Jerusalem, and sends the angel to the prophet, who speaks with him, Zech. i. and ii.; by Malachi, as 'the Messenger of the Covenant,' greatly longed for by the people, whose return to His Temple is promised, Mal. iii. 1. It nowhere occurs in the O. T. that an angel speaks as if he were God (since in Daniel, Gabriel, and in Zechariah, the angel who talks with the prophet, clearly distinguish themselves from Jehovah); while this

Angel of the Lord, in the passage under consideration, and often elsewhere in the O. T., speaks as Jehovah, and His appearing is regarded as that of the Most High God Himself. Nay, God says expressly of this Angel, 'My Name—i. e. My revealed Being—is in Him,' Ex. xxiii. 21. His name, 'Messenger,' or 'Angel,' is to be taken in a general signification, and by no means as if it denoted a class of higher created beings, of angels, which He had taken; comp. Heb. ii. 16. In the N. T. the expressions 'the Word,' 'Son,' 'Express Image,' 'Brightness,' denote the same, viz. the countenance turned to man, the Revealer of the Invisible God. The expressions which our Lord frequently uses, 'He who hath sent me,' 'I am sent from the Father,' particularly refer to this name, as in Heb. iii. 1 He is called 'the Apostle' of our Profession. The future appearance on earth of the God-man is gradually prepared for in the O. T. in two ways: on the one hand there is promised a mighty and glorious Human Ruler over all (in later times called 'Messiah'—the Anointed of the Lord), to whom at the same time in His human nature, Divine names, attributes, and works are ascribed (ch. xlix. 10; Ps. ii. cx; Isa. ix. 5; Mic. v. 1);

on the other hand, the personal distinction in the Godhead, the Revealer of the Invisible God as a separate [rather, *distinct,* "this word *distinction* is by the schoolmen conceived more commodiously applied to this mystery," *Barrow*] person, is more and more clearly made known (*v. Gerlach*). Consult, as defending in detail this view of the Angel of the Lord being the manifestation of the Second Person of the Trinity, Waterland, *Works,* Vol. I. p. 291; Bp. Bull, *Defence of the Nicene Faith,* I. i. § 10—20; *Primitive and Apostolical Tradition of the Divin. of Jesus Christ,* c. VI. § 6; Hengstenberg, *Christology of the O. T.* Vol. I. p. 107.—SHUR] A place to the east of Egypt bordering on the desert which extends to Palestine; Gen. xx. 1; xxv. 18; 1 Sam. xv. 7; xxvii. 8; according to Josephus, Pelusium, but better placed at Suez. The desert extending from the borders of Palestine to Shur, called the desert of Shur, is now called the desert *el Jofar* (*Gesenius*). As the road to Egypt led through the wilderness of Shur, Hagar seems to have attempted to regain her own country.

vers. 10—12. It is not merely the minute accuracy of this prediction, but especially *the long-continued fulfilment* of it, which stamps it as the offspring of the Divine foreknowledge. "The Arabians have occupied one and the same country. They have roved like the moving sands of their deserts; but the race has been rooted whilst the individual has wandered. That race has neither been dissipated by conquest, nor lost by migration, nor confounded with the blood of other countries. They have continued to dwell 'in the presence of all their brethren,' a distinct national family, wearing, upon the whole, the same features and aspect which prophecy first impressed upon them. The wildness which is incident only to a certain stage of man's social nature has been permanent with them; and although they have been compacted and embodied as a nation for more than three thousand years, they have resisted those changes of habit which it is the effect of civil union, so long continued, to induce. Plainly there is something unusual and remarkable in their case" (Davison, *Discourses on Prophecy*, p. 482).

ver. 10. I WILL MULTIPLY THY SEED] Arabia, the population of which, for the most part, consists of the descendants of Ishmael, is an abundant source of the human family, from whence have issued streams far and wide towards the east and west (*Ritter in v. Gerlach*). The conquests of Mahomet and his followers spread the Arabs over the south of Western Asia, North Africa, and Spain, the south of which they possessed for 700 years.

ver. 12. A WILD MAN] Lit. *an ass of men*, i.e. a wild man (*Wright*). For a description of the wild ass, see Job xxxix. 5—8. The whole verse accurately describes the unbridled love of liberty, and the wild, roaming, and lawless habits, characteristic of the Bedouin Arabs.—IN THE PRESENCE OF] The expression describes the wide and almost indefinite extent of territories through which the Bedouins roam, so that they seem to be everywhere 'before the eyes of' their brethren (*Kalisch*). Or it might be translated *to the east of his brethren*. See note on ch. xxv. 18 (*Knobel*).

vers. 13, 14. THOU GOD SEEST ME] i.e. *regardest me in my misery*.—HAVE I ALSO HERE LOOKED AFTER HIM THAT SEETH ME?] i.e. *Have I not even here* (in this wilderness where I am forsaken); or, *have I not indeed seen him after his seeing me?* When the angel vanished she perceived that it was God who had spoken to her. In memory of this expression, the well was called *the well of the Living One who sees me* (*Delitzsch*). And thus *in general* the passage is taken by Sept., Vulg., Ainsworth, Kid., Pat., Kurtz. A different interpretation is adopted by many expositors. *Thou art a God of vision,* i.e. a God who lets Himself be seen by man without destroying him; *for she said, Do I even still see?* i.e. live, *after the vision* of God? *Wherefore the well was called, The well of the life of vision,* i.e. the well where her life was preserved after seeing God (*Knobel, Hengstenb., Gesen., v. Gerl., Rosenm., Wright*). Mr Rowlands considers Moi-lâhi (*moi = water*), on the road from Beersheba to Jebel es-Sur, to be identical with Beer lahai-roi. Near it is a ruin called *Beit Hagar,* Hagar's house.

ver. 15. ISHMAEL] *Heard of God.*

Chapter XVII.

As yet the Lord had made no express mention of Sarai, as the mother by whom Abram was to obtain the seed of promise. He now reveals His purpose fully. To assure Abram and Sarai of the certainty of His making them to be the parents of the promised seed, He gives them both new names. At the same time He institutes the rite of circumcision by which Abram is brought into covenant with God (see note on ch. xv. 9, 10), and is also reminded of the spiritual nature of the race to whom God gives His blessing. The use of the divine names in this chapter is very peculiar. The difficulties it presents to the advocates of the various document-hypotheses can be removed only by their supposition of the spuriousness of v. 1. Hengstenberg's explanation of the occurrence of the names El-Shaddai and Elohim appears satisfactory. "Ex. vi. furnishes us with a key to the correct view. In v. 3 there is a verbal reference to v. 1 of this chapter, and in v. 4 to vv. 7, 8, of this chapter. The time of promise, as belonging to El-Shaddai, is contrasted with the time of fulfilment, as belonging to Jehovah. When Jehovah made the covenant with Abraham, &c., to give them the land of Canaan, the land of their pilgrimage, he was still El-Shaddai. When he fulfilled this covenant, he became Jehovah, but not in the fullest sense, till the last point of promise, the blessing on all the nations of the earth, came into fulfilment. In this point of view all difficulty vanishes. The author begins with Jehovah, to show that the God who appeared to Abraham was relatively, in relation to those who preceded him, already Jehovah. He then uses Elohim through the chapter, in order to intimate that the God, who at that time was Jehovah to Abraham as compared with the rest of mankind, was still even to him but Elohim, in comparison with later revelations of Himself."

ver. 1. THE ALMIGHTY GOD] Heb. *El-Shaddai*, meaning the *strong, mighty, God;* or the *All-sufficient God.*—BE PERFECT] i.e. place implicit confidence in me alone; comp. Deut. xviii. 13, 14 (*De Sola*).

ver. 4. FATHER OF MANY NATIONS] See note

on ch. xii. 2. The use made of this promise by St Paul (Rom. iv. 16, 17) proves that for the fulfilment of it we are to look, not to Abraham's descendants by Hagar and Keturah, not even to the Israel after the flesh *as such*, but to that great multitude of all nations and ages who shall have washed their robes, and made them white in the blood of the Lamb. Comp. Rom. ix. 6—9; Gal. iii. 8—14, 26—29.

ver. 5. NEITHER SHALL THY NAME] The change of the names of Abram and Sarai is, as it were, a *symbol* and an *earnest* of the new thing which the Lord is about to bring forth. For the name indicates the character (*Kurtz*).—ABRAM] *Exalted father.*—ABRAHAM] *Father of a multitude.*

ver. 6. KINGS SHALL COME OUT OF THEE] Rev. v. 10, 'And hast made us unto our God kings and priests: and we shall reign on the earth.'

ver. 7. AN EVERLASTING COVENANT] God makes with Abraham and his posterity an *everlasting* covenant; since this covenant of grace was the first germ of the new covenant in Jesus Christ [Gal. iii. 16, 'He saith not, and to seeds, as of many; but as of one, and to thy seed, which is Christ'] ... The eternal possession stands, in the first instance, in contrast to the present temporary abode of Abraham in Canaan. Yet at the same time is this land the visible pledge, the germ and prophetic type, of the new world, which belongs to the church of the Lord: it is therefore called emphatically, an 'Eternal Possession.' The same holds good of all the divine ordinances which in the O. T. are declared to be everlasting ordinances; and yet in the N. T. are in the letter abrogated, while in the spirit they have been really fulfilled. So it is with Circumcision, the Passover, the Priesthood, &c. (*v. Gerlach*).

ver. 10. THIS IS MY COVENANT] The general purport of the covenant was, that from Abraham there was to be generated a seed of blessing. There could not, therefore, be a more appropriate sign of the covenant than such a rite as circumcision—so directly connected with the generation of offspring, and so distinctly marking the purification of nature—the removal of the filth of the flesh—that the offspring might be such as really to constitute a seed of blessing. It is through ordinary generation that the corruption incident on the fall is propagated. Now, therefore, when God was establishing a covenant, the great end of which was to reverse the propagation of evil, he affixed to the covenant this symbolical rite, to show that the end was to be reached, not as the result of nature's ordinary productiveness, but of nature purged from its uncleanness—nature raised above itself, in league with the grace of God, and bearing on it the distinctive impress of His character and working (Fairbairn, *Typol.* I. 322). The spirituality and purity intimated by this sign of the covenant is often urged in the O. T. Comp. Deut. x. 16; xxx. 6; Jer. iv. 4; ix. 26; Ezek. xliv. 7. As woman since the fall was made dependent on man, through the relationship of wife and daughter she was admitted into covenant by what was done by man.

ver. 12. EIGHT DAYS] The number seven has in Scripture a peculiar and sacred import.

ver. 14. CUT OFF] This seems to imply an untimely death (Exod. xxxi. 14), and a punishment generally inflicted by God's hand, rather than that of the magistrate; Levit. xvii. 10; xx. 5 (*Kidder*). Comp. Exod. iv. 24.

ver. 15. SARAI] *Princess* (*Gesenius*).—SARAH] derived from a root meaning *to be fruitful* (*Kurtz*).

ver. 17. LAUGHED] *Rejoiced* (*Onkelos*). And the Hebrew word will bear it, ch. xxi. 6 (*Kidder*). That his laughter was not of unbelief, but of joy and wonder at the gracious promise, appears (1) from the fact that he is not reproved as Sarah afterwards was; (2) from the inspired comment in Rom. iv. 19—21, 'Being not weak in faith, he considered not his own body now dead, when he was about an hundred years old, neither yet the deadness of Sarah's womb: he staggered not at the promise of God through unbelief; but was strong in faith, giving glory to God, &c.;' (3) from the allusion made by our Saviour, Joh. viii. 56, 'Abraham rejoiced to see my day: and he saw it, and was glad.' Our Lord must have referred to some passage in Abraham's history familiar to the Jews. This is the only one to be found in which mention is made of Abraham's laughing or rejoicing. Our Lord's comment then on it shows, that his joy arose from seeing in Isaac (whom his faith enabled him to regard as existing already) the type and pledge of the coming Saviour, by whom we 'being delivered out of the hands of our enemies might serve Him without fear, in holiness and righteousness of life,' S. Luk. i. 73—75. See Bp. Andrewes, *Serm.* viii. *On the Nativity.*

ver. 18. O THAT ISHMAEL MIGHT LIVE BEFORE THEE] *Might be highly blessed and favoured by Thee.* Those who ascribe Abraham's conduct in the preceding verse to unbelief, take this as a wish that Ishmael should be the inheritor of the covenant-blessing. But that the prayer of Abraham was simply for the prosperity of Ishmael, appears from the Lord's answer in v. 20, 'As for Ishmael, I *have heard* thee: Behold, I have blessed him, &c.'

ver. 19. ISAAC] Heb. *one laughs;* so called from Abraham's joy. His name was a memorial of his father's faith, not of his mother's unbelief (*Kidder*).

ver. 20. The proofs from heathen writers of the punctual fulfilment of this prophecy or promise may be seen in Bp. Newton *On the Prophecies.* See ch. xxv. 16.

Chapter XVIII.

ver. 1. APPEARED] The manner of His appearing is detailed in v. 2.—THE PLAIN] Erroneous translation; it should be *the oaks*, or *oak-grove*.—MAMRE] Hebron, see note on ch. xiii. 18.—THE HEAT OF THE DAY] At noontide.

ver. 2. THREE MEN] As it is said in v. 1 that *the Lord appeared* to Abraham, and as throughout the chapter it is the Lord who converses with Abraham, it is natural to conclude, with most of the early Christian writers, that the *three men* were the Word, the Second Person of the Trinity, accompanied by two created angels. Thus Justin Martyr, Chrysostom, Hilary of Poictiers, Eusebius the historian, as cited in Forbes, *Instruct. Hist. Theol.* L. I. xiv. See this view defended in detail by Hengstenberg, *Christol.* I. p. 111. A few early writers, Ambrose and Augustine for instance, adopted the view afterwards maintained by the schoolmen, Alexander Halensis and Thomas Aquinas for example, that the three men were intended to represent the Trinity; see Forbes, as above.

ver. 4. WASH YOUR FEET] Even yet a customary mark of hospitality in Palestine; see Robinson, *Bib. Res.* II. 229.

ver. 6. THREE MEASURES] Lit. *three seahs* = one ephah = $1\frac{1}{12}$ English bushel (*Blackadder*).

ver. 8. BUTTER] The one Heb. word expresses butter and soured milk: either may be meant. The Arabs at the present day use melted butter (*semen*), and soured milk (*leben*). See Robinson, *Bib. Res.* II. 70. For the process of making butter, see Thomson, *The Land and the Book*, p. 255.

ver. 10. ACCORDING TO THE TIME OF LIFE] Lit. *as the time lives again*, after the winter, in which the year is, as it were, dead; next year about the present time (*Knobel*).

ver. 15. SHE WAS AFRAID] To this *sinful fear* or amazement of Sarah, which provoked her to falsehood, the Apostle alludes (1 Pet. iii. 6), when he proposes her as a pattern of obedience to women, and cautions them at the same time against the sinful fear by which she fell (*Kidder*).

vers. 17—19. Two reasons are here assigned for declaring to Abraham the Lord's counsel concerning the cities of the plain. (1) The doomed cities were a part of the land of Canaan, which was promised to Abraham. Hence the Lord explains to him why the cities in which he was so interested were destroyed. (2) To warn Abraham and his family, that it was only with those who 'kept the way of the Lord, to do judgment and justice,' that the Lord could deal graciously. "Throughout the O. T., the judgment on Sodom is held up to Israel as a type and prediction of future judgments, and, therefore, as a warning and call to repentance; see Deut. xxix. 23; Isa. i. 9; xiii. 19; Jer. xx. 16; xxiii. 14; xlix. 18; l. 40; Lam. iv. 6; Ezek. xvi. 46" (*Kurtz*).

ver. 19. FOR I KNOW HIM, &c.] This is better translated: *For I have known him*, i.e. regarded him with favour, chosen him, *to the end that he should teach his children after him, so as that they should walk in the way of the Lord* (*Michael., Gesen., Kal., Knob., Wright*). For this use of the word *to know*, as meaning *to choose, to care for*, see Am. iii. 2; Hos. xiii. 4.

ver. 20. THE CRY OF SODOM AND GOMORRAH] The cry concerning Sodom and Gomorrah (*Wright*).

ver. 21. I WILL GO DOWN...AND SEE] This he did by sending His two angels, whose treatment by the Sodomites was to be the test and proof of their immorality. God tempts people, or rather proves and puts them to the trial, by placing them in particular situations, not for the purpose of making them sin, but in order to bring out their true disposition, and to remove all cavil on men's part as to the justice of His dealings, 'that He may be justified when He speaks, and clear when He judges,' Ps. li. 4. Thus He is said to tempt Abraham, when He orders him to offer up Isaac, and from his conduct then He is said *to know* that he feared Him. Thus, Deut. viii. 2, He says, that He led Israel through the wilderness, *to prove him*, and *to know* what was *in his heart*. And, 2 Chron. xxxii. 31, in the matter of the ambassadors of Babylon, God is said to have 'left Hezekiah, to try him, that He might know all that was in his heart.'

ver. 22. THE MEN...WENT TOWARD SODOM] Comp. ch. xix. 1.—BUT ABRAHAM] He to whom it had been promised that he should be 'a blessing,' and that 'in him all nations should be blessed,' now comes forward to act in this capacity, and to intercede with God for the nations of the earth. It seems to be an unnecessary refinement to say that Abraham interceded for Sodom only of the five cities because in it dwelt his kinsman Lot. He interceded for it because it was Sodom which God was about to visit and prove first of all. And, *apparently*, God selected it for trial as having had, through the sojourn of righteous Lot, the chief opportunity of enlightenment, and therefore as being the one in which, if at all, would be found any remains of good.

ver. 33. THE LORD WENT HIS WAY] The Chaldee saith: the glory of the Lord was lifted up (*Ainsworth*).

Chapter XIX.

ver. 1. TWO ANGELS] Lit. *the two angels*, namely, those who were mentioned in ch. xviii. 22, as *going towards Sodom*. The Jewish tradition is, that no angel is sent on two separate missions. The first, therefore, of these two was sent to conduct Lot out of Sodom, and the mission of the other was to destroy the five cities.—SAT IN THE GATE] Dr Thomson, speaking of the *gates* of the cities of modern Palestine, says: "The gateway is vaulted, shady, and cool. This is one reason why people delight to assemble about it. Again, the curious and the vain resort thither to see and to be seen. Some go to meet their associates; others to watch for returning friends, or to accompany those about to depart; while many gather there to hear the news, and to engage in trade and traffic. I have seen—in Joppa, for example—the Kâdy and his court sitting at the entrance of the gate, hearing and adjudicating all sorts of causes" (*The Land and the Book*, p. 27).

ver. 2. NAY; BUT WE WILL ABIDE IN THE STREET] They would put Lot to the proof, since it was regarded as a mark of the corruption of morals in a place to allow a stranger to remain in the streets; Jud. xix. 15; Job xxxi. 32 (*v. Gerlach*).

ver. 4. BEFORE THEY LAY DOWN] to sleep.— FROM EVERY QUARTER] This translation is defended by Hitzig, Maurer, Knobel and Kalisch. Wright and Delitzsch adopt that of the Sept., *one and all, all in a body*. According to either translation the verse presents an awful proof of the appalling licentiousness of the people of Sodom.

ver. 8. I HAVE TWO DAUGHTERS] On this proposal made by Lot, may be consulted the remark of Bp. Sanderson, *Serm. on Rom.* iii. 8. Von Gerlach suggests that, as the daughters were betrothed to men of Sodom, Lot imagined that the people would not proceed to extremities. This suggestion depends on a disputed interpretation of ver. 14.

ver. 9. STAND BACK] This, which is the translation of the Sept. and Vulg., is defended by Gesenius, Tuch, Knobel, De Sola, and Delitzsch. But Fæsius and Maurer maintain that we should translate, *come here*.—HE WILL NEEDS

BE A JUDGE] From this it would appear that he had before this repeatedly attempted to restrain them in their wickedness.

ver. 11. BLINDNESS] They were not struck with actual and permanent blindness, but were dazzled and confused. The word itself occurs but once again, 2 Kin. vi. 18, where also it is used to express a temporary dazzling and confusion of the senses, so that objects appear distorted and confused (*De Sola*).

ver. 14. WHICH MARRIED] The words may be translated thus, in which case these two married daughters must be different from the two mentioned in ver. 7 (*Sept., Targ., Jon., Schumann, Knobel*); or they may be translated, *who were to be married to his daughters*, namely, the two referred to in ver. 7 (*Joseph., Vulg., Michael., Tuch, Delitzsch*). The first translation seems to be supported by ver. 15, 'thy two daughters, *which are here*,' lit. *which are at hand*.

ver. 16. AND WHILE HE LINGERED] All that the Scripture relates of Lot is characteristic of a mind naturally weak, and which selfishness and sensuality had still more enfeebled. Such a person must be quite incapable to act with promptitude and vigour in extraordinary circumstances (*De Sola*).

ver. 17. LOOK NOT BACK] as if reluctant to abandon it with its pleasures, and distrustful of the reality of God's threats against those remaining in it.—THE MOUNTAIN] of the country afterwards called Moab.

ver. 22. ZOAR] in Heb. means *smallness;* before this called Bela; see ch. xiv. 2. It was a town of Moab (Isa. xv. 5; Jer. xlviii. 34), and formed the southernmost boundary of the plain of the Pentapolis (Gen. xiii. 10; Deut. xxxiv. 3). I am disposed, says Dr Robinson, to assign its position to the mouth of the Wady Kerak, where the latter opens upon the isthmus of the long peninsula. In that spot Irby and Mangles found the traces of an extensive ancient site (*Bib. Res.* II. 107).

ver. 25. THE PLAIN] Lit. *the circle,* as in ch. xiii. 10. Gesenius, Knobel, and others, make the phrase, *the circle of Jordan,* to denote the whole of the *Ghôr,* the valley through which the river flows from the Lake Tiberias to the extremity of the Dead Sea. But a careful examination of the different passages where it occurs will show, that the phrase was applied only to the neighbourhood of the five cities where, before the catastrophe mentioned here, the mountains which hemmed in Jordan widened out, so as to give room for the broad and well-watered plain where these cities stood.

ver. 26. LOOKED BACK] This showed that the love of Sodom remained in her still; that though her feet were come from thence, her heart stayed there behind (Bp. Andrewes, *Sermon on Luke* xvii. 32).—AND SHE BECAME A PILLAR OF SALT] The language of the sacred text is quite indefinite, and tells us nothing more than the fact of her death by a divine judgment, and that the place where she was left dead became a heap of salt.

ver. 27. This may be the proper place to give a brief summary of what modern research has brought to light concerning the Dead Sea, and the locality of the five cities of the plain. The southern portion of Palestine is now bounded by the lake called by the various names of *the Salt Sea* (Gen. xiv. 3), *the Eastern Sea* (Ezek. xlvii. 18; Joel ii. 20), *the Asphalt Lake*, and *the Dead Sea* and *Bahr Lut*. In length about 39, and in breadth about 9 geographical miles, it lies sunk in a deep chasm, shut in on both sides by ranges of precipitous limestone rocks, and bounded on the south by the mountain of rock-salt called by the Arabs, Hajr Usdom. Until lately it was thought that it was brought into existence by a frightful convulsion of nature which accompanied the destruction of the cities of the plain, and which formed this chasm, and that up to that time the waters of the Jordan flowed through the 'Arabah into the Gulf of 'Akabah. But the observations of modern travellers, especially of Dr Robinson, have shown that the Jordan could never have flowed into the Red Sea; for the surface of the Red Sea is 1312 feet *above* the acrid waters of the Dead Sea, and 620 above the level of the Jordan even at Lake Tiberias. Instead of the land sloping down from the Dead Sea to the Gulf of 'Akabah, the incline is exactly the reverse, so that the waters of the 'Arabah itself, and also those of the high western desert far south of 'Akabah, all flow into the Dead Sea. Every circumstance goes to show that a lake must have existed in this place, into which the Jordan poured its waters, long before the catastrophe of Sodom. Before that event the lake must have covered a much smaller extent of surface than it does now. The cities which were destroyed must have been situated on or near the tract now covered by the southern portion of the lake. For Zoar, to which Sodom was so near, lay almost at the southern end of the present sea; see note on ver. 22. The fertile plain, therefore, which Lot chose as being well-watered, and which appears identical with or to have contained the vale of Siddim, with its bitumen-wells, lay south of the ancient lake. It would from this appear that, at the time of the destruction of Sodom, by volcanic action or other causes, the surface of the plain of the cities was lowered, and the waters of the lake poured over it from the north; at the same time may have been protruded those masses of rock-salt, exhibited in the Mount of Usdom, which have ever since embittered the waters of the lake. The following facts, lately brought to light, make this supposition very probable. A good *modern* map of the country will show that the lake is in a manner divided into two unequal portions by the peninsula el-Mesraa, which juts into it from the eastern side. The northern portion, which is about three-fourths of the whole, is throughout of great depth, as is proved by its soundings of from 1000 to 1227 feet. The southern portion, which is supposed here to occupy the ancient plain, is very shallow; in winter being 13 feet deep, and late in autumn so shallow as to be forded even by asses. It is on this portion, and on this only, that the bitumen is found floating; and it is into this southernmost end that those numerous living streams, noticed by Dr Robinson as more in number than can be found in any other locality in Palestine, make their way. In both these respects this shallow basin gives evidence of having been once the well-watered plain of Jordan, and the vale of Siddim, noted for its bitumen-pits. We are not obliged, however, to conclude that, along with the vale of Siddim, the four cities of the plain were submerged. They lay adjacent to the vale, ch. xiv. 3, 10; and several Scripture passages seem to intimate that in later sacred historical times the sites and ruins were visible. Comp. Deut. xxix. 23; Zeph. ii. 9. Josephus also mentions that the district Sodomitis, once a fruitful country containing many cities, lay along the Dead Sea (*Bell. Jud.* IV. 8. 4). Hence, it is argued by Kurtz, "as the Dead Sea is still bounded on the south by salt-pits (as described in the passages from Zeph. and Deut.), and as according to Gen. x. 19, these cities had formed the southernmost boundary of Canaan, we are warranted in supposing that the four cities had stood on the spot where now salt-pits surround the southern boundary of the Dead Sea." This note is derived from Robinson, *Bib. Res.* I. 502, &c.; II. 188, &c.; Kurtz, I. 137; Thomson, p. 622; Stanley, p. 287.

ver. 28. AND HE LOOKED TOWARD SODOM, &c.] Mr Stanley mentions a height on the east of Hebron as the traditional spot where Abraham saw the smoke of Sodom rising out of the deep gulf between the hills of Engedi and the mountains of Moab (*Sin. and Pal.* p. 101). Dr Robinson distinguished Kerak very clearly from the hill on the west of Hebron (*Bib. Res.* II. 85).

ver. 29. GOD] In visiting Sodom and the other cities with punishment, God displayed Himself as Jehovah, the righteous Ruler of man. He punished them for their sins. But though Lot was in moral condition raised far above the Sodomites, his conduct, when leaving the city, and more especially afterwards, vv. 30—35, proves that his religious feeling was but weak. In accordance with this we find the sacred narrative emphatically declaring that his supernatural deliverance was wrought only for Abraham's sake. Hence the sacred writer, when speaking of God's dealings exclusively towards a man who must have regarded God more in the light of the unearthly, the supernatural, than of the Righteous Everliving Being personally interested in his doings, properly speaks of God in the relation of Elohim.

ver. 30. CAVE] From its limestone formation the hills of Palestine abound in caves. Stanley, *Sin. and Pal.* p. 148.

ver. 31. THE FIRSTBORN SAID TO THE YOUNGER] Disappointment at the loss of their husbands, sensuality stimulated by the lusts of Sodom, seem to have excited them to their sin.

ver. 32. DRINK WINE] The mountains of Moab are full of spacious caves, in which the inhabitants of the plain used to store their abundant vintages. It was in such a cave that Lot took refuge, and used the wine which had now no owners (*De Sola*).

ver. 37. MOAB] which means, *he that is longed for* (*Kurtz*), *father's offspring* (*Gesen.*).

ver. 38. BEN-AMMI] Meaning, *son of my people*.

Chapter XX.

The use of the two names of God through this chapter is thus accounted for by Hengstenberg. For Abimelech God is Elohim; of Jehovah he knew nothing. Hence only as Elohim could He appear to him. What is told of that appearance is given from the account of Abimelech. Abraham used the name Elohim in conversation with Abimelech, that he might adapt himself to his religious position. For that reason he also prayed to Elohim—for the intercession was uttered in the hearing of the king to whom a prayer addressed to Jehovah would have been unintelligible. The second Elohim in v. 17, 'so Abraham prayed to Elohim; and Elohim healed Abimelech,' is a consequence of the first. On the other hand, Jehovah must stand in v. 18. For here the historian speaks in his own proper person, and not as a mere reporter of the views and words of other persons.

ver. 1. JOURNEYED FROM THENCE] From

Mamre, which from its proximity to the scene of the late catastrophe may have presented unpleasing associations to him.—BETWEEN KADESH AND SHUR] Probably at Beer-lahai-roi, which lay in that position, ch. xvi. 7, 14; and where Isaac lived, ch. xxv. 11.—GERAR] traced by Mr Rowlands in the name Joorf el-Gerar, three hours S.S.E. of Gaza. Near it he found traces of an ancient city, called Khirbet el-Gerar (the ruins of Gerar).

vers. 2—18. The transaction related in these verses, and the two similar occurrences in xii. 14—20, and xxvi. 6—11, are assumed by rationalist writers to be but the one and the same fact, presented by the variations of traditions in three different forms. In the prefatory note on ch. xxvi. it will be shown that there are fundamental differences between the occurrence mentioned there in relation to Isaac, and the similar passages in Abraham's history. And with regard to Abraham himself, those who have studied the character and relations of the East, can find no difficulty in such an event repeating itself in Abraham's history. Comp. Hævernick, p. 143; Ayre, p. 572. A special objection has been raised against the historical credibility of the present passage, on the ground of the great improbability that a woman, aged about ninety, could have offered any attraction. But the matter admits of ready explanation. Since the visit of the angels to Mamre, when Sarah was, through the creative agency of God, made capable of becoming a mother, her youth and beauty had returned. Comp. Kurtz, Nachmanides in De Sola's note.

ver. 2. ABIMELECH] A name, it would seem, common to all the kings of Gerar; see ch. xxvi. 8; Ps. xxxiv. *Title*, compared with 1 Sam. xxi. 10. Similarly, the national kings of Egypt were all called Pharaoh, and those of the Macedonian line, Ptolemy.

ver. 3. THOU ART BUT A DEAD MAN] With the reservation usually expressed or implied, *unless thou restorest Sarah.*

ver. 6. WITHHELD THEE] by visiting him and his household with some plague; see vv. 17, 18.

ver. 7. A PROPHET] Heb. *nabi*. The derivation is disputed. It is derived so as to signify either *a speaker*, or *one taught*, i.e. *inspired* (Davidson, *Introd.* p. 809). According to either derivation it cannot be restricted to express *only* a *foreteller* of things to come, but it must signify one commissioned or qualified to speak for God to man. As Abraham enjoyed direct intercourse with God, he was a prophet in the strict Scriptural sense of the word; Exod. iv. 15, 16; vii. 1. Comp. Fairbairn, *Proph.* pp. 5, 6; Lee, *Inspiration*, note K. It has been argued from 1 Sam. ix. 9, that the appellation of Abraham as a *nabi,* and not as a *seer, roeh,* is a proof that the present passage was written long after the time of Moses. The application of the title to him, on the contrary, proves that the passage must have been written long before the time of even Samuel. For the application of this term *nabi* to Moses (Deut. xviii. 15, 18), to Aaron (Exod. vii. 1), to the prophetic order in Moses' time (Deut. xiii. 1—3), to Miriam (Exod. xv. 20), to Deborah (Jud. iv. 4), proves that it was the genuine old designation of the prophetic order, which in the time of Samuel had fallen into disuse. When under David order was restored to Israel, and a regular line of prophets instituted, it appears that the theocratic title was revived. Comp. Ayre, *Introd.* p. 761; Hævernick, p. 169.

ver. 11. THE FEAR OF GOD] *the general principle of religion,* as we should now say. The name Elohim is appropriately and necessarily used. The result proved that Abraham was mistaken in thinking that the fear of *Elohim* was not there, and he acknowledges that. The fear of *Jehovah* was really not there (*Hengstenberg*).

ver. 16. A most difficult passage. Do the thousand pieces of silver denote the value of the presents given (ver. 14) to Abraham (*Knobel*), or a distinct gift to Sarah (*Tuch, Kalisch*)? To what does the pronoun which we translate *he, behold he is*, refer; to Abraham (*Kalisch*), or to *the gift of a thousand shekels* (*Knobel*, and most expositors)? What is the meaning of the *covering of the eyes;* is it *a veil* used only by married women (*Rosenm., v. Bohlen, Tuch, De Sola*), or *a protection* afforded by her husband (*Kalisch*), or *a gift to condone the injury* (*Gesen., Knobel, Wright*)? What is the meaning of, and what part of the verb is the word which we translate, *thus she was reproved?* is it to be translated thus (*Genesius*), or by, *thou hast justice done to thee* (*Maurer, Knobel, Delitzsch*)? If we adopt the translation of our version, the passage means that the gift of 1000 pieces of silver should be a proof to Sarah that Abraham was sufficient to protect her from the gaze of licentious eyes, and therefore she had gratuitously practised a deception. We are inclined to prefer the following translation: *I have given thy brother a thousand pieces of silver; lo, it is a condoning gift for all that has happened to thee and to all* (thy family, or handmaids); *and thou hast justice done to thee* (*Maurer, Knob., Del.*), or, *and she was reproved* (*Gesen.*).—COVERING OF THE EYES] by English expositors taken generally to denote a veil; as if he reproved her for going abroad unveiled in the guise of an unmarried woman. But the veil is not the peculiar mark of difference between married and unmarried women, which this explanation supposes. The expression, *to cover the eyes of a person* in the sense of *to cause him to pardon a wrong,* is not unusual in the Bible; see Job ix. 24; Ex. xxiii. 8; Deut. xvi. 19; comp. Ps. xxxii. 1; lxxxv. 2.

Chapter XXI.

ver. 1. THE LORD VISITED SARAH] It was not a general divine concurrence which attended the birth of Isaac, but strictly a peculiar operation of the living personal God, revealed to the chosen race, and in a peculiar sense their God, to whom it belonged to make and fulfil promises. Hence the subject requires the use of the name Jehovah (*Hengstenberg*).—VISITED] denotes the Providence of God, whereby He fulfils what He had promised. Sometimes it is to be understood of evils to be inflicted (Exod. xx. 5); at other times it denotes the bestowing mercies, as here, and Ps. viii. 4 (*Kidder*).

ver. 2. AT THE SET TIME OF WHICH GOD HAD SPOKEN TO HIM] See ch. xviii. 10. The reason which Hengstenberg gives for the use of Elohim, where from the reference we should expect rather Jehovah, is not satisfactory. It is used, he says, to "indicate the contrast between the word of God and the word of man, which is proved by the sequel." The use of the name throughout the chapter may be better explained on the principle pointed out in the prefatory note to ch. xvii. The sacred writer has in view the momentous transaction of the next chapter. By it, as we shall see there, was perfectly fulfilled to Abraham the promise of a son. The birth of Isaac was but the preparatory step to the full completion, which was effected when Jehovah restored Isaac to Abraham on Moriah with the promise now confirmed by an oath. Hence, from the natural birth of Isaac to the time of the sacrifice on Moriah, God is spoken of as Elohim to Abraham, because He was still such to Him comparatively with the revelation of Himself He was to vouchsafe to him there.

ver. 3. ISAAC] which means *laughter*. The name points to the contrast between the idea and the fact; in the first instance, to the contrast between the promise of God on the one hand, and the advanced years of Abraham and Sarah on the other hand. When, by the birth of a son this contradiction was removed, a new and no less decided contrast appears between the greatness of the blessing which the promise had attached to this son, and the weakness of the child which had just come into the world. The former contrast had caused the laughter of Abraham and Sarah, the latter that of Ishmael (*Hengstenberg, Kurtz, Drechsler*).

ver. 6. GOD HATH MADE ME TO LAUGH, &c.] God, she says, has made her to laugh with wonder and astonishment, by thus fulfilling His promise, notwithstanding her old age; and all who hear of it will join in laughter of wondering astonishment (*Hengstenberg*).

ver. 8. WAS WEANED] It is impossible to fix the exact time when he was weaned. From 2 Macc. vii. 27; 1 Sam. i. 23, 24; Joseph. *Ant.* II. 9, 6, it has been inferred that children were weaned at the end of three years. In 2 Chron. xxxi. 16, nothing is assigned for the provision of the priests and Levites until after three years of age, which renders it probable that they were not weaned sooner. Jerome says, that it was a Hebrew opinion that Isaac was five years old. It is still customary in Persia and India to celebrate the event with a feast.

ver. 9. MOCKING] For this S. Paul has substituted the stronger expression, *persecuted*, Gal. iv. 29. "Ishmael *laughs*, mocking the weak babe, about whom his parents make so much work, and with whom they connect such exceeding hopes" (*Kurtz, Hengstenberg*). See Alford on Gal. iv. 29.

ver. 12. IN ISAAC SHALL THY SEED BE CALLED] The promised seed to whom the great blessing belongs, shall not descend from Ishmael, but from Isaac (*Kidder*).

vers. 14—21. It is objected that this is but a repetition in a different form of the tradition before recorded in ch. xvi. 4—16. There is, however, no improbability in the belief that Hagar twice left Abraham's roof. Amid the simple relations of nomad life, as Keil observes, such an occurrence is not at all surprising. And in all the particulars narrated there is so much diversity, as to render it impossible to fit the two stories to one event (*Ayre*). Comp. Kalisch, p. 438.

ver. 14. A BOTTLE] Rather a *waterskin*, such as is to this day used; see Robinson, *Bib. Res.* I. 232; Thomson, *The Land and the Book*, p. 576. —AND GAVE IT, &c.] i.e. *putting the bottle on her shoulder he gave it to Hagar, and also gave her the boy*. There is no ground for the assertion of Schumann and v. Bohlen that the sacred writer, forgetful that Ishmael must now be at least fifteen years old, represents him as a little child still carried by his mother.

ver. 15. SHE CAST THE CHILD UNDER] The Heb. verb may be translated *lowered*, as in Jer. xxxviii. 6.

ver. 17. GOD] The use of the name in this passage is very striking, as in the parallel narrative, ch. xvi., we find *Jehovah*, and *the angel of Jehovah*. The variation is thus accounted for. Hitherto, as the circumcision of Ishmael proves, Hagar and Ishmael had formed part of the chosen family, and therefore shared in the relation to Jehovah: with the Almighty's declaration, v. 12, *In Isaac shall thy seed be called*, they were withdrawn from the jurisdiction of Jehovah, and placed under that of Elohim. The outward separation from the chosen seed was only a manifestation of that which had already taken place internally (*Hengstenberg*).

ver. 18. HOLD HIM IN THINE HAND] Lit. *join thy hand to him*, i.e. lay hold of him with your hand (*Gesen*). She was to lead the lad; he was therefore, in the writer's mind, not an infant who could be carried in the mother's arms.

ver. 19. OPENED HER EYES] Made her see a well at a short distance from her, which she had not noticed before. Wells in that arid tract are sedulously concealed by the roving Nomads from the intrusion of strangers (*De Sola*).

ver. 20. AND HE GREW, AND DWELT, &c.] Thus Kalisch and Kurtz. As he was at most aged seventeen, it could well be said that he grew after that age. Maurer and Knobel would translate, *and he was growing an archer*, i.e. acquired increasing skill in the use of the bow, *and he dwelt*, &c.

ver. 21. PARAN] The wilderness of Paran embraces the broad desert tract of table-land between Egypt, Palestine, and Mount Seir, which is now called by the Arabs the desert of et-Tih (*Kurtz*).

ver. 22. PHICHOL] The word, according to the Hebrew derivation, means *mouth of all*, i.e. *commander of all* (*Gesenius*). It seems to have been a general name for the chief captains of the kings of Gerar.—GOD IS WITH THEE IN ALL THAT THOU DOEST] The blessing of God which rested on Abraham moved reverence in these heathens. We have here an image of the blessing which, even in O. T. times, reached beyond the people of the covenant, and extended itself to the heathen (*v. Gerlach*).

ver. 28. SEVEN EWE-LAMBS] Seven is a peculiarly sacred number in Scripture, apparently meant to bear reference to the covenant of God. Hence Abraham gives Abimelech seven lambs in token of the covenant or oath passed between them. "The presentation," says Hengstenberg, "of seven lambs was an usual symbol at that time—the incorporation of the transaction and the oaths" (*Pentateuch*, I. 285). He gives no proof of the existence of the custom he mentions. Herodotus says that the Arabs, when pledging their faith, smeared blood drawn from their hands on *seven* stones (*Hist.* III. 8).

ver. 31. BEER-SHEBA] *The well of the oath* (*Gesenius*). The site was visited by Dr Robinson in 1838. Although it lies near the desert, the country about it is fit for pasturage. Near the ruins are two wells, called *Bir-es-seba*, the sides of which are sheathed with solid masonry of great antiquity. The water in both is pure and sweet and in abundance. *Bib. Res.* I. 203.

ver. 33. A GROVE] Rather *a tamarisk*, a tree which grows to a considerable size in Palestine.

Chapter XXII.

This chapter records the most important event in Abraham's career. The references to it in the New Testament (Heb. vi. 13—17; xi. 17; Jas. ii. 21) point to it as the climax of all the trials and leadings of his life. Once he has passed beyond it, his life is spent untroubled and unmoved. The inquiry naturally presents itself, why did his trial take this peculiar form? The satisfactory answer seems to be this. The promise was made to Abraham of a blessed race, and of a son Isaac through whom this race was to be derived to him (ch. xvii. 19; xviii. 10; compared with Rom. ix. 7, 8). It might be thought that the promise was fulfilled in the birth of Isaac; but, in Heb. vi. 13—17, it is declared that the promise was not fulfilled to him until the offering was made on Mount Moriah; comp. also Heb. xi. 17, *whence he received him.* For though born by the creative working of God, Isaac was still the naturally born son of Abraham, linked to him solely by the tie of fleshly sonship. The rite of circumcision brought both father and son only outwardly and in a symbolic way into the spiritual lineage by which they were united in one family to one another and to God. To effect this, and to make Isaac the son of promise and blessing to Abraham as well as the son born of the flesh, a fresh trial is laid on Abraham. As formerly he had sacrificed father and mother and kindred and country, so now he is called on to surrender up the life of his only son in whom the promises seemed to centre. His complete dependence and reliance on God stands the trial, and is proved by it. He receives back his son, and with him the sworn, and therefore irrevocably fixed, promise of God, that he himself should be the father of a blessed race, which was to issue from him through Isaac. The trial has its bearing on Isaac also, for, as arrived at an age when he could bear the wood for the sacrifice, he could have resisted the will of his father; but even as the father's will is so conformed to the will of God as to sacrifice his son, so the son's will is so moulded into likeness with the father's as to be obedient to him even unto death. Thus is proved a true spiritual affinity between them; and Abraham receives his son back with the seal of God's promise of being the channel through which he was to be made the father of nations. The sonship of Isaac is therefore perfected. Viewing the transaction in this light we can see the true typical relationship which connects it with Christ's sacrifice. Abraham was by it made the human father of the multitude of blessed nations, and Isaac the son through whom the multitude of nations were to trace their lineage to Abraham. This was the human basis essential in the divine counsels to the Incarnation of the Son of God. And as it was arrived at through denial and sacrifice of the will in compliance to the will of God, it was the fit antecedent of that perfect sacrifice of the Son of God who came to do the will of God, and therefore took on Him the form of a servant, and so perfectly brought His human will into subjection to the Divine will as to become obedient even unto death. See especially Kurtz, I. p. 263. That the offering of Isaac and the sacrifice of Christ are typically connected, was always discerned by our old divines; yet through failing to observe the true ground of the relation, and through their tendency to run into minute applications, they have for the most part placed it too much in the light of an accidental parallelism between two unconnected events. Of all of them Jackson has come nearest the truth, *Works*, Vol. VIII. pp. 151, 370, 396. Comp. Pearson, *On the Creed*, Art. IV; Mede, *Disc.* XIII. We are thus prepared to discern the accurate use of the divine names. From the time of the natural birth of Isaac up to the time that he is restored to Abraham on Moriah, Elohim is used; after that point is reached, Jehovah appears. For in the first period God was in the sacred writer's eyes unto Abraham only Elohim, in comparison with the fulness of revelation of Himself, as the Personal God blessing His people, vouchsafed to Abraham when God perfectly fulfilled the promise of giving him a son. See pref. note to ch. xvii.

ver. 1. GOD DID TEMPT] or *try*. Throughout all Scripture, the *trials* which God exposes men to are represented as means to strengthen faith, and consequently as a divine benefit. The temptation or trial here was, whether Abraham's faith was of such self-renouncing power as to enable him to sacrifice for the Lord that in which centred his affections and his hopes. Though it was only the implicit surrender of his son in *mind* and *heart* that was required of Abraham, yet it was necessary to be effected in this shape, in order to avoid all mental reservation and self-delusion on his part. When the mental sacrifice was thoroughly accomplished by Abraham, then God interposed and prevented the actual sacrifice, which was not requisite. Thus Kurtz. For the objections to the transaction on the part of the old English deistical writers, see Waterland, *Works*, IV. 199; and for those of later German rationalist writers, Hævernick, p. 172.

ver. 2. WHOM THOU LOVEST] He is to offer up the son whom he had hoped and waited for twenty-five years, and on whose life hung all the precious and glorious promises which held out such unspeakable blessing and salvation itself to all nations. And yet Abraham was to preserve his faith, and his confidence in him who had given them. This was the testing-point in the temptation (*Kurtz*). Heb. xi. 17—19.—LAND OF MORIAH] The name would lead us to conclude that the mountain was the same with that on which Solomon built the temple (2 Chron. iii. 1). This inference is rendered more probable when we find the distance between Beer-sheba and

Jerusalem, as represented by Dr Robinson, to be just such as Abraham might have traversed in three days. Dr Robinson travelled with camels from Beer-sheba to Jerusalem in twenty hours and twenty-five minutes; Abraham, *who travelled with asses*, took three days to reach his destination. But Gerizim, near Sychem, which Mr Stanley, following the Samaritan tradition, maintains to be the Moriah of Genesis, was a journey of thirty-five hours to the American traveller. This alone proves that it would have been impossible for Abraham to have reached Gerizim in three days. See this argument strongly confirmed by the experience of Dr Thomson, *Land and Book*, p. 475. The name Moriah, here applied to *the country*, was in the time of Solomon confined to the Temple Mount: various explanations, founded on various derivations, have been given of it: *That which is shown of, appearance of Jehovah* (Hengstenberg, Kurtz); *chosen by Jehovah* (Gesenius); *shown by Jehovah* (v. Gerlach); *country rich in springs* (Ebrard).

ver. 5. AND COME AGAIN TO YOU] This declaration proves that Abraham 'accounted that God was able to raise up Isaac from the dead;' Heb. xi. 17—19.

ver. 14. JEHOVAH-JIREH] i.e. *the Lord sees* or *provides;* in reference to his own answer in v. 8, *God will provide himself a burnt-offering.*—AS IT IS SAID TO THIS DAY, IN THE MOUNT OF THE LORD IT SHALL BE SEEN] or, *so that it is said to this day, In the mount of the Lord provision shall be made;* i.e. The Lord is ever present in His holy mountain with His ready help (*Wright*). The strong hold that this event took of the memories of Abraham's immediate descendants is proved by the allusion made by Moses (Ex. xv. 17), where he gives the people prophetic promise of this mountain being the place of the sanctuary. Hengstenberg labours to trace a connexion between the name *Moriah* (as if it were given to the mountain from this transaction) and the name given by Abraham here. But certainly from the reference to the name Moriah in v. 2, it appears to have been in existence before this, and to have been applied *not* to the *mountain* but to the *country*, and hence to have no connexion with the name applied by Abraham to the mountain alone.

ver. 16. HAVE I SWORN] God's *oath* imports more than His *word* merely. Blessings promised, but not confirmed by oath, were conditional, and the promise revocable. The oath of God was always an infallible argument that the thing which He swore was immutable. Thus Dean Jackson, *Works*, Vol. VIII. p. 399, &c.

ver. 17. POSSESS THE GATE] i.e. conquer the cities.

ver. 20. The account of Nahor's family is here inserted as a necessary introduction to the relation of Isaac's marriage with Rebecca, to prove that she was of his kindred (*De Sola*).

Chapter XXIII.

ver. 1. SARAH] The only woman, remarks Lightfoot, the length of whose life is related in Scripture.

ver. 2. CAME TO MOURN, &c.] There is something formal in this remark, but it is in perfect accordance with present customs. Should such a person die here to-morrow, there would be a solemn mourning and weeping,—not as indicating the grief of the family so much as in honour of the dead (Thomson, *Land and the Book*, p. 577).— CAME] either from his own tent, or from some other place in the neighbourhood where he happened to be.

ver. 6. A MIGHTY PRINCE] Lit. *a prince of God*, blessed by God.—IN THE CHOICE OF OUR SEPULCHRES BURY THY DEAD] A mere Oriental compliment. There has always been the utmost exclusiveness in this country in regard to tombs. Abraham regarded the offer in its true light (*Thomson*).

ver. 7. STOOD UP AND BOWED] Another act of respect in accordance with modern manners (*Thomson*).

ver. 8. INTREAT FOR ME TO EPHRON] There is scarcely anything in the habits of Orientals more annoying than this universal custom of employing mediators to pass between you and those with whom you wish to do business. Nothing can be done without them (*Thomson*).

ver. 9. MACHPELAH] a proper name. Dr Robinson considers the tradition accurate which marks the very ancient enclosure of masonry surrounding the Great Haram at Hebron as the sepulchre of Abraham (*Bib. Res.* II. 79). A description of the enclosure, of the mosque and the cave beneath the mosque, is given by Dr Thomson from observations of himself and other travellers (*Land and Book*, p. 581).

ver. 11. THE FIELD GIVE I THEE] One of the usual exaggerations of Oriental politeness; and thus it was understood.

ver. 15. SHEKELS] in weight, not in coin; see next verse, and note on ch. xxxiii. 19.

ver. 16. AND ABRAHAM WEIGHED, &c.] As Jeremiah, by the purchase of the field of Hanameel, proved his conviction of the return of Israel from the captivity, so the Patriarch evinces his belief that his descendants will possess the land by this act.

ver. 17. AND THE FIELD, &c.] The *specifications* in the contract are just such as are found in modern deeds. It is not enough that you purchase a well-known lot; the contract must mention everything that belongs to it (*Thomson*).

Chapter XXIV.

ver. 1. OLD] about 140 years; comp. ch. xxi. 5, and xxv. 20.

ver. 2. SERVANT] generally understood to be Eliezer of Damascus.—PUT THY HAND UNDER MY THIGH] He commands him to put his hand there, that being mindful of the promise of circumcision he might not defile his master's race with a foreign marriage (*Theodoret*). The other ancient writers and the Jewish Rabbins similarly refer the gesture to the covenant sign; and rightly, since its use is confined to the patriarchs. Kurtz explains the symbol as referring to the thigh as the seat of power. Why then was the custom not more general? Aben-Ezra takes it as a sign of subjection of the servant to the master; yet Jacob used it in the case of his son Joseph.

ver. 3. THOU SHALT NOT, &c.] The reason of Abraham's precaution will be found in the command afterwards given to Israel (Deut. vii. 3).

ver. 7. THE LORD] That throughout the narrative of Isaac's marriage the name Jehovah should be most prominent, is exceedingly natural. The writer's design is not to show, by a single example, the agency of Divine Providence in the marriage institution; in such a case Elohim would have been suitable. His design is rather to show how the special Providence of the God of revelation superintends the chosen race (*Hengstenberg*).

ver. 10. TEN CAMELS] Such an expedition would not now be undertaken from Hebron with any other animals, nor with a less number. The most direct route would be along the west side of Jordan and the lakes, into the Buk'ah, and out through the land of Hamath to the Euphrates, and thence to the city of Nahor (*Thomson*).— MESOPOTAMIA] Heb. *Aram-naharaim*, Aram or Syria of the two rivers, the country between the rivers Euphrates and Tigris. Padan-Aram, the abode of Bethuel, was a district of Aram-naharaim.

ver. 11. CAMELS TO KNEEL] The action is literally kneeling.— WITHOUT THE CITY BY A WELL] In the East the people prefer to have the well outside the city, to avoid the noise, dust, and confusion always occurring at it. It is around the fountain that the thirsty traveller and the wearied caravan assemble. It was perfectly natural, therefore, for Eliezer to halt there (*Thomson*).—THE EVENING, EVEN THE TIME THAT WOMEN GO OUT TO DRAW WATER] True to life. At that hour the peasant returns home from his labour. Cool fresh water is then demanded, and of course there is a great concourse around the well. About great cities men often carry water; but in the country *women only* go to the well (*Thomson*).

ver. 15. HER PITCHER UPON HER SHOULDER] The Egyptian and the negro carry on the head, the Syrian on the shoulder or hip (*Thomson*).

ver. 16. WENT DOWN TO THE WELL] Nearly all the wells in the East are in wadies [hollows between hills], and many of them have steps down to the water (*Thomson*).

ver. 19. I WILL DRAW WATER FOR THY CAMELS ALSO] As we might infer from Eliezer's prayer, this was an unusual act of kindness. For although Dr Robinson on one occasion found people ready to offer to draw water for the animals of his party (*Bib. Res.* II. p. 22), Dr Thomson often found it difficult to get his horse watered even for money (*Land and the Book*, p. 593).

ver. 20. THE TROUGH] several of which are generally at the wells (Robinson, II. 26).

ver. 22. GOLDEN EARRING] more properly,

nose-ring, an ornament still worn by women in the East.

ver. 30. WHEN HE SAW THE EAR-RING, HE SAID, COME IN, &c.] The greediness of gain, which the subsequent history shows to have characterized Laban, here appears prominently.—THOU BLESSED OF THE LORD] We might feel tempted to attribute Laban's use of the name Jehovah to the remains of a deeper knowledge of God which was retained in the family of Nahor; but the exact reference of ver. 31 to ver. 27 is against this opinion. Laban's *Come in, thou blessed of Jehovah,* is a mere echo of the servant's *Blessed be Jehovah.* Also in vers. 51, 52, no independent knowledge of Jehovah is manifested, but only the reception of what the servant had said of him (*Hengstenberg*).

ver. 32. STRAW AND PROVENDER] that is, *tibn,* and some kind of pulse and grain. There is no *hay* in the East (*Thomson*).

ver. 50. LABAN] In those ancient days the brothers appear to have had even a stronger right of protection and care over their sisters than the fathers over their daughters; comp. ch. xxxiv. 13. There are still traces among the modern Arabs of this custom (*Rosenmuller*).

ver. 55. A FEW DAYS, AT LEAST TEN] Thus

most modern expositors translate in preference to the translation of some Jewish interpreters adopted by Patrick, *about ten months.*

ver. 59. NURSE] Deborah; ch. xxxv. 8.

ver. 63. TO MEDITATE] This translation is supported by Sept., Vulg., Rosenmuller, Maurer, Tuch, Baumgarten. The other translations proposed are: *to pray* (*Onkelos, Saadias, Luther*); *to converse* (*Aquila, Symmachus, v. Bohlen*); *to walk* (*Aben-Ezra, Kimchi*); *to mourn* for his mother (*Knobel*).

ver. 64. WHEN SHE SAW ISAAC, SHE LIGHTED OFF THE CAMEL] It is customary for both men and women, when an emeer or great personage is approaching, to alight some time before he comes up with them. Women frequently refuse to ride in the presence of men (*Thomson*). An instance of women dismounting until the man passes is found in Niebuhr's travels, as cited by Rosenmuller.

ver. 65. TOOK A VAIL] In the East the bride is brought veiled to her husband.

CHAPTER XXV.

ver. 1. KETURAH] *Katura* is the name of a tribe in the neighbourhood of Mecca.

ver. 2. ZIMRAN] Perhaps the *Zemareni* of Plin. VI. 32 (*Delitzsch*). Knobel sees a resemblance to the word in *Zabram*, the royal city of the Kinædokolpitæ of Ptol. VI. 7. 5, 20, 23.—JOKSHAN] The *Kassanitæ* of Ptol. VI. 7. 6, who dwelt by the Red Sea to the south of the Kinædokolpitæ.—MEDAN AND MIDIAN] *Modiana* on the east coast of the Œlanitic Gulf, and *Madiana* a district to the north-east of it. The two races seem to have been united; for the *Midjanim* are called Medanim, ch. xxxvii. 28, 36.—ISHBAK] or *Jischbak*, perhaps appears in *Schobek*, a place in the land of Edom. See Robinson, II. 123.— SHUAH] may be compared with the Arab tribe *Syayhe*, on the east of Aila; or with the place *Schyhhan* in Moabitis. Bildad, the friend of Job, was of this tribe; Job ii. 11.

ver. 3. SHEBA] Neighbours of the Nabathæans, according to Strab. XVI. p. 779; alluded to in Job i. 15, vi. 19 (*Knobel*).—DEDAN] the *banu Dudan* in Hegaz or Hedjaz.—ASSHURIM] the powerful and warlike races of the *Asyr*, dwelling in the south of Hedjaz.—LETUSHIM] the *banu Leits* in Hedjaz.—LEUMMIM] the tribe of the *beni Lam*, who were spread as far as Babylonia and Mesopotamia. The plural forms of these last names are well adapted to widely diffused and dispersed tribes (*Knobel*).

ver. 4. EPHAH] named in Isai. lx. 6 after Midian, as a tribe which brought gold and incense to the Hebrews.—EPHER] Probably the *banu Ghiphar*, belonging to the tribe Kenana in Hedjaz. —HANOCH] *Hanakye*, three days' journey to the north of Mecca.—ABIDAH AND ELDAAH] The *Abida* and the *Wadaa*, two important tribes near the Asyr. The preceding notices are derived from the commentaries of Knobel and Delitzsch.

ver. 6. CONCUBINES] Hagar and Keturah.

ver. 8. WAS GATHERED TO HIS PEOPLE] An expression which shows that death was not regarded in those times as the termination of existence. Comp. note on ch. xv. 15.

ver. 11. GOD BLESSED ISAAC] Elohim appears, because the blessing here referred to was only of an earthly temporal character.

vers. 12—15. NEBAJOTH AND KEDAR] thus connected not only in Isa. lx. 7, but also in Pliny (*H. N.* VI. 32, *Nabatœi et Cedrei*). *Kaidhâr* and *Nabt* or *Nabit* appear in the Arabian genealogies as descendants of Ishmael. The Nabathæans were a powerful people who possessed great part of Southern Arabia. Three centuries before Christ they took Petra from the Edomites, and occupied almost all of the original country of that nation. According to Delitzsch, the language of the Nabathæans was quite Aramaic. Kedar, or the Cedreni, dwelt between Arabia Petræa and Babylonia.—DUMAH] Hence is derived the name of the town *Dumath al Djendel* in the district of *Djof* or *Gof*, between the Syrian Desert and Arabia Proper, about six days' journey from Damascus, and thirteen from Medina.— MASSA] perhaps the *Masani* of Ptolemy, v. 19. 2. (*Kalisch*).—TEMA] A trace of the ancient abode of this tribe may be found in the little castellum Thaima, near the border of the Syrian desert, about three days' journey from Medina—JETUR] The *Itureans*, who occupied the north-east of Palestine to the east of Mount Hermon. Nothing can be said with any degree of certainty about the remaining tribes mentioned here.

ver. 18. THEY DWELT FROM HAVILAH UNTO SHUR, THAT IS BEFORE EGYPT, AS THOU GOEST TOWARD ASSYRIA] *They dwelt from Havilah*, or Chaulan in the south, *to Shur, the eastern boundary of Egypt*, in the north-west, *as thou goest toward Assyria*, i. e. all along from Shur in the west to Assyria in the east and north-east. Or we might understand by Havilah, the place Huäle on the Persian Gulf, and compare with it the Chaulotæi (Strabo, XVI. p. 767), or Chaulasii (Dionys. *Perieg.* 956), or Avalitæ (Plin. *H. N.* VI. 32), though this tribe dwelt more to the north-west. In this case the Ishmaelites would be represented as extending first from the south-east to the north-west, and from that to the north-east (*Knobel*). Comp. notes on ch. x. 7, 29.

ver. 20. SYRIAN] Lit. *Aramean*, inhabitant of Aram.—PADAN-ARAM] Aram, which means highland, is the general name for Syria. Aram-naharaim, or Aram of the two rivers, is Mesopotamia; while Padan-Aram (*Padan* = cultivated land, from *Padah* = plough) is the name of some particular fertile district in it (ch. xxiv. 10 = xxv. 20), where Nahor took up his abode.

ver. 21. BARREN] for twenty years.

ver. 22. SHE WENT] This shows that it was

not in vision or in dream that she inquired of the Lord. *Whither* or to *whom* she went Scripture says not.

ver. 23. TWO NATIONS] The prophecy was in reference not to the individuals, but to the races which were to spring from them, and which, as elsewhere in Scripture, are regarded as included in the fathers.—THE ELDER SHALL SERVE THE YOUNGER] The promise of the seed of blessing is limited to the race of the younger son. The servitude of the elder to the younger refers to the universal rule which Christ as man merited by His obedience to death (Heb. i. 2, Phil. ii. 10, Eph. i. 22), and to that dominion which His glorified Church is to enjoy with Him (Rev. v. 10).

ver. 26. ESAU] *Hairy (Gesenius).* The birth of Esau and Jacob, though mentioned after the death of Abraham, occurred fifteen years before it. The order of time is sometimes not observed (*Kidder*).

ver. 27. JACOB] *He who takes by the heel, trips up, a supplanter.*

ver. 28. HE DID EAT OF HIS VENISON] or, *venison was according to his taste,* venison was his favourite food (*Delitzsch, Wright*).

ver. 29. FAINT] In the next chapter a famine

is mentioned. We may perhaps thus account for Esau's eagerness for food.

ver. 30. THAT RED POTTAGE] Lit. *that red, red;* a repetition expressive of eagerness. The pottage was made of the *'adis* or lentiles, still prepared in Palestine for food. "The pottage generally is made of the brown or bronze-coloured, and not of the red kind. I can testify that when cooking it diffuses far and wide an odour extremely grateful to a hungry man" (Thomson, p. 587). Comp. Robinson, I. 166.

ver. 31. BIRTHRIGHT] The external rights of primogeniture gave at least a double inheritance (Deut. xxi. 17), if not more (Gen. xxv. 5, 6); and implied primacy over the family (Gen. xlix. 3). With the latter a third advantage was connected in the family of the patriarchs, viz. the transference of the promised blessing (*Kurtz*).

ver. 32. I AM AT THE POINT TO DIE] The words in the Hebrew do not mean, as the translation intimates, that Esau was at the point of death through hunger, but that his life as a hunter led him into constant dangers (*Knobel, Wright*). Or, it means, *I must one day or other die,* what do I want then with the inheritance? He considered himself only and not his posterity, and preferred what was tangible and present, to that which was invisible and in the future (*Delitzsch*). The epithet *profane* applied to Esau in Heb. xii. 16 is quite justified by this language of his. Provided that his desires were satisfied in the present time he did not care to hear of spiritual blessings. Though Jacob's desire to take advantage of his brother's folly is not to be excused, his conduct we see is not so bad as is represented by our version.

Chapter XXVI.

The marked similarity between the contents of this chapter and certain passages in Abraham's life has led rationalist writers to affirm that it is only a reproduction of part of Abraham's history. But, notwithstanding the apparent similarity of events, there is a real dissimilarity, having its foundation in the *differences of character* of the two patriarchs. "Abraham takes refuge in Egypt, and Isaac is about to imitate him. But Abraham learns only by the complications and dangers in which he is involved, that this device was contrary to the will of God. On the other hand, Isaac, whose greater weakness of character would not have been equal to the dangers which there threatened him, or whose softness could not have resisted the peculiar attractions of the land, is by divine intervention preserved from following the device which he had at first conceived. What Abraham could not experience, Isaac learned by the hundredfold harvest which he reaped, viz. that even in a year of famine and failure the land of promise would yield a blessing, and manifest the reality of the promise given him. Analogous and not less apparent is the difference between Abraham and Isaac under those circumstances which had led to another fall of Abraham. That patriarch *loses* his wife. The protection of God does not spare him this trial, although it delivers him from dangers which might thence have resulted. The weaker Isaac is spared this trial, and the protection of God manifests itself in this, that the falsehood of his pretence appears before it is too late. The similarity of their nomadic occupations, and the continuance of former circumstances, account for the fact that in both cases we read of the same stations and wells, and of another alliance with Abimelech. But what a contrast between the personality of Abraham, who commands respect, and the patient yielding of Isaac. People do not interfere with the rights and privileges of Abraham, but Isaac must give place before continual hostilities and interferences" (*Kurtz*).

ver. 1. ABIMELECH] Abimelech, like Phichol, was a name of office, not of person. All the kings of Gerar were called Abimelech; see note on ch. xx. 2. We are therefore not obliged by the identity of name to infer the identity of person here and in ch. xx. Still, considering the age that the people at that period lived to, the chronology does not forbid this inference, which is rather confirmed by the conduct of Abimelech on this occasion. He who earlier in life had not hesitated to seize the beautiful Sarah, now, when age had quelled his passions, is only fearful lest any of his subjects should insult Rebekah.—UNTO GERAR] In the time of scarcity it was very natural for Isaac to take refuge in the plains of Philistia, which are described by Dr Thomson as exceeding in fertility the richest parts of America. "Without manure, and with a style of ploughing and general culture which would secure nothing but failure in America, this vast plain continues to produce splendid crops every year; and this too, after forty centuries of such tillage" (*The Land and the Book*, p. 557). He includes Gerar in this description.

ver. 2. THE LORD] used appropriately in this chapter. Hitherto Isaac had prospered through God's general providence, ch. xxv. 11. A famine occurring, as he could not hope, according to the natural course of things as thus regulated, to find support in Palestine, he seems to have designed to go to Egypt. At the command of Jehovah, who reveals Himself and renews the blessing of Abraham, he continues in the country of the Philistines, and (ver. 12) is rewarded by the extraordinary return that the land makes to him, not in the natural course of things, but by the blessing of Jehovah. Even the heathens (ver. 28) saw a special interposition of the God whom Isaac worshipped. Comp. Hengstenberg, *Pent.* I. 352.

ver. 8. A WINDOW] Heb. *the challon;* the aperture in the parapet round the roof of Abimelech's palace, through which the king could look down on the houses in the town, and see what took place in the domestic privacy of their inner courts. Compare 2 Sam. xi. 2 (*v. Bohlen*).

ver. 10. THOU SHOULDEST HAVE BROUGHT GUILTINESS] He had in mind the punishment incurred by the outrage committed in Sarah's case.

ver. 12. Isaac is taught that even in a time of famine the Lord can provide for His own who obey Him.—IN THE SAME YEAR] In Palestine the harvest is reaped in less than four months after sowing in the same year.—AN HUNDREDFOLD] No improbability in this enormous yield, as is shown by Dr Thomson, p. 83.

ver. 20. ESEK] The reason of this name being assigned is seen by translating the verse: *He called the name of the well,* CONTENTION (*Esek*), *because they contended with him.*

ver. 21. SITNAH] which means *enmity.*

ver. 22. REHOBOTH] *space, extension.* The name is still preserved in the Wady er-Ruhaibeh, midway between Gerar and Beer-sheba, at the fork of the two main roads to Gaza and Hebron. On the hill to the left of the valley are ruins covering twelve acres in extent (Robinson, I. 196).

ver. 24. Forced from the place where in time of famine he had found plenty, he is comforted by a renewed assurance of the Lord's protection.

ver. 25. DIGGED A WELL] apparently in addition to that already sunk by Abraham. It is remarkable that there are *two* wells sheeted with masonry of great antiquity at Beer-sheba.

ver. 26. AHUZZATH, ONE OF HIS FRIENDS] His chief minister and counsellor; comp. 1 Kin. iv. 5; 1 Chron. xxvii. 33.—PHICHOL] an official title, it would seem, like the name Abimelech, as *mudir* or *mushir* in the modern Palestine. "If one of these officers is spoken of, his name is rarely mentioned; I indeed never knew any but the official titles of these Turkish officers" (Thomson, p. 560).

ver. 33. Rationalist writers find here a proof that the narrative of Isaac's covenant with Abimelech is only the transaction of ch. xxi. in a different shape. But "that the Philistine king made a covenant with Isaac is probable; that Isaac then received the first intelligence of the well which his servants digged, and that he named it Shebah, in commemoration of the sworn covenant, is possible; finally, that Beer-sheba is named from two wells, in allusion to the two covenants made between Abimelech, and Abraham, and Isaac, is confirmed by the two ancient wells which Robinson found there. As we find that Isaac renewed the old names of the wells in other places, it is rendered probable that in thus naming the well, he alluded to the naming by his father of the other well which lay near" (*Delitzsch*).—SHEBAH] meaning *oath*.

ver. 34. Fresh proof of Esau's *profanity*. Careless of the religious hopes and promises of the chosen family, he marries into a Canaanitish family.

Chapter XXVII.

The conduct of Isaac, Rebekah, and Jacob, as narrated in this chapter, has been made the ground of objection to the moral teaching of the Bible, but very incorrectly. There would indeed be matter for objection if the conduct of these personages was held forth as worthy of approbation; but the narrative has been so framed as to express, not indeed by words but by the equally expressive testimony of the issue of events, God's disapprobation of actions, which He permitted but yet overruled so as to bring out His own purposes. Isaac finds his ill-devised attempt to favour Esau recoil on himself and breed dissension between his sons. Jacob has to flee from his home and endure years of exile and hardship among kinsmen, who overreach him as he overreached his brother. Rebekah is obliged to drive her best-loved son from her presence in order to secure his safety. Thus the punishment which the transaction brings down on each of the offenders is the sure proof of the light in which their conduct was regarded by the Almighty Overruler of events.

The explanation given by Hengstenberg of the use of the divine names in this chapter, and in the first four verses of the next, is not satisfactory. The following is proposed. Isaac, thinking that death was at hand, proposed to confer a solemn blessing on his son Esau. Although the words, 'that I may bless thee *before the Lord,*' were used by Rebecca when repeating to Jacob what he had said, it is not improbable that Isaac may have used the expression 'before the Lord.' When about to implore a blessing on his son, he might well have had in mind God under that character in which He held forth so splendid a future to his descendants, and who had assured to Abraham and to Isaac the certainty of His promises by immediate marks of favour. For the same reason Jacob would, in v. 20, use the words *the Lord thy God.* In v. 27 Isaac is obliged to use the name Lord, because the garden of the Lord, or Paradise, supplied to him the image of that earthly abode which he desired for his son. In the blessing contained in vv. 28, 29, the name Jehovah would have been misplaced. None of the Patriarchs could take on themselves to single out the particular person who was to be the inheritor of the blessing of Abraham. Hence, neither Isaac when blessing the supposed Esau, nor Jacob when blessing Joseph, used the name Jehovah. Nay, the use of the name Elohim, leads me to think that Isaac had not at all the blessing of Abraham in view; but that he only, out of the fulness of his partiality for Esau, desired to secure his temporal welfare without any thought of Jacob. In the unexpected result he recognises the hand of God marking out Jacob as the inheritor of the hopes of the family. For this reason, in ch. xxviii. 3, by a solemn benediction he acknowledges him as such. He uses the name El-Shaddai, which God had Himself used, in ch. xvii. 1, when giving the promise to Abraham, and beseeches God, in that character, to use His Almighty power in controlling and disposing all events, so that, notwithstanding natural improbabilities, the promises might be fulfilled to Jacob. Hengstenberg certainly is mistaken in taking El-Shaddai as conveying a conception of God equivalent to that denoted by Elohim. In ch. xvii. 1, xxviii. 3, xlix. 25, El-Shaddai denotes the Personal God overruling by His might all things to the accomplishment of His promises, and to the good of His servants.

ver. 2. DEATH] Isaac, however, did not die for upwards of forty years after this; see ch. xxxv. 28.

ver. 4. SAVOURY MEAT] The most esteemed dishes of the Orientals are saturated with butter or fat, highly seasoned with salt, spices, garlic, onions, sharpened with vegetable acids, and sweetened with honey or vegetable sweets (*Pict. Bible*). It appears strange that, before pronouncing the blessing, Isaac should have demanded *meat* such as he loved. We cannot regard the meal as a *covenant-feast*, for in that case both parties must have joined in it. Nothing, therefore, remains but to suppose that Isaac had wished to excite his animal spirits, and to predispose himself for pronouncing a blessing, by partaking of savoury meat and drinking wine, just as Elisha wished to encourage and excite himself for prophetic inspiration by music. This appears the more likely as, irrespective of its acceptableness, the gift desired was one of *love*, an expression of the attachment of the son to his father; just as the blessing was an expression of the tenderness of the father to the son (*Kurtz*).

ver. 12. I SHALL BRING A CURSE UPON ME] He is not afraid of deceiving his blind father, only of being detected.

ver. 15. GOODLY] His *finest* or *best* clothes, worn on especial occasions (*Knobel, Wright*).

ver. 16. SKINS OF THE KIDS] The black silky hair of the eastern camel-goat was used by the Romans for false hair (*Tuch*). In Sol. Song iv. 1, the bride's hair is compared to that of goats (*Rosenm.*).

ver. 27. THE SMELL OF MY SON IS AS THE SMELL OF A FIELD, &c.] Many parts of Arabia and Palestine exhale a most delicious odour (Herod. III. 113); after a refreshing rain especially the air is perfumed with a fragrance inexpressibly sweet (Plin. XVII. 5). Thus the garments of Esau, the man of the field, were redolent of the scent of aromatic herbs; they called up in Isaac's mind the pictures of freshness, health, and abundance (*Kalisch, Tuch*).—A FIELD WHICH THE LORD HATH BLESSED] He speaks of a field like that of Paradise, resplendent with traces of the Deity— an ideal field, bearing the same relation to an ordinary one as Israel to the heathen—a kind of enchanted garden, such as would be realized in a later period in Canaan, as far as the fidelity of the people permitted it (*Hengstenberg*).

ver. 28. THEREFORE GOD GIVE THEE] This promise is at first annexed to things seen at present, hence it rises to the unseen future. The summit and centre of the blessing is contained in the words, 'Be Lord over thy brethren,' since thereby was signified that he alone was bearer of the blessing,—the others only shared the advantage through him. The lordship over the whole race consisted externally in the dominion which the Israelites exercised, in a great measure, over those descended from Esau, but *spiritually* in the rule of the Messiah which was to last for ever (*v. Gerlach*).—FATNESS OF THE EARTH] i.e. fertile meadows (*Wright*).

ver. 33. TREMBLED] He sees that without knowing it he had blessed, not according to his own will, but by the authority and according to the will of God (*Kurtz*).

ver. 38. WEPT] But, Heb. xii. 17, 'He found no place for repentance, though he sought it carefully with tears.'

ver. 39. THY DWELLING SHALL BE THE FATNESS OF THE EARTH, &c.] Most modern expositors adopt the translation, *Thy dwelling shall be without fatness of the earth, and without the dew of heaven.* "It may indeed be true, as Burckhardt has it (Vol. II. p. 702), that 'the declivities of Mount Seir are covered with corn-fields and orchards,' and as Robinson remarks (Vol. II. p. 154), that 'the mountains in the East appear to enjoy a sufficiency of rain, and are covered with tufts of herbs and occasional trees. The wadys too are full of trees and shrubs and flowers; while the eastern and higher parts are extensively cultivated, and yield good crops.' But it is equally true that Seetzen (Rosenmüller, *Antiq.* II. 1, p. 156), from personal observation, describes the country as 'perhaps the most desolate and sterile mountain in the world.' And Robinson himself expressly states that the western mountains 'are *wholly desert and sterile.*' And this must have been the general impression produced by a sight of the country, as the prophet Malachi says in the name of Jehovah, i. 3: 'I hated Esau, and laid his mountains and his heritage waste for the dragons of the wilderness.' Under the circumstances, Isaac is only disposed prophetically to regard the sterile aspect of the land of Esau" (*Kurtz*).

ver. 40. BY THY SWORD SHALT THOU LIVE] Unlike Jacob, who was to draw his support from the peaceful cultivation of a productive soil, Esau was to owe all to the sword.—AND SHALT SERVE, &c.] Isaac prophesies "a continuous and not unsuccessful, though ultimately vain, reaction on the part of Esau against the blessing of Jacob. And in point of fact the historical relation between Edom and Israel was one of continual alternation, of submission, of rebellion, and of renewed submission" (*Kurtz*). At first, and for a long time, the Edomites remained independent; then Saul subdued them (1 Sam. xiv. 47). David made them subject (2 Sam. viii. 14). Solomon made a navy of ships in Ezion-Geber, the harbour of Edomites on the shore of the Red Sea (1 Kin. ix. 26). In still later times were they under the dominion of the kingdom of Judah (2 Kin. iii). They revolted against Joram (2 Kin. viii. 20); Amaziah smote them and took Selah (2 Kin. xiv. 7); Uzziah also defeated them (2 Chron. xxvi. 2); but under Ahaz they made themselves independent (2 Chron. xxviii. 17). After they had been subjected to the Chaldæans, Persians, Greek-Syrians, they pushed as far as Hebron, and possessed it (1 Macc. v. 65); so that the whole southern part of Palestine was named Idumæa after them. About 100 B.C. John Hyrcanus entirely subdued them, and compelled them to receive circumcision; since which time they formed one people with the Jews, so much so, that even an Idumæan, Antipater, and his son, reigned in Judæa (*v. Gerl*). However, as the true fulfilment of the prophecy concerning Jacob is to be sought in the Messianic kingdom, so we may regard Edom as the representative of the God-hating heathen world which was to be put under the feet of the true king of Israel.—WHEN THOU SHALT HAVE THE DOMINION] This would seem to be better translated, *when thou shalt roam at large* (*Maur., Gesen., Knob., Del.*). Other translations are: *when thou shakest it* (*Kurtz*); *when thou art rebellious* (*Tuch, Wright*); *when thou desirest it* (*Kalisch*).

ver. 41. DAYS OF MOURNING, &c.] This translation is supported by Tuch, Knob., Del.; but Kalisch and Wright propose, *days of grief are at hand for my father, for I will slay*, &c.

ver. 42. DOTH COMFORT HIMSELF] Thus Maurer and Delitzsch; otherwise translated, *will revenge himself on thee by slaying thee* (*Gesen., Kalisch, Wright*).

ver. 45. DEPRIVED OF YOU BOTH] namely, of

Jacob murdered by his brother, and of Esau slain for his fratricide, according to ch. ix. 6.

ver. 46. This verse is asserted to contradict vv. 42—45, where a different reason is assigned for Jacob's departure. But, as Keil remarks, the one motive does not necessarily exclude the other; Esau's threatening to slay his brother, and Rebekah's wish that Jacob should marry one of his own kindred, were two separate causes which jointly brought about the one effect. Besides this, we can well imagine that with a woman's forethought she would naturally hide from Isaac the anxiety produced by the strife of her children, and assign for Jacob's departure another reason. Comp. Keil, *Einl.* p. 72; Ayre *Introd.* p. 564; Kurtz, I. 301.

Chapter XXVIII.

ver. 2. PADAN-ARAM] meaning *the level* or *plain Aram*, is not identical with *Aram-naharaim* or Mesopotamia, by which name the *whole* country between the Euphrates and Tigris was designated. Padan-aram denotes only a district of Mesopotamia, namely, the neighbourhood of the city Haran, which lay in a spacious plain surrounded with mountains. *Aram-naharaim* is mentioned in the Pent., only in Gen. xxiv. 10, and in Deut. xxiii. 4. In the former passage the country in general from which Isaac's wife was to be taken had at first to be mentioned, while the exact place in this country is named as the 'city of Nahor;' but afterwards, when the reader is acquainted with the country and the particular locality in it, the place might well be mentioned by the special name of *Padanaram*, as in Gen. xxv. 20; xxviii. 2, 5, 7; xxxi. 18; xxxiii. 18; xxxv. 9; xlviii. 7. But in Deut. xxiii. 4 Padan-aram could not be used, because

Balaam came from Mesopotamia, but not from Padan-aram (Keil, *Einl.* 87). By this notice is overthrown the argument for the different authorship of different portions of Genesis and of the remainder of the Pentateuch based on the use of these two geographical designations.

ver. 3. GOD ALMIGHTY] *El-Shaddai.* See pref. note on the last chapter. The name represents God as removing by His might the natural difficulties which opposed the fulfilment of His purposes of grace.

ver. 9. On the difficulties connected with the names of Esau's wives, see note on ch. xxxvi. 2.

ver. 11. The central route of Palestine winds through an uneven valley, covered, as with gravestones, by large sheets of bare rock; some few here and there standing up like the cromlechs of Druidical monuments. It is impossible not to recall, in this stony territory, the wanderer who 'went out from Beer-sheba, and went toward Haran; and he lighted upon a certain place...and he took of the stones of that place, and put them for his pillows, and lay down in that place to sleep.' Then arose the visions of the night. The stones around seemed to form themselves into the steps of a vast '*staircase,*' 'whose foot was set upon the earth,'—on the bare sheet of rocky ground on which the sleeper lay,—'and whose top reached to heaven' (Stanley, *Sin. and Pal.* p. 218).

ver. 12. Jacob as he lies on the earth, a fit representative of sinning helpless humanity, sees heaven and earth connected by a ladder which is traversed by angels 'sent forth to minister for them who are heirs of salvation.' At the same time the voice of God reaches his ears promising His ever-present protection, and announcing that in his seed all the nations should be blessed. Viewing this vision in the light of the declarations of the New Testament (comp. Joh. i. 51; xiv. 6; Eph. i. 9, 10; ii. 18; Heb. ix. 8; x. 19), we see that by the ladder between earth and heaven was represented the incarnate Son of God. "All intercourse between heaven and earth, God and man, is in and through Him. If any grace come from God to us, it is by Christ; if any glory come from us to God, it is by Christ too" (*Bp. Sanderson*). Comp. Dean Trench's *Huls. Lect.* p. 195.

ver. 16. THE LORD IS IN THIS PLACE; AND I KNEW IT NOT] This exclamation marks (says Hengstenberg) the internal difference of Jehovah and Elohim. Here Elohim could not be used, for the insertion of it would attribute to Jacob a childish notion of God, irreconcileable with a belief in the Divine Omnipresence. He must have known that Elohim was in every place with him; but that Jehovah should have revealed Himself to him when separated from the household of the chosen family, and from the place where Jehovah appointed the family to worship Him,—this was the fact which filled Jacob with astonishment and gratitude.

ver. 17. THIS IS THE HOUSE OF GOD] Why then does not Jehovah stand here? The reason appears to be this. In the later books of the O. T. it will be seen that the expression, *House of the Lord*, denoted the *one* place where the Lord met His people, and where they worshipped Him publicly. While Isaac was living, such a Lord's house would be only in the places where, by God's appointment, he and the chosen family resided. After his death even Jacob, though heir of the blessing, could not of himself fix *a House of the Lord*. He could therefore only regard the place of the vision as a Beth-el, a place sanctified in his recollections by this appearance of the Lord.

ver. 18. FOR A PILLAR] Heb. a *matzebah*.

On account of the idolatry which was afterwards connected with these *pillars*, the erection of them was forbidden in the law (Lev. xxvi. 1; Deut. xvi. 22), and the children of Israel were commanded to destroy those that they found (Ex. xxiii. 24; xxxiv. 13; Deut. xii. 3). "It was a general custom of remote antiquity to erect a stone as a memorial of remarkable events, and to consecrate it by a libation of wine, or by anointing it with oil. They were called *Bætylia*" (*Tuch*). The Bætylia appear to have been different from these commemorative pillars, as generally they seem to have been meteoric stones, which were regarded as having been sent by some deity, and were worshipped as that deity. It is rash at any rate to derive the worship of these Bætylia from this action of Jacob, on account of the resemblance between the names *Bætylia* and *Beth-el;* for he was evidently only acting in conformity with an old established custom.—OIL] This forms an important and most necessary part of the provision for travellers in the East to carry, not only for food, but also at night to anoint their limbs, which have been scorched and stiffened by the sun, and blistered by the burning sands (*Rosenm.*).

ver. 19. BETH-EL] *House of God.*

vers. 20, 21. The translation of the verses which is given in our authorised version is supported by Delitzsch and Knobel. But Hengstenberg (who is supported by Tuch, Kalisch, and Wright) translates : *If God will be with me, and will keep me in the way that I go...so that I come again to my father's house in peace, and Jehovah is my God; so shall this stone be a house of Elohim,* &c. His reasons for this translation are : (1) the vow can only relate to some *external act.* Wherever in the O. T. a vow is mentioned, it never treats of something internal, but of the embodying of gratitude by some external act. (2) Jacob's words refer to v. 13, and mean, *if Jehovah shall be to me what He was to Abraham and to Isaac, then will I,* &c.

Chapter XXIX.

ver. 1. WENT] Lit. *raised his feet*. Strengthened by the vision of the night he proceeds on his journey with a light and rejoicing heart (*Delitzsch*).

ver. 2. A WELL] Not the one at which Eliezer met Rebekah; for that was a spring, to which she descended to get water, and this was a well or cistern dug in the ground, and covered with a large stone. The former was directly without the town, and the present one was in the pasture-grounds at some convenient distance from the town (*Raphall*).—A GREAT STONE] Cisterns are very generally covered with a large slab, having a round hole in it large enough to let down the leather bucket or earthen jar. Into this hole a heavy stone is thrust, often such as to require the united strength of two or three shepherds to remove. The same is seen occasionally over *wells* of living water; but where they are large and the supply abundant, no such precaution is needed (Thomson, p. 589). Comp. Robinson, I. 490.

ver. 3. This verse is introduced to explain why the three flocks were waiting at the well.

ver. 5. SON OF NAHOR] instead of grandson of Nahor, by a free use of the word 'son,' not uncommon in the Bible.

ver. 7. HIGH DAY] Early in the day.

ver. 8. WE CANNOT] When a well is private property, it is, in neighbourhoods where water is scarce, sometimes kept locked, to prevent the neighbouring shepherds from watering their flocks fraudulently from it: and even when left unlocked, some person is so far the proprietor, that the well may not be opened, unless in the presence of himself, or of some of his household. *Chardin*, the celebrated traveller, conjectures that the well spoken of here belonged to Laban's family; and that therefore the shepherds could not, i.e. dared not open this well, until Laban's daughter came with her father's flock (*Raphall*).

ver. 12. BROTHER] *Kinsman*, as ch. xiv. 16.

ver. 17. TENDER-EYED] She had weak eyes, a great defect according to the Oriental idea of female beauty.

ver. 18. I WILL SERVE THEE] This offer is explained by the custom which has always prevailed in the East. As the services which the daughter renders the father are equivalent to those of a domestic, he sustains a loss through her marriage. For this loss the suitor is bound to compensate the parents, either by a stipulated sum of money, or, if unable to do this, by his own servitude for a fixed period. Such in both respects are still the customs of the East, among the Arabs, Curds, &c. as appears in Niebuhr's and Burckhardt's travels (*Tuch*).—SEVEN YEARS] The law of Moses, many of the commandments of which were re-enactments of long recognised customs, ordered that the servitude of a Hebrew bondman should terminate in seven years.

ver. 23. HE TOOK LEAH HIS DAUGHTER] The deceit of Laban became possible by the custom of leading the bride veiled into the dark bridal chamber. This imposition is the Nemesis that overtakes Jacob, and must have reminded him of the similar wrong which he had been guilty of. As instead of the beloved son he had brought to Isaac him whom he had despised and neglected, so Laban substitutes the despised Leah for the beloved Rachel (*Kurtz*).

ver. 27. FULFIL HER WEEK] The marriage festivities were kept up for seven days; comp. Jud. xiv. 12. When the seven days were expired Jacob married Rachel.

ver. 31. THE LORD] Hengstenberg thus accounts for the interchange of the divine names in the account of the birth of Jacob's children. Leah was suffering injustice, and out of health. Her hardhearted and jealous sister bore the principal blame of her husband's aversion to her, and made use of this aversion to ridicule and depreciate her. Under these circumstances Leah acknowledged, and with her the historian agreed, that the offspring granted to her was not merely the effect of a general operation of Providence, but specially an act of the living, personal, righteous, and rewarding God. But as to the children of the handmaid no notice is taken of the divine agency, either by Leah or the historian. There was nothing singular or out of the ordinary course of nature either attending or preceding their birth. In the birth of the fifth and sixth sons the divine hand is acknowledged, yet that special importance which was attached to the birth of the first four was no longer felt. Leah's devotional feelings are less strongly excited; her eye is chiefly directed to natural causes, and she acknowledges only an indistinct divine co-operation. On the other hand, Rachel had no motive to raise herself to Jehovah, she would rather dread him as a judge and avenger. Not till the birth of her firstborn, in which she acknowledges a gift of the divine favour, did she become more courageous and confident. She then ventured to ask a son of Jehovah; she forgot there was still cause for fear, since she had persisted in her unjust conduct towards her sister; so the son whom she asked of Jehovah was given by Jehovah, but as a son of sorrow.—HATED] i.e. *loved less* (Luk. xiv. 26; Matt. x. 37).

vers. 32—35. REUBEN] meaning *Behold, a son.* The birth of a son she appeals to as proof of God having regarded her in her affliction.—SIMEON] *Hearing.*—LEVI] *Attachment.*—JUDAH] *He for whom God is praised* (Del.).

Chapter XXX.

ver. 2. IN GOD'S STEAD] who, as the Author of life and death, alone can accomplish your wishes.

ver. 3. BEHOLD MY MAID BILHAH, &c.] Such things happen to this day in India and China, often at the request of the lawful wife, when she is herself sterile, or when her children are dead (*Pict. Bibl.*).—BEAR UPON MY KNEES] i.e. the child which she bears I will take to my bosom, and treat as my own (*Knob.*)

ver. 6. DAN] *A judge.*

ver. 8. WITH GREAT WRESTLINGS] Lit. *with wrestlings of God;* i.e. wrestlings regarding God and His favour: *In godly emulation I have wrestled with my sister.* She describes herself and Leah as engaged in the struggle for the possession of God's favour (*Hengstenberg, Knobel*). Our translation, *great wrestlings*, though supported by Rosenm. and Schumann, is incorrect; since *Elohim* or *God* is "never used in this way

merely to add emphasis to an expression" (*Hengst.*).
—NAPHTALI] *My wrestled for* (*Raphall*).

ver. 9. WHEN LEAH SAW SHE HAD LEFT BEARING] though only for a time, see ver. 17.

ver. 11. A TROOP COMETH] The clause is now generally rendered, *with good fortune*, or, according to the Masorah, *good fortune hath come.*—GAD] *Good fortune.*

ver. 13. ASHER] *Happy, Prosperous;* comp. the names, Felix, Prosper.

ver. 14. THE DAYS OF WHEAT-HARVEST] which in Palestine comprises about the whole month of May.—MANDRAKES] the apples of the *Mandragora vernalis.* "It is in wheat-harvest that they are still found ripe and eatable in the lower ranges of Lebanon and Hermon. The apple becomes of a very pale yellow colour, partially soft, and of an insipid, *sickish* taste. The Arabs believe them to be stimulating and exhilarating even to insanity" (Thomson, p. 577). In the East at the present day the fruit is thought to help conception: hence Rachel's eagerness to get it.

ver. 18. ISSACHAR] meaning *there is reward*, or *he brings reward.* She regards this her own fifth son as the recompense of her self-denial (*Del.*).

ver. 20. ZEBULUN] which means *dwelling*.

ver. 21. DINAH] *judged, vindicated*.

ver. 23. REPROACH] as barren; comp. Isa. iv. 1; Luk. i. 25.

ver. 24. JOSEPH] It has been thought that there is a double allusion in this name: *she bare a son and said, God hath taken away (asaph) my reproach; and she called his name Joseph; and said, The Lord shall add (joseph) to me another son.* The real derivation of the name is evidently to be sought in the word of ver. 24, *shall add* (*joseph*), while there *may* be an allusion to the expression of ver. 23, *God hath taken away*. Comp. Hævernick, *Introd.* p. 75; Keil, *Einl.* p. 72; Ayre, *Introd.* p. 565. As Joseph was born before the fourteenth year of servitude had elapsed, and as the marriage had taken place in the seventh year, twelve children must have been born during the seven intervening years. The text, however, does not mean to convey that these children were born in succession. The first four children of Leah were born within the shortest possible intervals of time. Before Leah felt her temporary barrenness Rachel had already given Bilhah to Jacob, and whenever Leah imagined that she was to bear no more children she gave Zilpah to her husband.

Soon after she again conceived; and before the seven years were elapsed bore other three children. It is not necessary to suppose, with Lightfoot, that Zebulun and Dinah were twins. The occurrence connected with the mandrakes took place immediately before Leah conceived for the fifth time; and it is not improbable that Reuben, a child of about four years, should have been taken to the fields, and have been attracted by the beauty of the fruit (*Kurtz*).

ver. 30. SINCE MY COMING] Lit. *at my foot*, i.e. *wherever I went* (*Kal., Del., Wright*).

vers. 32—35. The agreement between Jacob and Laban depends on the fact that in the East the sheep are commonly white and the goats black, while speckled and spotted animals are rarely seen. All spotted and dark sheep, and all speckled goats, are removed from the flock intrusted to Jacob, and led over to the flocks intrusted to the sons of Laban, so that only sheep of pure white colour, and goats of pure black colour, remain. All in that flock which should bear different colours were to become the hire of Jacob; and as in the ordinary course of nature, anything of the kind expected by Jacob was scarcely to be anticipated, Laban agrees to the demand, selfishly rejoicing over what he believes the folly of his nephew (*Kurtz*).

ver. 33. SO SHALL MY RIGHTEOUSNESS ANSWER FOR ME] Rather: *and my righteousness shall bear witness against me,* i.e. I shall be self-condemned (*Wright*).—WHEN IT SHALL COME FOR MY HIRE] Rather: *when thou shalt come to inspect my hire (which is) before thy face* (*Wright*).

ver. 37. The peculiar weakness of Jacob's character appears in full light here. Instead of leaving the result to the Lord, he has recourse to artifice. He takes advantage of the fact that any impression on the imagination at the time of conception, or during pregnancy, has frequently effect on the offspring. (For proofs of this see the authorities in Kurtz, I. p. 318.) First he put rods of various trees of a peculiarly white wood, strakes of which he had peeled away, into the watering-troughs, where the flocks would be sure to see them. When speckled animals appeared through this device, he separated the animals which were of one colour from those which were spotted, and placed them so that the former must look towards the latter, while the latter never saw the former (*Kurtz*).

ver. 41. WHENSOEVER THE STRONGER CATTLE DID CONCEIVE] The text, without mentioning any period of the year, simply says that Jacob used his artifice with the stronger, and not with weak cattle. There is little need of inquiring whether the lambs conceived in spring (as Bochart asserts), or those conceived in autumn (as Pliny and Columella, according to Patrick, affirm), were the stronger.

ver. 43. HAD MAID-SERVANTS, &c.] Von Bohlen asks, 'Whence could Jacob acquire all these objects, as his gains were limited to sheep and goats?' The words, *current money with the merchant*, ch. xxiii. 16, prove that trade and traders were familiarly known long before the days of Jacob, who, either by barter, or by sale and purchase, would find no difficulty in converting his cattle into whatever he was desirous of possessing (*Raphall*).

Chapter XXXI.

ver. 3. THE LORD] The command given to Jacob to return to Canaan is properly attributed to Jehovah, for the whole journey was under the guidance of Jehovah (*Hengstenberg*). The Lord does not tell Jacob to return by stealth. But Jacob has yet to learn by more bitter lessons the uselessness of his own crafty contrivances, and the necessity of leaving to the Lord to carry out His promises.

ver. 7. TEN TIMES] a round number. Or, as the number denotes completeness, it may mean that his wages had been changed as often as possible. The changes referred to differences in the marks of the flocks; v. 8.—GOD] This name of God is used by Jacob in addressing his wives, not because Jehovah was unknown to them, but because He stood at a distance from them, so that they could only elevate themselves to Him in some solemn moments, of which the preceding section furnishes instances (*Hengstenberg*).

vers. 11—13. Von Gerlach thinks that Jacob joins together two visions: the one alluded to in ver. 3, and another which he experienced when he first bargained with Laban about the partition of the sheep. The division is needless. There was but the one vision, viz. that of ver. 3, in which the Lord, to encourage Jacob to trust to Him and to obey Him, tells him that the increase of his flocks was owing solely to the blessing of the Lord, and not to his own artifices.

ver. 13. THE GOD OF BETHEL] with especial reference to the protection there promised to Jacob, and the vow he had there made (*Tuch*).

ver. 14. The daughters of Laban considered their father's bargain with Jacob as very disadvantageous to them, inasmuch as it quite overlooked the provision of a settlement, which is usually made for females at the time of marriage. Laban's bargain had been exclusively for his own personal advantage (*Pict. Bible*).

ver. 19. SHEAR] As the shearing was accompanied with much festivity and rejoicings (ch. xxxviii. 12; 1 Sam. xxv. 4; 2 Sam. xiii. 23), Jacob could readily steal away while Laban's attention was thus occupied.—IMAGES] Heb. *Tera-*

phim. All that we can gather from the Bible of these is, that they were images in the form of man (1 Sam. xix. 13), used by idolaters as oracles: "For the Jews and others agree that they were small images made under a certain constellation, which they used to consult both in things doubtful and things future. And therefore we read (Ezek. xxi. 21), that the king of Babel, among other divinations, consulted also of Teraphim" (*Mede*). As we find that the use of them was considered, though wrongly, not inconsistent with the worship of Jehovah (Jud. xvii, xviii; Hos. iii. 4), the conjecture of Lud. de Dieu is probable, that they were representations of angelic powers. However, the use of them is always represented in the Bible as idolatrous; Gen. xxxv. 4; 2 Kin. xxiii. 24; Zech. x. 2.

ver. 20. STOLE AWAY UNAWARES TO] Lit. *stole the heart of,* i.e. deceived.

ver. 21. THE RIVER] Euphrates.

ver. 23. THE MOUNT GILEAD] Not "the mount Gilead in the narrower sense, viz. the modern Djebel Djelaad, which lay south of the Jabbok" (*Knobel*). As the name was applied to the entire mountain region between the Arnon and Batanæa, the mount Gilead of the present passage refers to some mountain north of the Jabbok in that region.

ver. 24. EITHER GOOD OR BAD] A proverbial phrase, meaning not *to interfere* or *meddle with*. Comp. ch. xxiv. 50; 2 Sam. xiii. 22.

ver. 34. CAMEL'S FURNITURE] or, *saddle* used by Arab women, which consists of a heap of carpets and woollen cloaks rising about eighteen inches above the pack-saddle. These are always taken off at the end of a day's journey, and used to lie or sit on. Dr Thomson says, that it is still very usual for the Arabs to hide stolen property under the padding of their saddles; *The Land and the Book*, p. 370. Dr Kitto takes the furniture to denote the high wooden saddle of the camel, the concavity of which would form a hiding-place for the teraphim; but it is not customary to remove these saddles at the end of a day's journey.

ver. 40. IN THE DAY THE DROUGHT CONSUMED ME, AND THE FROST BY NIGHT] Chardin writes: "I have travelled in Arabia and Mesopotamia both in winter and summer, and have found the truth of what the Patriarch said. The contrariety in the qualities of the air in twenty-four hours is extremely great in some places; one would imagine they had passed in a moment from the violent heats of summer to the depth of winter" (*Raphall*).

ver. 42. FEAR OF ISAAC] Whom Isaac feared; Ps. lxxvi. 11; Isa. viii. 13.

ver. 43. WHAT CAN I DO, &c.] They are so dear to him, that in injuring them he would be injuring himself.

ver. 45. PILLAR] A lasting monument of this covenant.

ver. 47. JEGAR-SAHADUTHA] The Aramaic or Syriac for *Galeed = heap of witness*, which afterwards became Gilead.

ver. 49. MIZPAH] *Watch-tower.*

ver. 53. THEIR FATHER] Terah.

ver. 54. OFFERED SACRIFICE] or *killed beasts.* He offered sacrifice to invoke God to be present at this covenant, and enforce its observance.— THEY DID EAT BREAD] As we have no proof of the existence of peace-offerings before the Sinaitic legislation, it is safest to take this literally, viz. that after offering burnt-offerings to the Lord, they feasted together in token of amity.

Chapter XXXII.

ver. 1. THE ANGELS OF GOD MET HIM] As an assurance of God's protection from any violence on the part of Esau or others. Comp. 2 Kin. vi. 17, where we find Elisha similarly protected.

ver. 2. MAHANAIM] *two hosts* or *camps*. The name was continued in that of the Levitical city in the territory of Gad, to the north of the Jabbok. On Dr Robinson's map is a place *Mahneh*, which Delitzsch is inclined to identify with Mahanaim.

ver. 3. SEIR, THE COUNTRY OF EDOM] This passage, which makes Esau to have already located himself in Edom, is said to be contradicted by ch. xxxvi. 6, &c., where Esau is described to have settled in Seir *subsequently* to Jacob's arrival. But the summary account in ch. xxxvi. 6 does not state that Esau went to Seir for the first time after Jacob's return from Mesopotamia and Isaac's death; and in this passage neither the time nor the reason of Esau's withdrawal from Canaan to Seir is given (Keil, *Einl.* p. 72). It is moreover possible, as Dr Davidson remarks, that Esau may have sojourned in Seir more than once (*Introd.* p. 597). However it is not improbable that the true reason why Esau did not withdraw his family and possessions to Seir until after Isaac's death, ch. xxxvi. 6, is, that he had not till then completely subdued the Horite inhabitants. As Delitzsch remarks, the fact of his being accompanied by four hundred men shows that he had yet to maintain himself against the primitive inhabitants of Seir whom he had not thoroughly subdued.

ver. 4. MY LORD ESAU; THY SERVANT JACOB] He disclaims all pretence to *earthly* supremacy over his brother.

vers. 9, 10. The long and bitter discipline which Jacob had undergone at last had its effect on him. When in obedience to God's commands he tremblingly prepares to meet his brother, he throws himself entirely on the protection of the Lord. He now acknowledges the errors and mistakes of his past life, and ascribes his return in prosperity to Canaan not to his own strivings and plannings, but to God's mercy alone.—On the use of the name Jehovah in this address

Hengstenberg remarks: "Jehovah, who had promised to do him good, who had by the hitherto glorious fulfilment of His promise given him a pledge for the future, was alone the ground of his comfort and hope. The danger was too great for a mere general faith in a general Providence to sustain his confidence."

ver. 11. THE MOTHER WITH THE CHILDREN] Similarly, Hos. x. 14 (*Delitzsch*); or, *the mother bending over her children to protect them* (*Knobel*).

ver. 13. WHICH CAME TO HIS HAND] Rather, *that which had come to his hand*, what he had acquired; i.e. he took of his own possessions (*Knob., Del.*). Our translation would mean, that he gave what was in his power to present him. His wealth consisted in flocks and herds only; from them only therefore could he select his gift.

ver. 15. MILCH CAMELS] Nothing was more delicious in those countries (as Bochart observes out of Aristotle, Pliny, and many other authors, *Hierozoic.* II. 2) than camels' milk (*Patrick*).

ver. 22. JABBOK] A river flowing from east to west, and meeting the Jordan about midway between the lake of Gennesareth and the Dead Sea. Now called the Zerka.

vers. 24—30. The twenty years' exile which Jacob had brought on himself by trying to supplant his brother has now drawn to its close. The Lord by this long period of trials, labours, and disappointments, mixed up still with instances of His goodness, was disciplining and purifying His servant before He replaced him in the promised land. From ver. 9—13 we can see that this long and hard training had at length produced some effect. It had broken down the old man in him, had destroyed the reliance on his own cleverness, and had taught him the hard lesson of waiting in patience on the Lord. He who before thought ever to prevail by deceit, now in a sense of his own utter helplessness, and in a spirit of dependence on God, betakes himself to prayer and supplication to the Lord to carry him over his difficulties. That same night, as he is rejoining his company whom he had sent over the brook before him, his way is checked by a solitary foe. Not discerning him then to be more than man, he grapples with him and wrestles with him. For a time his attempts to prevail are permitted, until towards dawn his antagonist discloses his supernatural might by disabling him with a single touch. Jacob now finding his helplessness, and from it discerning that it was God he had been striving against, clings in prayer and supplication to Him for His blessing. The man therefore was God, who met him in this guise to teach him that hitherto his life had been a self-reliant opposition to God. The day-break betokens the new career that was to be opened out to Jacob when humbled before God. His thigh, the place of strength, is put out of joint by a touch of Him who had suffered him so long to wrestle with Him, to betoken the destitute helpless state he was reduced to by the course which God had permitted him to follow, but had so overruled and directed as to oblige him to throw himself unreservedly on God's mercy. At this very time, he was reduced to the greatest strait, hemmed in on all sides by enemies whom he had himself raised up, and whom he, by the case of Laban, saw to be restrained from violence only by God's interposition. This view of the transaction, which is in the main that of Kurtz, is confirmed by the use made of it by Hosea, in ch. xii. 3—7, where the connexion is thus traced by Umbreit: "That which attaches to the people as its especial guilt—*deceit and a contest with God*—had already appeared in their ancestor.

Even in the womb Jacob held his brother Esau by the heel to prevent him as the first-born; and when he had attained to the age of maturity he contends against God. But nothing can be thus gained from God. If man is to prevail with Him, he must weep and entreat. Thus Jacob also obtained the pre-eminence only in the way of humiliation and sincere prayer."

ver. 28. ISRAEL] The meaning of this word is now generally conceded to be *wrestler against* or *with God* (*Hengst., Kurtz, Knob., Del.*). As this name betokens only the change of character and disposition which had been effected in Jacob, it is not strange that his old name still adheres to him and is used with the new one. In this respect his change of name differs from that of Abraham. As the name Abraham was given to denote the *official* character of the Patriarch, it supplanted the old name at once and for ever. As that of Israel marked the change of individual character, the old name was at times applied just as the old *man* broke out in Jacob.

ver. 29. TELL ME, I PRAY THEE, THY NAME] He felt that God was known to him in a higher style than El or Elohim; for the new fact he wished to have a new form. He desired that

God would announce to him a name which would serve henceforth as a constant representative of the nature of God. But the time was not yet come. The name would have been then comparatively a title without the reality. Had God replied He would have said Jehovah, but the event was deferred till the Exodus (*Hengstenberg*). Comp. Jud. xiii. 17, 18.

ver. 30. PENIEL] which means *face of God*. In the next verse the place is called *Penuel*. Jacob appears to have slightly modified the old name so as to make it allude to the foregoing incident.

ver. 31. HE HALTED] Plain proof that the contest of Jacob took place neither in *dream*, nor in *vision*, nor in the *ecstatic state*, but in outward reality.

ver. 32. THE SINEW] From Mr De Sola we learn that the Jewish tradition has always regarded the *ischiatic nerve* as the interdicted sinew. The Jews, he also informs us, avoid using the hind legs or quarters, whenever there are not at hand properly qualified persons to remove this nerve.

Chapter XXXIII.

ver. 2. RACHEL AND JOSEPH HINDERMOST] In the place of greatest safety.

ver. 3. BOWED HIMSELF] Jacob, who in his contest the night before had prevailed by prayer and entreaty, now also prevails by humility and modesty against Esau (*Kurtz*).

ver. 5. GOD HATH GIVEN] Jacob, who had before praised Jehovah as the author of his prosperity, now ascribes it to Elohim when conversing with Esau, above whose superficial religion Jehovah was far exalted (*Hengstenberg*).

ver. 10. AND JACOB SAID, &c.] i.e. if I have found grace in thy sight, take this present from me, for therefore (i.e. because I have found favour with you) I have seen thy face, as though I had seen the face of God. Rightly regarding the change in his brother's feelings towards him as having been brought about by God, in the friendly countenance of his brother he beholds a reflection of the divine goodness towards himself (*Kidder, Delitzsch*).

ver. 11. MY BLESSING] i.e. this present which has been brought to thee to express my desire for your being blessed and prosperous.

ver. 13. TENDER] Joseph and Dinah were only about six or seven years old.—WITH YOUNG] or *giving suck*, as the Heb. signifies, 1 Sam. vi. 7 (*Kidder*).

ver. 17. SUCCOTH] signifying *booths*, a place evidently to the *east* of the Jordan and to the south of the Jabbok; comp. Josh. xiii. 27; Jud. viii. 4, 5. Dr Robinson, *Bib. Res.* III. 310, labours to prove the identity of Succoth with *Sâkut* to the west of Jordan, and considerably to the north of Penuel and Shechem. His view is opposed by the probabilities of Jacob's route, the comparison of the other Scripture notices of the place, and the testimony of Jerome.

ver. 18. CAME TO SHALEM] This translation is by Dr Robinson supposed to be confirmed by his discovery of a small village named Sâlim near Nablous (*Bib. Res.* II. 279, *note*). But most modern expositors, following the Jewish authorities and the old versions, with the exception of the Sept. and Vulg., translate, *and Jacob came in safety to the city of Shechem*. There will thus be a manifest reference to ch. xxviii. 21; xxxii. 9.

ver. 19. HE BOUGHT A PARCEL OF A FIELD] The land appears to have been now more thickly occupied by the Canaanites than in Abraham's time. He had only to purchase a burying-place. —PIECES OF MONEY] Heb. *Kesitah*. Neither of the usual interpretations, *lambs* given in barter, or *coins* stamped with the figure of a *lamb*, can be maintained. The signification given to *Kesitah*, viz. *lamb*, is not supported by etymology or by the cognate dialects (*Gesenius*); and coined money seems to have been unknown to the Hebrews before the captivity. The nations with whom they had intercourse, though highly civilized, appear not to have had coined money in use. "Among the numerous remains of Egyptian and Assyrian antiquity, not a single coin has been found" (Rawlinson, *Herodotus*, Vol. I. p. 684). "No Phœnician coins have the appearance of such antiquity as attaches to a large number of specimens belonging to Greece and Lydia" (*Ib.* p. 685). Commercial dealings among these nations appear to have been carried on by weights of the precious metals. We are therefore led to the conclusion that the *Kesitah* was a certain known weight of silver or gold.

ver. 20. EL-ELOHE-ISRAEL] *God the God of Israel.* The name attached to the altar would recall to his posterity the result of those leadings in his life by which Jacob had become Israel (*Kurtz*).

Chapter XXXIV.

WE have in this chapter the account of the transaction which caused Simeon and Levi to lose the birthright after it had been forfeited by the firstborn Reuben. On examining the narrative, we may discern these three points prominently brought out. (1) At the very beginning of the history of the race the carnal tendency of Israel to intermix with the idolatrous Canaanites displays itself in the case of Dinah, who rashly enters into social intercourse with the daughters of the land. (2) In the sons of Jacob we perceive the same self-reliant spirit, the tendency to have recourse to human plans and human power for self-deliverance, rather than to trust to their God, which characterised their father Jacob before he became Israel, and which Israel after the flesh so often manifested. (3) We see how God overrules and turns to His own ends the efforts of these headstrong men. Their temptation appears to be, to forget their peculiar calling, and by intermixing with the nations to become lost among them. By giving way to that Dinah exposes herself to insult; in revenging the insult done to their blood, the brothers, by their deed of treachery and cruelty, raise a barrier between themselves and the nations they have to dwell among.

ver. 1. DINAH] She was at this time not far from seventeen. From ch. xxx. 21—25, she appears to have been about Joseph's age, or a little older. She was therefore about seven when her father met Esau (ch. xxxiii. 13). The next date we find is that of ch. xxxvii. 2, which tells us that Joseph, when sold by his brethren, was seventeen. Now as no events requiring any length of time are recorded as intervening between the slaughter of the Shechemites and the selling of Joseph; and also as nothing is recorded which obliges us to think that the slaughter of the Shechemites was perpetrated immediately, or even shortly after Jacob's interview with Esau; we may place that event not long before Joseph's misfortune, or, in other words, not long before Dinah reached her eighteenth year. It is well known that in the East females are marriageable as early as their twelfth year.—WENT

OUT TO SEE] It is not necessary to think that this was the first time she had done so.

ver. 2. DEFILED] Lit. *humbled her*. The word seems to intimate his *violence*, as well as her *dissent* (*Kidder*).

ver. 3. SPAKE KINDLY] Lit. *spake to the heart of the damsel*. Comp. Isa. xl. 2, where the same expression is well translated, *comforted*.

ver. 5. AND JACOB HELD HIS PEACE UNTIL THEY WERE COME] Professor Blunt notices this as characteristic of the mingled timidity and duplicity which Jacob elsewhere displays. However, it may be explained differently. "In the Eastern countries it is thought that a brother is more dishonoured by the seduction of a sister than a man by the infidelity of his wife: for, say the Arabs, a man may divorce his wife, and then she is no longer his; while sister and daughter remain always sister and daughter" (*Michaelis*). We see this exemplified by Absalom's conduct, when his sister was ill-treated by Amnon, 2 Sam. xiii.

ver. 7. BECAUSE HE HAD WROUGHT FOLLY IN ISRAEL] The phrase is used several times with reference to disgraceful sins affecting the great principles of morality, and staining Israel as a community; see Deut. xxii. 21; Jud. xx. 10; Jer. xxix. 23 (*Kalisch*). Knobel sees an anachronism in the use of the phrase, which, though appropriate in the Mosaic and later times, was not appropriate at this time, when there was not a people of Israel. The expression may possibly be Mosaic (Hævernick, p. 200), but certainly it might well be used at this time of the family of Jacob, who with his sons, numerous servants and retainers, ch. xxxii. 10, presented as much the appearance of a community as the Shechemites, vv. 21, 22.

ver. 12. DOWRY AND GIFT] It was the custom among many nations, that the bridegroom should pay to the father of a girl a certain sum, as a sort of compensation for the loss of her services. Besides this *dowry* (*mohar*), certain presents, or *gift* (*mattan*), were given to the bride, the value of which was probably well ascertained by custom, and proportionate to the condition of the parties. This is still in use among the Arab tribes (*De Sola*).

ver. 25. DINAH'S BRETHREN] i.e. by the same mother. We are to suppose that they took their armed servants to assist them in the attack on the town, which could not have been a very large one. It evidently did not exist in Abraham's time, as it is then called the place of Shechem, see ch. xii. 6.

ver. 30. AND JACOB SAID TO SIMEON AND LEVI, &c.] From ch. xxxv. 5 we see that Jacob's apprehensions were well founded, and that it was only by God's interposition that he and his family were preserved from the consequences of the cruel and perfidious conduct of Simeon and Levi. It should be observed, that we are not to infer from the silence of the sacred narrative on the subject here, that either Jacob or the sacred writer approved of the transaction. In ch. xlix. 5—7, we see from the manner in which Jacob speaks of it, how deeply he had taken to heart his son's misconduct. And the curse which the prophetic Spirit uttered then by his lips, shows how it was regarded by Him through whose inspiration the book of Genesis was written.

Chapter XXXV.

In the narrative of the foregoing chapter we see how closely the chosen family had been drawing to the idolatrous Canaanites, and what little difference there must have been in the religious sentiments of two communities which had been on the point of amalgamating themselves into one. This leads us to the conclusion, that in his prosperity Israel had been falling back into the old Jacob. The position of danger in which he finds himself arouses him. In obedience to a revelation from God he prepares to go to Bethel, to keep the vow he had made there thirty years before; and preparatory to doing so, in order that indeed 'the Lord should be his God,' he commences by purifying his household from idolatry. On this, as proof of God's approval, the name Israel is again solemnly given to him.

ver. 1. WHEN THOU FLEDDEST, &c.] These words remind him of the protection vouchsafed to him by God ever since.

ver. 2. THEN JACOB SAID] We may find in this the reason of Jacob's long delay in fulfilling his vow after entering again the land of Canaan; as yet he had not been able to bring himself to render to God the undivided homage and devotion which that vow required.—THE STRANGE GODS] Perhaps among these were the *images* or *teraphim* which Rachel had brought from Canaan.—BE CLEAN, AND CHANGE YOUR GARMENTS] Their purification was by washing or bathing themselves, as appears from Numb. viii. 6, 7, 'Take the Levites from among the children of Israel, and cleanse them. And thus shalt thou do unto them, to cleanse them: sprinkle water of purifying upon them, and let them shave all their flesh, and let them wash their clothes, and so make themselves clean.' This was to betoken the necessity of the inward purification of heart before approaching God.

ver. 3. DAY OF MY DISTRESS] When he fled from his father's house in fear of Esau; comp. v. 1.

ver. 4. EARRINGS] which seem to have been used as amulets or charms; comp. Jud. viii. 24—27; Hos. ii. 13.—UNDER THE OAK] A tree not likely to be suddenly digged up, being sacred in the esteem of idolators (*Kidder*).

ver. 5. TERROR OF GOD] i. e. inspired by God; comp. Ex. xxiii. 27.

ver. 7. EL-BETH-EL] *God of Beth-el;* the place was thus named to commemorate the faithful fulfilment of the promises given by God at Beth-el.

ver. 8. BENEATH BETH-EL] which was built on the point of a low hill; Robinson, *Bib. Res.* I. 448.—ALLON-BACHUTH] *Oak of mourning.*

ver. 11. GOD ALMIGHTY] El-Shaddai; comp. prefatory note on ch. xxvii., and on the use of the name Elohim, pref. note on ch. xvii.

ver. 14. A PILLAR OF STONE] See note on ch. xxviii. 18.

ver. 16. EPHRATH] The situation of Ephrath cannot justly be doubted; the obscure passage in 1 Sam. x. 2 can in no way be used to assign to Rachel's grave a much more northern position (between Ramah and Gibeah), and to overthrow the traditional opinion which, from very remote antiquity, placed it in the neighbourhood of Bethlehem (comp. Matt. ii. 18). The assertion that the words 'which is Bethlehem,' are in v. 9, and in xlviii. 7, a later interpolation, is perfectly unfounded. The town Bethlehem is sometimes called, with a certain completeness, Bethlehem-Ephratah (*Kalisch*). The passage in Jer. xxxi. 15

says nothing of Rachel's grave; it therefore cannot be alleged to prove the contiguity of this place to Ramah in the tribe of Benjamin.

ver. 18. BEN-ONI] *Son of my sorrow.*—BENJAMIN] *Son of my right hand* (*Del., Knob.*); *son of my old age* (*Raphall*).

ver. 20. RACHEL'S GRAVE] Its site was well known in Samuel's time; 1 Sam. x. 2. The place assigned to it by tradition agrees, according to Dr Robinson, with the description of the sacred narrative. It is about twenty-five minutes distant from the north of Bethlehem (*Bib. Res.* I. 218, 469).

ver. 21. TOWER OF EDAR] i.e. tower of the flock.

ver. 22. Reuben commits the sin for which he is deprived of the birthright. The remark made in the note on xxxiv. 30 is strictly applicable to this case.

ver. 29. As Isaac's death did not occur till about ten years before Jacob's descent to Egypt, it is evidently mentioned here, in order to avoid breaking the thread of the narrative by the insertion in its true chronological place of an event of comparatively little importance.

Chapter XXXVI.

vers. 2, 3. We may here consider the difficulties connected with the different statements regarding the names and descent of Esau's three wives. (1) Esau is represented, in ch. xxvi. 34, to have married Judith the daughter of Beeri the Hittite, and Bashemath the daughter of Elon the Hittite, and in ch. xxviii. 9, Mahalath the daughter of Ishmael. In this chapter these wives are called respectively Aholibamah, Adah, and Bashemath. This difference in the *names* of the wives is easily explained by a reference to the Oriental custom, mentioned by Chardin (Hengstenberg, *Pent.* II. 226), of people, and especially women, changing their names on any remarkable occurrence. (2) The same custom explains how the Hivite who, in ch. xxxvi. 2, is called *Anah*, should, in ch. xxvi. 34, be designated by the name *Beeri* (= *man of the springs*), which was given to him when he discovered *the hot springs* in the wilderness; see note on v. 24. (3) Lastly,

Beeri or Anah is evidently the same individual who is called in ch. xxvi. 34 the Hittite, in ch. xxxvi. 2 the Hivite, in ch. xxxvi. 25 a *Horite*. But neither do these variations involve contradictions. He was a *Horite* or *cave-dweller*, as being one of the Canaanitish clan which got that name from dwelling in caves in Mount Seir; he was a *Hivite*, inasmuch as the Horites were an off-shoot from the Canaanite nation of the Hivites; and as a Canaanite he could be called *Hittite*, for though that name originally denoted a single Canaanitish tribe, yet do we find it in Scripture applied to the Canaanites in general; see Josh. i. 4; 1 Kin. x. 29; 2 Kin. vii. 6; Ezek. xvi. 3. Comp. Hengstenberg, *Pent.* II. 222; Keil, *Einl.* 72.

ver. 2. DAUGHTER OF ANAH THE DAUGHTER OF ZIBEON] i.e. the daughter of Anah and the granddaughter of Zibeon.

vers. 9—14. An account of Esau's family after he took up his abode in Mount Seir, from which he expelled the Horites.

ver. 12. AND TIMNA WAS CONCUBINE TO ELIPHAZ ESAU'S SON] We have here one of those minute and undesigned coincidences which abound in the Bible, and form a strong evidence of its truth.

Before Esau left his father's house, the Horites were so influential a tribe that he married the daughter of a Horite prince. In Deut. ii. 12, 22, it is recorded that Esau conquered the Horites, and dwelt in Mount Seir their possession. Now no direct mention is made here of the subjugation of the Horites; but we find in the record of Timna, the sister of the Horite duke Lotan, being thought worthy of no higher rank than that of concubine of Esau's son Eliphaz, an indirect proof of the degraded and inferior position which the Horites held in the time of the generation immediately succeeding Esau. "The concubines whom we read of in the Pentateuch were of the class of handmaids, and that Timna was a female slave appears from the circumstance that her son is numbered, in vv. 12, 13, with the sons of Adah" (*Hengstenb.*).—AMALEK] The founder of the warlike tribe of the Amalekites.

vers. 15—19. DUKE] Heb. *Alluph, leader of a thousand.* In these verses there is given an account of the tribes into which the Edomites were divided, each of which, like the Israelitish tribes, took their names from one of the sons of Esau. It appears from vv. 31—39, that above these dukes or *alluphim*, there was an order of kings who were appointed by election, and not by hereditary descent. This mode of government by heads of tribes or dukes, under an elective king, was in existence in Moses' time; see Ex. xv. 15, and Numb. xx. 14; and is found so late as the time of the Babylonish Captivity; see Ezek. xxxii. 29.

vers. 20—30. It is evident that these *sons of Seir* are only his descendants in various degrees of affinity, who raised themselves to the dignity of independent chiefs. Judging from the fact of Anah being of an age to be father to the wife of Esau, we may conjecture that the sacred historian gives a list of the Horite chiefs, and their respective families, at the time of the conquest by Edom. If this be so, Zibeon and Anah were inserted on account of their relationship with Edom.

ver. 24. THIS WAS THAT ANAH THAT FOUND THE MULES] Modern commentators are generally agreed that the correct translation is, *this is that Anah that found the hot springs*. In the district inhabited by the Horites, to the south-east of the Dead Sea, are the warm springs of Callirrhoe, which have been described by Legh in remarkable agreement with the accounts of the ancients. This traveller speaks of "the enclosed situation of the place. At the edge of a precipice was hewn out a narrow zigzag path, which led to a thicket of reeds, thorns, and palms, growing out of the clefts of the rocks, and here bubbled forth the numerous warm springs which they sought." And if the treasure was so hidden, it is explained more easily why Anah, from the discovery, got the name of *Beeri* = *man of the springs* (*Hengstenb.*).

vers. 31—39. THESE ARE THE KINGS] None of these kings was succeeded by his son, and the seat of royalty was not confined to any one city. Hence we infer that the monarchy was elective, not hereditary.—BEFORE THERE REIGNED ANY KING OVER ISRAEL] The sacred historian, who had just before recorded the promise made to Israel, 'kings shall come out of thy loins,' ch. xxxv. 11, remarks the mystery of the divine arrangements in bringing to pass His will. The family of the outcast Edom could boast of a long line of kings, while the family with whom the promise rested were only on the point of reaching the land of promise, and had still to look forward in expectation to the time when they should be gathered into one great nation under one great king! It is much to be regretted that Mr Rawlinson should have lent the weight of his authority to the assailants of the integrity of the Pentateuch by asserting that this passage, ch. xxxvi. 31—39, " cannot have been written by Moses" (*Bampt. Lect.* p. 322). There is nothing in it which could not have been written by him. The words, *before there reigned any king in Israel,* are capable of a simple and very natural interpretation. The enactments made and recorded by Moses in the Pentateuch show that he expected the fulfilment of the promise, 'kings shall come out of thy loins.' The number of the kings of Edom which he records is not too great for the period intervening between Esau and Moses. A period of 400 years is surely quite sufficient for the reigns of eight kings, especially when it is remembered that they were elective. There is also internal evidence that this is not an interpolation by a writer living after there had been kings in Israel. From the notice of Hadar in this list, it is evident that he was *living* when the passage was written; for no mention is made *of his death,* and his wife's family is given with exactness. But when we turn to the corresponding passage in 1 Chron. i. 50, 51, copied evidently from the old record in Genesis long after there were kings over Israel, we find this significant addition, "Hadad died also." The only remaining argument against the genuineness of this passage is that very trivial one made out of the similarity of the names of one of these kings of Edom and the adversary to Solomon, whom the Lord raised out of Edom. Because both have the name of Hadad, they must be the same! But (1) Hadad of Genesis is said to have smitten Midian in the field of Moab. Now Midian appears to have vanished as a nation after its complete overthrow by Gideon; it never figures in the sacred history after that. And (2) we have seen that the monarchy spoken of in Genesis was an elective one; it was not so in the days of David when the Edomites were subdued, for the Hadad of that time is spoken of as "of the king's seed in Edom," 1 Kin. xi. 14. A thorough examination of the entire question will be found in Hengstenb. *Pent.* II. Art. Edom.

ver. 37. BY THE RIVER] Euphrates. "On the right bank of the Euphrates, at the north-western extremity of the plain of Shinar, three and a half miles south-west of Mayadin, are extensive ruins round a castle still bearing the name of Rehoboth" (*Col. Chesney*).

vers. 40—43. After the lists of dukes and of kings there is given an account of the chief localities or districts into which Edom was divided, and which were presided over by their dukes or *alluphim* (*Hengstenberg*). The truth of this explanation is confirmed by the peculiar phrases used in these verses—'after their places,' 'after their habitations,' 'in the land of their possessions,'—all local expressions, leading to the inference that the passage details the districts or feoffs of these electoral heads of clans, or dukes. The difficulty of there being only *eleven* districts for the *fourteen* dukes of vv. 15—19, is naturally solved by the supposition of Kurtz, that in vv. 15—19 the original number of dukes is given, but that vv. 40—43 give the territorial distribution as it existed at the time of Moses.

Chapter XXXVII.

ver. 1. AND JACOB DWELT] This statement stands in intimate connexion with ch. xxxvi. 8. While Esau 'dwelt in Mount Seir,' Jacob the heir of the promise, although 'a stranger,' still remained in the promised land. In that land, which was thus held solely by faith and hope, none of the collateral branches were to reside. Elsewhere they might soon find a home, and found a race, but not there; it was the patrimony of the believing, who here, as elsewhere, through much tribulation enter the kingdom (*Blackadder*).—A STRANGER] This expression illustrates the remark made in note on ch. xxxvi. 31, that the historian seems desirous of drawing attention to the seeming delay in the fulfilment of the promises to Abraham's seed. Comp. also ch. xxiii. 4.

ver. 2. THESE ARE THE GENERATIONS OF JACOB] Having completed the history of Isaac by an account of his death and the descendants he left after him, the historian commences a new section, which contains the history of Jacob. And just as the actions of Isaac's sons, and more especially of Jacob, occupied the chief portion of the family history of Isaac, so here also the family history of Jacob is chiefly concerning the actions of his sons. The fragmentary and unconnected appearance which the section assumes, when taken as the history exclusively of Joseph, vanishes at once, when we observe the rule in accordance with which the historian has framed the successive histories of the generations of the different patriarchs, and consider it as the family history of Jacob, in which Joseph is the leading but not the sole actor.

ver. 3. COAT OF MANY COLOURS] or, as most modern expositors translate, *a sleeved robe reaching to the ankles;* evidently a badge of rank (2 Sam. xiii. 18). By this distinction Jacob seems to have desired to transfer to Joseph the privileges of the birthright, and thus to have excited the jealousy of the other sons.

vers. 5—10. The first dream refers to the brothers only, the second includes the parents. The former typifies only Joseph's wealth and worldly position; the latter promises eternal fame and universal homage: for sheaves of corn are an emblem of a prosperous and a peaceful life spent in comfort (Job v. 26), while the heavenly bodies are the symbols of dominion and imperishable renown (*Kalisch*). Comp. also Ps. cxxvi. 6.

ver. 9. HE DREAMED YET ANOTHER DREAM] We descry for the first time a prophetic anticipation that the salvation which was to issue from this family should be such that its members, and even its ancestors, should bend before it and worship (*Kurtz*).

ver. 17. DOTHAN] The name signifies, *double cistern*. It was the scene of the great miracle wrought in preservation of Elisha, 2 Kin. vi. 13. From this chapter it is seen to have been on the regular route from Gilead through Samaria into Egypt. Eusebius and Jerome place it 12 Roman miles from the city Samaria. In this very situation Dr Robinson discovered in 1852 a green and well-marked tell or mound bearing the name Dothan, at the foot of which was a fountain. The plain around was well adapted for pasturage; and through it passed the great road from Beisan to Ramleh and Egypt, along which the Ishmaelites would naturally have travelled from Gilead (Robinson, *Bib. Res.* III. 122).

ver. 22. CAST HIM INTO THIS PIT] The pit was probably one of those narrow-mouthed ancient cisterns, shaped like a demi-john, and smooth as glass within, which are mentioned by Dr Thomson as existing by thousands in Upper Galilee (*The Land and the Book*, p. 287). His description agrees perfectly with that given by Diodorus Siculus (XIX. 94) of the cisterns made by the Nabathæan Arabs. Dr Robinson lighted on several near Hableh in the district of Nablous, which he pronounces to be of great antiquity (*Bib. Res.* III. 136). These descriptions all show that these cisterns could be used as prisons, as in the cases of Joseph and, long afterwards, of Jeremiah (Jer. xxxviii. 6).

ver. 25. A COMPANY OF ISHMEELITES] When mentioned more particularly in ver. 28, and ver. 36, they are called Midianites. The Midianites, with the other nomadic tribes sprung from Abraham, seem, except when exact accuracy was required, to have been designated by the name of Ishmael, the chief and most powerful of their race. See especially Judg. viii. 24, where of the Midianites conquered by Gideon it is said, 'For they had golden ear-rings, because they were Ishmaelites.' Similarly we have seen already (note on ch. xxxvi. 2) that all the Canaanitish nations were denominated often by the name of the most powerful of the kindred nations, the Hittites.—SPICERY] Probably the gum exuding from the stem and boughs of the *Astragalus Tragacantha*, still found in Lebanon (*Kal., Knob.*). The general Heb. derivation shows that the substance was *pulverized*, pounded *small*. Mr Osburn remarks, as an instance of the particular care taken by the Egyptians in triturating their spices, that "in a mummy opened at Leeds not a particle could be discovered larger than the rest" (*Israel in Egypt*, p. 63.)—BALM] The gum exuding from incisions in the bark of the *Balsamum*, indigenous in Palestine and especially in Gilead, and much prized in Egypt.—MYRRH] The gum collected from the shoots of the shrub anciently called *ledon*, and by modern botanists *cistus ladaniferus*, found in Arabia, Syria, and Palestine; used in the embalming of mummies.—GOING TO EGYPT] The great highway from Gilead to Egypt still passes by Dothan. The caravans come up the Ghor Beisan, pass by Zer'in and Lejjûn, enter the hill-country of Samaria by the Wady of Dothaim, and thence go on to Ramleh, Gaza, and Egypt (Thomson, p. 466).— EGYPT] There is remarkable accuracy in this specification of the commodities brought by these Midianites to the Egyptian market. In Homer's time, Egypt was famed for its infinite number of drugs (*Od.* IV. 229); Jeremiah alludes to its use of medicines (ch. xlvi. 11); Herodotus speaks of the fame of its physicians (II. 84; III. 1, 132); and the process of embalming must have entailed an enormous consumption of drugs. In the readiness of the Midianites to purchase a slave for sale, we can see, what is fully proved by the Egyptian remains (Osburn, *Israel in Egypt*, p. 21), that a traffic in slaves was also carried on with that country.

ver. 28. TWENTY PIECES] From Lev. xxvii. 1—7, we learn the recognised value of a slave according to the variation of sex or age. In vv. 2 and 5 it is said, 'When a man shall make a singular vow, the persons shall be for the Lord by thy estimation ... And if it be from five years old even unto twenty years old, then thy estimation shall be of the male twenty shekels, and for the female ten shekels.' Joseph, who is only seventeen years old, is sold for twenty shekels.

ver. 29. REUBEN RENT HIS CLOTHES] Luther's conjecture is not unnatural, that Reuben had been humbled by his fall, and so was less hardhearted than his brethren.

ver. 35. DAUGHTERS] Under this word may be included the wives of his married sons.—THE GRAVE] Heb. *Sheol*, the state or place of the dead, as it often signifies, and particularly in Isa. xiv. (where the king of Babylon is expressly denied the honour of a grave, vv. 19, 20) *Sheol* is said *to be moved for him*, and *to meet him*, and *to stir up the dead for him*, ver. 9 (*Patrick*).

ver. 36. AND THE MIDIANITES SOLD HIM INTO EGYPT] An argument for the early commencement of trade by caravans with Egypt is furnished by the fact, that the king Amun-m-gori II., of the 16th dynasty, erected a station in the Wady Jasoos to command the wells which furnish water for those passing through the desert (Hengstenberg, *Egypt*).—POTIPHAR] The Septuagint version gives the more exact Egyptian form of the name, *Petephres;* a name found frequently on the monuments, and meaning *belonging to, devoted to, the sun*, the local God of On, or Heliopolis.—AN OFFICER] Heb. *saris*, a title of constant occurrence in the tombs of the magnates of Egypt (Osburn,

p. 22). The same word is applied to the chief butler and the chief baker (ch. xl. 2). Hebrew scholars make the word in its primary sense to denote a eunuch, and then, as this class were much employed in Oriental courts, to have, as here, the secondary meaning of royal officer. Sir G. Wilkinson (*Ancient Egypt*, II. 61), asserts that eunuchs were not employed in Egypt. His opinion is confirmed by the fact that monogamy was the rule in Egypt in the times of the monuments (Wilkinson, *Her.* Vol. II. p. 148), and by the higher social position and superior treatment which women enjoyed in that country.—CAPTAIN OF THE GUARD] It is evident from Herodotus that the kings of Egypt had a guard, who, in addition to the regular income of a soldier, also received a separate salary. In the paintings of marches and battles on the monuments, these royal guards are commonly seen about the person of the king, and are distinguished by a peculiar dress and weapons. During the reign of the Ptolemies, who in general adhered to the usages of the ancient Egyptians, the office of the commander of the body-guard was a very important one. They possessed the confidence of the king, and were often employed in the most important business transactions. Finally, the superintendence of executions belonged to the most distinguished of the military caste (Hengstenb. *Egypt*, p. 23). The last sentence will account for the Hebrew appellation which we translate *chief of the guard*, viz. *chief of the slaughtermen, or executioners.*

Chapter XXXVIII.

This chapter occupies an important place in the history of the family of Israel. The birth of Pharez, who held the place of firstborn of Judah, forms the central point of the chapter. The history of Judah and of his house is of such importance, because to Judah Jacob assigned the sceptre of principality among the tribes of Israel; and the primogeniture of Pharez is brought out prominently, because Nahshon, the eminent prince in Israel during the journey in the wilderness, was a descendant of Pharez. But as we not merely say that Moses has written this account, but also that the Holy Ghost has written it, we perceive in it a glance into ages yet to come. We call to mind that David sprung from Nahshon, and that Jesus was the Son of David. We are therefore now tracing the lineage of Jesus Christ, and looking forward to him who is both the commencement and the end (*Kurtz*).

Von Bohlen represents the chapter as an episode conceived in a thoroughly Jewish spirit. The essential historical connexion of the chapter we have seen; and so far from its betraying a Jewish spirit of glorifying the line of David, it rather depreciates the royal tribe, by recording plainly the Canaanitish alliances of the founder of the tribe, and the punishments which he and his family drew down on themselves from God. Comp. Hævernick, p. 204; Kurtz, I. 358; Baumgarten, I. 313.

ver. 1. ADULLAMITE] Adullam, a town in the plain of Judah, south-west of Jerusalem, mentioned together with Jarmuth and Socoh (Josh. xv. 35), or with Libnah and Makkedah (Josh. xii. 15), one of the most ancient of cities, and which enjoyed an existence of unusual duration. For in the time of the Hebrew conquest it was the seat of a Canaanitish king; a cave in its neighbourhood was the refuge of David from the persecution of Saul, and here he was joined by his relatives and followers; it was fortified by Rehoboam (2 Chron. xi. 7); in Micah's days counted among the important cities of Judah (Mic. i. 15); it was still inhabited after the captivity (Neh. xi. 30); and existed even at the time of the Maccabees (2 Mac. xii. 38) (*Kalisch*).

ver. 5. CHEZIB] Generally considered the

same as Achzib, which was in the plain of Judah, Josh. xv. 44, and mentioned by Micah, together with Adullam, Mic. i. 14, 15.

ver. 7. Judah is soon punished for his impious connexion. His two sons are cut off for their wickedness, and he himself drawn into incest.

ver. 14. We see in this story how *one* interest—that for their families, and the preservation of them—overpowered every other feeling, even the sense of shame in a woman (*v. Gerlach*).—AN OPEN PLACE] Lit. *the door of eyes*, or *of Enayim*. If, as is probable, Enayim be a proper name, it would seem to be the same as the city *Enam*, mentioned in Josh. xv. 34.— TIMNATH] or *Timna*, a city not far from Ekron; in the time of the Judges possessed by the Philistines, who got possession of it again in the days of Ahaz (2 Chron. xxviii. 18); of some importance in the time of the Romans; identified by Dr Robinson with the modern *Tibnch* (*Bib. Res.* II. 17).

ver. 18. THY SIGNET AND THY STAFF] Herodotus (I. 195) mentions that every Babylonian used to carry "a seal and a walking-stick, carved at the top into the form of an apple, a rose, a lily, or an eagle, or something similar." The seals referred to by him were, as recent discoveries show, cylinders of various composition, "hollow, and pierced from end to end either for the purpose of being worn strung upon a cord, or perhaps to admit a metal axis by which they were rolled upon the clay so as to leave their impression on it" (Rawlinson, *Herod.* Vol. I. p. 336).—BRACELETS] The Heb. word is derived from a root signifying to twist, and is by Gesenius, Knobel, and Delitzsch, interpreted, *the string from which the signet was suspended.* "Most of the Arabs of the towns have each his signet-ring either worn on the finger or suspended from the neck, the impression of which serves as a signature" (Robinson, *Bib. Res.* I. 36). The impression is made by smearing the seal with ink, and then impressing it on the paper.

ver. 21. THE HARLOT] Heb. *Kedesha, dedicated* to the goddess Asherah, to whom these dedicated women devoted the wages of prostitution. Tamar appears therefore to have assumed the guise of a Kedesha. This view is confirmed by her asking a kid of the goats for her reward, for goats were chiefly sacrificed to this goddess (*Kurtz*).—OPENLY] Lit. *at Enayim.*

ver. 26. SHE HATH BEEN MORE RIGHTEOUS] He intended not to commend himself as *righteous*, but to signify that he had been more to blame in that matter than she, as having defrauded her of Shelah, who ought to have married her (*Waterland*).

ver. 29. The remarkable circumstances attending Tamar's delivery form no valid objection to the credibility of the narrative. The medical authorities referred to by De Sola and Kurtz prove that the fact related here, though extremely rare, is credible.—THIS BREACH BE UPON THEE] that is, the breach is thine, thou hast made it, and shalt carry the name of it. Pharez (by interpretation, *breach*) was so named upon this fact of his. He violently took the dignity of the birthright from his brother; is set before him in the genealogy (Numb. xxvi. 20; 1 Chron. ii. 4, 5); and became father of Christ after the flesh (Matt. i. 3), (*Ainsworth*).

ver. 30. ZARAH] Heb. *Zarach, to shine;* from the bright red colour of the thread tied to his hand (*De Sola, Delitzsch*); or *risen, sprung up*, as the sun is said to rise, because he should first have risen or been born (*Ainsw., Knob.*).

Chapter XXXIX.

ver. 1. AN EGYPTIAN] Why is the national origin of an officer holding rank in the court of a king of Egypt thus accurately specified? We are led by this notice to conclude that a monarch of one of the shepherd, or Hycsos, dynasties occupied the throne at this time. Comp. Osburn, *Isr. in Eg.* p. 29.

ver. 2. THE LORD WAS WITH JOSEPH] The monuments present many proofs of the general ill-treatment of Egyptian slaves (Hengstb. *Eg.* p. 24, note). The sacred writer accounts for the exceptional treatment of Joseph by the remark that Jehovah, not Elohim, was by a special Providence watching over him.

ver. 4. OVERSEER] Among the objects of tillage and husbandry (says Rosellini) portrayed in the Egyptian tombs, we often see a steward, who takes account and makes a registry of the harvest before it is deposited in the storehouse.

And the same author remarks, in reference to a painting in a tomb, 'In this scene, a man carrying implements for writing—the pen over his ear, the tablet or paper in his hand, and the writing-table under his arm—either follows or goes before the servants.' According to the inscription, this is the overseer of the slaves or the steward (Hengstb. *Egypt*, p. 24).

ver. 6. SAVE THE BREAD WHICH HE DID EAT] This exception may be accounted for by the national horror of strangers, in consequence of which they would not eat of the flesh of an animal cut up with the knife of a foreigner. See note on ch. xliii. 32.

ver. 7. HIS MASTER'S WIFE CAST HER EYES UPON JOSEPH] The truth of this narrative has been cavilled at as being inconsistent with the seclusion in which women are kept in the *East*. But the Egyptian monuments prove that in Egypt women were not under the restraint now usual in the East. The delineations of Egyptian social life represent men and women as mingling together with much of the freedom of modern Europeans. In the *Cambridge Essays* for 1858, there is given an analysis of an Egyptian tale founded on an incident similar to the temptation of Joseph. It is entitled, 'The tale of the two brothers,' and has been translated from a papyrus which dates about B.C. 1314.

ver. 9. AGAINST GOD] Joseph to an Egyptian naturally speaks of God, not of Jehovah.

ver. 20. THE PRISON] Lit. *house of roundness*, a tower or circular building used as a prison. From ch. xl. 3 it is seen that the prison was part of the house of Potiphar, as captain of the guard. In our own days the state prison forms part of the house of that functionary in the East (*Kurtz*), as it did in the days of Jeremiah; Jer. xxxvii. 15.

ver. 21. THE KEEPER OF THE PRISON] Potiphar's subordinate officer, who is therefore distinct from him. Knobel and Tuch confound the two functionaries, in order to introduce an appearance of discrepancy into the sacred text. See Davidson, *Introd.* p. 598; Ayre, *Introd.* p. 566; Keil, *Einl.* p. 73; Delitzsch, p. 540.

Chapter XL.

ver. 1. THE BUTLER] or *cup-bearer;* an office held by Rabshakeh and Nehemiah, and therefore of some distinction.

ver. 4. THE CAPTAIN OF THE GUARD] Potiphar had committed Joseph to the custody of his subordinate, *the keeper of the prison;* but when the two high officials were by royal command cast into prison, we can readily understand that he would take charge of them himself. Knowing by experience the capability of Joseph, he might naturally commit them to his care, the more so as the keeper of the prison had probably reported to Potiphar his aptness for such duties (*Kurtz*).

ver. 5. EACH MAN ACCORDING TO THE INTERPRETATION OF HIS DREAM] Each man had a dream with a peculiar interpretation belonging to it; the dream of each had its own peculiar import.

vers. 9—11. Resting on some statements of Herodotus and Plutarch, Von Bohlen and Tuch assert that this passage proves the recent age of the narrative, inasmuch as up to the time of Psammetichus, consequently to the time of Josiah, the culture of the vine was unknown, and the use of wine forbidden as sacrilegious, in Egypt. It is only an evasion of this objection to say (Hævernick, p. 216), that in the dream only the unfermented juice of the grape, and not wine, is given to Pharaoh. For the imagery of such a dream would only present those leading features that were necessary to the delineation of the information to be conveyed. Nor is this explanation necessary. The soil and climate of Egypt, except in a few parts, is adapted to the growth of the vine (Wilkinson, *Herod.* Vol. II. p. 126; Osburn, *Isr. in Eg.* p. 35); and, to pass over the statements of classical writers as referring to times subsequent to Psammetichus, the monuments of the oldest dynasties give ample proof that the vine was generally grown, its produce made into wine, and the wine used in Egypt in the oldest ages. Not only is the entire process of the vintner's art, from the planting and tending of the vines to the storing of the expressed and fermented juice in jars, represented; but the monuments give sad proof also of the wine being drank to excess by men and women. Comp. Hengstenberg, *Eg.* pp. 13, 25; Rawlinson, *Herod.* Vol. II. pp. 27, 103, 104, 126.

ver. 13. SHALL LIFT UP THINE HEAD] *Shall restore thee to thy dignity* (*Maurer, Wright*); *shall lift thine head* (i. e. *thyself*) *up out of prison* (*Knob., Gesen.*).

ver. 16. The same accurate agreement with the monumental representations of Egyptian life is found in the imagery of the baker's dream.— THREE WHITE BASKETS] This should be: *three baskets of white* (bread) (*Gesen., Knob., Del.*); or, *three wicker-baskets* (*Rosenm., De Sola*). Similar wicker-baskets, flat (which the circumstance that three are placed one on the other requires), and open, for carrying grapes and other fruits, are found represented on the monuments (Hengstenberg, *Eg.* p. 27).—ON MY HEAD] When the sons and daughters of the princes of Egypt served their parents at table, they carried on their heads three baskets, one piled upon the other, and in the uppermost are the bake-meats (Osburn, *Isr. in Eg.* p. 37).

ver. 17. BAKEMEATS] Rosellini says, after describing the kitchen-scenes upon the tomb of Rameses IV. at Biban el Moluk : "From all these representations, it is clear that the Egyptians were accustomed to prepare many kinds of pastry for the table, as we see the very same kinds spread out on the altars and tables which are represented in the tombs. They made even bread in many and various forms. These articles are found in the tombs kneaded from barley or wheat, in the form of a star, a triangle, or disk, and other such things" (Hengstenberg, *Egypt*, p. 27).

ver. 18. THIS IS THE INTERPRETATION] The essential difference between the two dreams consists in this, that in the second the birds of prey take the place of Pharaoh (*Kurtz*).

ver. 20. PHARAOH'S BIRTHDAY] The birthday of the reigning king of Egypt was a high festival at all periods of its history. One of the objects of the Rosetta inscription is, to decree the observances to take place on the birthday of Ptolemy Epiphanes (Osburn, *Isr. in Eg.* p. 38).

Chapter XLI.

ver. 1. PHARAOH] See note on xii. 15.—THE RIVER] Nile; the source of all the fertility of Egypt. Its periodical inundations supply the want of rain. Its rise is watched with the greatest anxiety, as a few feet under the regular height of inundation will produce a famine.

ver. 2. The imagery of Pharaoh's dreams is quite Egyptian. The cow was to the Egyptians the symbol of the goddess Isis, the personification of the earth and of productiveness. In dream, then, Pharaoh beholds seven of these symbols of fertility rising out of the Nile, the source of all the fertility of the land. But the lean as well as the fat kine are aptly depicted as rising from the same Nile, because on it depended the sterility as well as the fertility of the land.—A MEADOW] Heb. *Achu*, the Nile-grass; an Egyptian word for an Egyptian thing (*Hengstenberg*). The aquatic plants of the Nile were so valuable in Egypt, that they were reaped in as regular a harvest as the flax and corn (*Taylor*).

ver. 5. SEVEN EARS OF CORN UPON ONE STALK] The Egyptian wheat, *triticum compositum*, bears several heads on one stem.

ver 6. BLASTED WITH THE EAST WIND] This also, it has been said, betrays ignorance of Egypt, inasmuch as the east wind never is felt there. In answer to this it is to be observed that the Hebrew language has terms only for the four principal points of the compass; the term *Kadim* here used includes therefore all winds of an *easterly* direction. Now travellers declare that the south-east wind, called Asiab or Chamsin, blows frequently in Egypt, and that its effects are most destructive. "The grass withers, so that it entirely perishes, if this wind blows long" (Ukert, in *Hengstenb. Egypt*).

ver. 8. THE MAGICIANS OF EGYPT] Heb. *The Chartummim;* which signifies, according to the derivation given by Gesenius, *sacred scribes,* or men skilled in *the sacred writing.* "We find in Egyptian antiquity an order of persons to whom this is entirely appropriate, which is here ascribed to the magicians. The priests had a double office, the practical worship of the gods, and the pursuit of that which in Egypt was accounted as wisdom. The first belonged to the so-called prophets, the second to the holy scribes. These last were the learned men of the nation; as in the Pentateuch they are called *wise men*, so the classical writers named them *sages*. These men were applied to for explanation and aid in all things which lay beyond the circle of common knowledge and action. Thus in severe cases of sickness, for example, along with a physician a holy scribe was called, who from a book and astrological signs determined whether recovery was possible. The interpretation of dreams, and also divination, belonged to this order. In times of pestilence they applied to magic arts to avert the disease" (Hengstb. *Egypt*, p. 28).

ver. 14. HE SHAVED HIMSELF] Herodotus, II. 36, mentions it among the distinguishing peculiarities of the Egyptians, that they commonly were shaved, but in mourning they allowed the beard and hair to grow. The sculptures also agree with this representation. "So particular (says Wilkinson) were they on this point, that to have neglected it was a subject of ridicule and reproach; and whenever they intended to convey the idea of a man of low condition or a slovenly person, the artists represented him with a beard." "Although foreigners (says the same author) who were brought to Egypt as slaves had beards on their arrival in the country, we find that, as soon as they were employed in the service of this civilized people, they were obliged to conform to the cleanly habits of their masters; their beards and heads were shaved, and they adopted a close cap" (Hengstb. *Egypt*, p. 30). The Hebrews, far from shaving the beard, regarded this as a sign of disgrace or mourning (2 Sam. x. 4; Isa. xv. 2; Jer. xli. 5; xlviii. 37).

ver. 40. ACCORDING UNTO THY WORD SHALL ALL MY PEOPLE BE RULED] Lit. *according to thy mouth shall all my people dispose themselves*, i. e. they shall be ruled by thy order (*Rosenm., Maur., Del., Wright*). Gesenius and Knobel would translate, *all my people shall kiss thy mouth*, i. e. shall honour thee as their lord. But as Maurer remarks, only the hands and feet were kissed as a sign of reverence.

ver. 42. HIS RING] At the present day public documents in the East are more frequently authenticated by the royal signet than by the sign manual; the seal, however, is a stamp giving an impression with ink, and is rarely used to give an impression on wax, or any similar substance. The bestowing of the seal on Joseph was equivalent to intrusting him with the charge of the administration; because its impression attached to any document gave it as much authority as if it had been signed by the king's own hand (Taylor, *note on Hengstenb. Egypt*, p. 31).—VESTURES OF FINE LINEN] or *of byssus*. Garments of linen and cotton were regarded by the Egyptians as pure and holy. The priests were obliged to dress in garments made of these materials only. It would appear, therefore, from Joseph being thus arrayed, that Pharaoh not only *naturalized* him, but also enrolled him in the priestly order.—GOLD CHAIN] An ornament, as the monuments show, peculiar to kings or persons of high rank.

ver. 43. BOW THE KNEE] Heb. *Abrech;* in all probability an Egyptian word, meaning *bowing down*, or *falling down*. "At the present day *abrek* or *berek* is the name applied to the kneeling of a camel" (Rawlinson, *Herod*. Vol. II. p. 132).

ver. 45. CALLED JOSEPH'S NAME] By this change of name he was naturalized.—ZAPHNATH-PAANEAH] The Septuagint translation gives us the exact Egyptian form of the name, viz. *Psonthomphanech, Supporter* or *Preserver of the world*. The name when formed for Hebrew pronunciation was slightly changed so as to have also a Hebrew signification, viz. *Revealer of secrets*.—AND GAVE HIM

TO WIFE THE DAUGHTER OF POTI-PHERAH PRIEST OF ON] Notwithstanding the intolerant and exclusive character of the Egyptian hierarchy, there is nothing incredible in this marriage of the shepherd Joseph with the daughter of the priest of On; for the marriage was formed in obedience to the command of the king, who was himself of the highest sacerdotal order, and after Joseph had been naturalized (ver. 42), and, as Jacob says of him (ch. xlix. 26), 'separated from his brethren.' —ASENATH] explained by Gesenius to signify *belonging to Neith*, the goddess of Sais, answering to Athene or Minerva.—ON] the city Heliopolis, or *City of the sun*, the Hebrew name of which is by Gesenius derived from the Coptic *Un* or *On*, which signifies *light* or *the sun*. According to Wilkinson, the name of Heliopolis was 'ci-n-re,' *the abode of the sun*, from which the Heb. *On* or *Aon* was taken. It was one of the oldest cities of Egypt (Rawlinson, *Her.* Vol. II. p. 10, note 7), and noted for the numerous and learned priesthood attached to its celebrated temple of the Sun (Herod. Bk. II. 3; Strabo, XVII. p. 806). The ruins of it are still to be seen near the modern village of Matariyeh, about two hours N. N. E. from Cairo, occupying a space of about three quarters of a mile in length, by half a mile in breadth (Robinson, *Bib. Res.* I. 25).

ver. 48. LAID UP THE FOOD IN THE CITIES] The paintings upon the monuments show how common the storehouse was in ancient Egypt. In the tomb of Amenemhe, at Beni-Hassan, there is a painting of a great storehouse, before the door of which lies a large heap of grain, already winnowed. The measurer fills a bushel, in order to pour it into the uniform sacks of those who carry the grain to the corn-magazine. The carriers go to the door of the storehouse and lay down the sacks before an officer who stands ready to receive the grain: this is the overseer of the storehouse. Near by stands the bushel with which it is measured, and the registrar who takes the account. At the side of the windows there are characters which indicate the quantity of the mass which is deposited in the magazine. Compare with this the clause of ver. 49, "Until he left numbering" (Hengstenberg, *Egypt*, p. 36).

vers. 51, 52. MANASSEH] *Forgetting.*—EPHRAIM] *Fruitful.*

ver. 54. THE DEARTH WAS IN ALL LANDS] On account of this statement the author of Genesis is charged by Von Bohlen with ignorance of the natural condition of Egypt. He argues that as the fertility of Egypt depends on the overflowing of the Nile, and that of Syria and Palestine on the fall of rain, the two countries could not be visited simultaneously with a famine. But the inundations of the Nile depend on the rains which fall on the high mountains of Abyssinia (Somerville, *Phys. Geog.* p. 244; Wilkinson, *Herod.* Vol. II. p. 29); and these rains depend on the same causes as those which fall in Palestine. The industry of Hengstenberg, *Egypt*, p. 37, has collected instances of famine visiting not Egypt alone, but Egypt simultaneously with the adjoining countries. Comp. *Kurtz*, Vol. I. p. 368.

Chapter XLII.

ver. 4. BENJAMIN JACOB SENT NOT] Jacob's reluctance to part with Benjamin leads to the surmise that he suspected that Joseph had met with foul play at the hands of his brothers.

ver. 7. SPAKE ROUGHLY UNTO THEM] We need not ascribe Joseph's treatment of his brothers to vindictive feelings. His object seems to have been to prove whether they had repented of their selfish jealousy of him.

ver. 9. YE ARE SPIES; TO SEE THE NAKEDNESS OF THE LAND YE ARE COME] The nakedness of the land, i.e. the defenceless part of the country. The sons of Jacob in coming from Canaan must have entered Egypt by its northeast frontier, the side on which it was most exposed to invasion from a foreign enemy.

ver. 11. WE ARE ALL ONE MAN'S SONS] A father would not be likely to expose so many of his sons at once to such a risk (*Delitzsch*).

ver. 15. BY THE LIFE OF PHARAOH] Men naturally swear by what they regard as most powerful, most precious, or most sacred. In despotic countries, therefore, where the king is not only the sum total of worldly power, but where he is worshipped rather than served, the most solemn oath is that taken by the head or the hearth and throne of the monarch (*Kalisch*).

ver. 21. They come to sound the depth of their brother's misery: their close imprisonment shows them what it was to have cast their brother into a desolate pit; their woful experience of this governor's implacable mind in their perplexity, gives them to know what deep impression the heavy designs of their impenetrable hearts had wrought in the tender heart of their afflicted brother; and justly do they fear, lest their present misery be farther extended, until it answer in every point unto the just quantity of the mishaps which have since befallen their brother. That which I would thence commend to our imitation, when like troubles shall befall us, is, their speedy humiliation under the powerful hand of God: they ascribe all unto God, who had found out their wickedness (Jackson, *Works*, XI. 246).

ver. 24. WEPT] moved at the sight of the wholesome remorse of his brethren. But still he goes on to try the thoroughness of their repentance, to prove whether it would stand the trial of seeing their young brother made the object of a father's partiality and of the powerful Egyptian's favour.

ver. 24. SIMEON] The cruelty and perfidy displayed by Simeon in the matter of Shechem makes it not improbable that he had shown most heartlessness when Joseph was sold, and that for that reason he was now the one detained.

ver. 25. JOSEPH COMMANDED TO RESTORE EVERY MAN'S MONEY TO HIS SACK] He was unwilling to take money from his own flesh and blood for what was to sustain life.

ver. 27. INN] Lit. *place where travellers pass the night, halting-place*, either under cover or in the open air.

Chapter XLIII.

ver. 11. TAKE OF THE BEST FRUITS IN THE LAND] Lit. *the song of the land*, the most praised or prized productions of the land. The custom of making presents to a superior is so very common in the East, that it is refining too much, to represent this proceeding of Jacob as an instance of his timid prudence. Of these *fruits of the land*, the *balm, spices, and myrrh*, have been treated of in the notes on ch. xxxvii. 25.—HONEY] Heb. *D'bhash*, not the bee-honey which abounds in Egypt, and therefore would be of little value as a present, but the *grape-honey*, by the Arabians called *dibs* (Robinson, *Bib. Res.* III. 40), by the Persians *Dushab*, prepared from the juice of the grape boiled down to a jelly (Robinson, II. p. 81). Ezekiel, ch. xxvii. 17, speaks of it as an article of merchandise which Judah carried to Tyre. In modern times large quantities are brought from the neighbourhood of Hebron into Egypt.—NUTS] Heb. *botnim*. The nuts of the pistachio-tree, valued by the Orientals as a delicacy, and also for their supposed medicinal properties, being considered an antidote to the bite of serpents and to poison, and generally useful in strengthening the stomach. The tree, which is not found in Egypt, grows in Palestine and Syria.—ALMONDS] The nut of the *Amygdalus communis*.—Von Bohlen represents the gift of these presents of the fruits of Canaan as contradicting the statement of the land having been visited with famine. It is sufficient to remark, that the productiveness of fruit-trees depends on causes very different from those which affect the grain-crops. And supposing that there might have been a dearth of these *fruits* of the land, which might prevent their being treated as articles of *commerce*, this itself would enhance their value as *presents*.

ver. 16. SLAY AND MAKE READY] The historian is taxed by Von Bohlen with ignorance of Egyptian habits. According to his representation, the Egyptians in general partook of flesh-meat only in the shape of consecrated flesh-offerings; the higher classes, and especially the priests to whose class Joseph belonged, abstained entirely from animal food; and neat cattle, goats, and sheep, were accounted inviolable. But not only do the kitchen-scenes and delineations of feasts on the monuments prove the abundant use of animal food; but the ancient authors also alleged by Von Bohlen support the Scriptural account. Porphyry says that *at certain times* the priests abstained from animal food. Herodotus (B. II. 18) says that *cows*, not *oxen*, were inviolable; so that (II. 168) a ration of beef was received daily by the warriors, and (II. 37) by the priests. Comp. Hengstenberg, *Eg.* p. 8.

ver. 32. THEY SET ON FOR HIM BY HIMSELF] The arrangement of the guests agrees exactly with the indications of the pictures in the tombs. The heads of the house and their children and dependents sat at separate tables (Osburn, *Isr. in Eg.* p. 70; Hengstenberg, *Eg.* p. 39).—BECAUSE THE EGYPTIANS MIGHT NOT EAT BREAD WITH THE HEBREWS, &c.] See note on xlvi. 34.

ver. 33. THEY SAT] Many of the Eastern nations *reclined* on couches at their meals, as did the Romans and Greeks; but the Egyptian monuments prove that, while couches or sofas were in use for rest, the Egyptians *sat* on chairs or stools when eating their meals. From the expression in ch. xviii. 4, "rest yourselves," Hengstenberg infers that the Hebrew custom was to recline at meals. If this inference be correct, the minute accuracy of the Hebrew writer of Genesis, in depicting Egyptian habits, is still more striking.—AND THE MEN MARVELLED ONE AT ANOTHER] Was Joseph's care in ranging them after their age an *inadvertence* on his side nearly betraying him to his brethren, as Dr Taylor supposes (Hengstenb. *Eg.* p. 77)? or was it designed by him, in furtherance of his plan relating to Benjamin, in order to make his brethren to regard him with awe as one possessed of extraordinary and almost supernatural gifts? See xliv. 15. The latter is Dr Kalisch's view.

ver. 34. BENJAMIN'S MESS WAS FIVE TIMES SO MUCH AS ANY OF THEIRS] He wished to try whether the repentance and remorse of his brethren would stand this additional test of seeing, without jealousy, their father's favoured son made the object of the great Egyptian governor's peculiar favour.

Chapter XLIV.

ver. 2. THE SILVER CUP] The Egyptians, says Herodotus, Book II. c. 37, universally used *brazen* cups for drinking out of (*Hævernick*). The monuments, however, show that the wealthy Egyptians used glass, porcelain, and gold, sometimes inlaid with a coloured composition resembling enamel, or with precious stones (Rawlinson's *Herod.* Vol. II. p. 61).

ver. 5. WHEREBY INDEED HE DIVINETH] The ancient Egyptians, and still more the Persians, practised a mode of divination from goblets. Small pieces of gold or silver, together with precious stones, marked with strange figures and signs, were thrown into the vessel; after which certain incantations were pronounced, and the evil demon was invoked; the latter was then supposed to give the answer, either by intelligible words, or by pointing to some of the characters on the precious stones, or in some other more mysterious manner. Sometimes the goblet was filled with pure water, upon which the sun was allowed to play; and the figures which were thus formed, or which a lively imagination fancied it saw, were interpreted as the desired omen: a method of taking auguries still employed in Egypt and Nubia. The goblets were usually of a spherical form, which is even confirmed by the etymology of the Hebrew name used here, *gabhiya* (*Kalisch*).

ver. 18. JUDAH] who had taken on himself the responsibility of Benjamin's safety.

ver. 29. THE GRAVE] See note on ch. xxxvii. 35.

ver. 34. In these moving words of Judah we perceive what a change of character had taken place in Joseph's brethren, since the most faithful conscientiousness and filial love towards their father are expressed therein. This it was which Joseph desired to see; and so with these words, when the anguish and perplexity of his brethren have reached their height, there comes in the turning-point of the history (*v. Gerlach*).

Chapter XLV.

ver. 1. CAUSE EVERY MAN TO GO OUT FROM ME] He was not willing that any should be witnesses of his own passion, or his brethren's former faults (*Kidder*).

ver. 5. FOR GOD DID SEND ME BEFORE YOU TO PRESERVE LIFE] His words on another occasion explain this, ch. 1. 20: 'But as for you, ye thought evil against me; but God meant it unto good, to bring it to pass, as it is this day, to save much people alive.' "We ought to distinguish between the action of Joseph's brethren which was evil, and the passion [i.e. suffering] of Joseph, which was good. God willed and predefined the sufferings of Joseph, and disposed them to his own glory, and the good of His Church. God sent Joseph before; how? dispositively, *to preserve life*. But He willed not, nor predefined the action of his brethren, otherwise than permissively, or at the most occasionally, by doing good, which they made an occasion of doing evil, or in respect of the order of their evil act" (Archb. Bramhall, *Castigat. of Mr Hobs, Works*, p. 741).

ver. 6. NEITHER BE EARING NOR HARVEST] Earing is old English for ploughing. "The passage points out the cause of the famine. The ploughing in Egypt takes place just as the waters of the inundation reach the field. In these disastrous years the water scarcely rose above its wonted level; there was consequently no ploughing and no harvest" (Osburn, p. 77).

ver. 8. FATHER TO PHARAOH] Counsellor or prime minister to Pharaoh. This title of honour was applied to the king's chief minister among the Persians, Esth. iii. 13. LXX.; and the Syrians, 1 Macc. xi. 32 (*Knobel*).

ver. 10. THE LAND OF GOSHEN] a district of Egypt between the Delta and Canaan (ch. xlvi. 28, 29); at no considerable distance from the royal city where Joseph lived (xlv. 10); adjacent to the Nile where Pharaoh's daughter bathed (Ex. ii. 3, 5); and from which the Israelites supplied themselves with fish (Num. xi. 5); yet distinct from the country inhabited by Egyptians (ch. xlvi. 34); well adapted for tillage, and most productive (ch. xlvii. 6; Num. xi. 5), and irrigated artificially from the overflowing waters of the Nile (Deut. xi. 10); yet equally well adapted for the pastoral occupation of the Israelites (ch. xlvi. 34, xlvii. 4). All these notices point to the tract of country extending from Heliopolis on the south-west towards the north-east, bounded on the west by an eastern (perhaps the Pelusiac, or, as Kurtz and Robinson think, the Tanaitic) arm of the Nile, comprehended within the modern province of Esh-Shurkiyeh, which in situation, richness, and general physical condition, corresponds with the land of Goshen. Comp. Robinson, *Bib. Res.* I. 52; Hengstb. *Eg.* p. 42; Kurtz, II. p. 14.

ver. 16. PHARAOH'S HOUSE] The name of the royal city of the Pharaohs in Joseph's time is not mentioned. Hengstenberg, Baumgarten, and Kurtz, consider it to have been Zoan or Tanis. But the passages they appeal to, Numb. xiii. 22; Ps. lxxviii. 12, 43, refer only to the time of Moses, when the capital might have been, and probably was, changed. Delitzsch decides for Memphis. Joseph's marriage with a daughter of a priest of On renders it probable that On, or Heliopolis, was the capital of the Pharaoh to whom Joseph was minister.

ver. 19. NOW THOU ART COMMANDED, THIS DO YE, &c.] i.e. Now thou art commanded [to say to thy brethren], this do ye, &c. (*Maurer*).

ver. 23. TEN ASSES LADEN WITH THE GOOD THINGS OF EGYPT, AND TEN SHE ASSES LADEN WITH CORN AND BREAD, &c.] He and she asses appear in great numbers on the monuments. The former were commonly used for riding—we find them represented with rich trappings—*the latter as beasts of burden.* A single individual is represented on the monuments as having 760 of them, which makes it evident that they were numerous (*Hengstenberg*).

ver. 24. FALL NOT OUT BY THE WAY] He fears that remorse for the wrong they had committed might lead them to mutual recriminations (comp. ch. xlii. 22), and then to quarrels; or that the necessity of divulging the whole crime to their father might lead to disputes as to their relative participation in the guilt (*Knob., Delitzsch*). The translation adopted by Gesen., Maur., Tuch, Baumgarten, *fear not, go on your way with confidence,* has little to recommend it. For it is not likely that the brothers would have much reason for fear on a road they had already travelled three times.

ver. 27. WHEN HE SAW THE WAGONS] which were a present evidence of the truth of the almost incredible tidings.

Chapter XLVI.

We stand now at the threshold of a fresh era in the history of the Kingdom of God, for which everything since ch. xxxvii. had been preparing—the going down of Jacob and his family into Egypt. Had the Israelites remained any longer in Canaan, they must have merged themselves in the Canaanites, or at all events have lost their united family character. They could only preserve their unity any further under the peculiar circumstances in which they went into Egypt. Here, at first treated with great favour, they obtained room enough to spread. Here they were objects of religious avoidance as herdsmen, at the same time that they were enabled to participate in the riches and high cultivation of the people among whom they sojourned. And here they came into close contact with a people, the most renowned of all heathens for the profoundness and symbolism of their religion, and for the extensive influence that it exercised (*Von Gerlach*). Comp. Davison, *Prophecy*, pp. 100—103.

ver. 1. CAME TO BEER-SHEBA, AND OFFERED SACRIFICES] Although everything tended to convince him that the divine arrangements were drawing him away from the land of promise, he does not venture to leave it without consulting the will of the Lord. His sacrifice was offered at Beer-sheba, either because it was his last halting-place in Canaan on the road to Egypt, or because it was there (ch. xxvi. 24) the Lord appeared to confirm Isaac in remaining in Canaan in defiance of opposition or adversity.

ver. 2. JACOB, JACOB] According to Nachmanides, he is in this vision styled Jacob, not Israel, because, in his going down to Egypt, he and his descendants were not, for a time at least, *to prevail*, but were to enter on the period of bondage predicted to Abraham (*Raphall*).

ver. 5. IN THE WAGONS] The sacred writer has here been again charged with ignorance of the nature of the country between Beer-sheba and Hebron, on account of his describing the wagons of Pharaoh to have traversed a road which Dr Robinson has pronounced impassable for wheeled carriages. But the American traveller was merely speaking of the direct road between the two places, by which he himself travelled, and he afterwards adds: "We were convinced that wagons for the patriarch could not have passed by that route. Still, by taking a more circuitous route up the great Wady el-Khulil more to the right, they might probably reach Hebron through the valleys without great difficulty" (*Bib. Res.* I. 214).

ver. 7. ALL HIS SEED BROUGHT HE WITH HIM INTO EGYPT] A remarkable parallel to the description of the arrival of Jacob's family in Egypt is furnished by a scene in a tomb at Beni Hassan: "strangers" who arrive in Egypt. They carry their goods with them on asses. The number 37 is written over them in hieroglyphics. The first figure is an Egyptian scribe, who presents an account of their arrival to a person in a sitting posture, the owner of the tomb, and one of the principal officers of the reigning Pharaoh. The next, likewise an Egyptian, ushers them into his presence, and two of the strangers advance, bringing presents. Four men with bows and clubs follow leading an ass, on which there are two children in panniers, accompanied by a boy and four women. Last, another ass laden, and two men, one of whom carries a bow and club, and the other a lyre, which he plays with a plectrum. All the men have beards contrary to the custom of the Egyptians (Hengstb. *Egypt,* p. 40).

vers. 8—27. THESE ARE THE NAMES OF THE CHILDREN OF ISRAEL, WHICH CAME INTO EGYPT... ALL THE SOULS OF THE HOUSE OF JACOB, WHICH CAME INTO EGYPT, WERE THREESCORE AND TEN] The sacred writer does *not* mean to assert that all these descendants of Jacob were born before the removal into Egypt. His intention evidently is to give, at this important epoch, an exact list of those who became *heads of families* in Israel, and in making it he evidently regards Jacob's immediate descendants who were born in Egypt as having come in the persons of their fathers into Egypt. The arguments which prove that he does not give an historical account of the individuals who came in Jacob's company to Egypt are these: (*a*) When Jacob's sons were preparing for their second journey to Egypt, Reuben had evidently only *two* sons (ch. xlii. 37); here four sons are given to him, two of whom must have been born in Egypt. (*b*) Since Joseph was now about thirty-nine years old (ch. xli. 46; xlv. 6), Benjamin could not have been more than twenty-four years old; and consistently with this the previous narrative throughout represents him as a youth; here ten sons are given him, who therefore must have been born after the removal from Canaan. (c) The sons of Pharez (ver. 12) must also have been born in Egypt. The whole period of Jacob's sojourn in Canaan, after his return from exile, was only about thirty years. This interval is too brief to include the marriage of Judah, the birth of a son Pharez after the sons by his first marriage had reached maturity, and the births of grandchildren, the children of Pharez. The birth of Pharez must be placed a very short time before the removal from Canaan. (d) In ver. 5, and in xliii. 8, mention is made only of Jacob, his sons, and their little ones; in this list Jacob's great-grandchildren are mentioned as well. (e) In Numb. xxvi. where the list of heads of families is given, not a single grandson of Jacob is mentioned in addition to those mentioned here; it is against all probability that no more sons should have been born to Jacob's sons after they had entered Egypt. On the other hand, that the writer speaks of the yet unborn grandsons and great-grandsons of Jacob as entering Egypt in the persons of their fathers appears from the following considerations: (*a*) In ver. 27 it is said, "All the souls of the house of Jacob which came into Egypt were threescore and ten." Among these he reckons the two sons of Joseph, who were certainly born in Egypt. Another instance of this mode of speaking is found in Deut. x. 22. (*b*) The grandchildren of Jacob are spoken of as the children borne by his wives; e.g. (ver. 15) 'These be the sons of Leah, which she bare unto Jacob in Padan-Aram ... all the souls of his sons and his daughters were thirty and three.' Here the grandchildren are viewed as existing in their fathers. (*c*) A similar conception is found in ver. 4, 'I will go down with thee into Egypt, and I will also surely bring *thee* up again.' Comp. Hengstenb. *Pent.* II. 290; Kurtz, II. 6; Delitzsch, p. 563.

ver. 10. CANAANITISH WOMAN] This particular notice seems to intimate that Judah and Simeon alone had married Canaanites. The others may have intermarried with the families descended from Abraham. One of the children of Manasseh was by an Aramitess or Syrian (1 Chron. vii. 14).

ver. 28. AND HE SENT JUDAH, &c.] He sent Judah before himself unto Joseph, that he (Joseph) might direct him (Judah) to Goshen, before his (Jacob's) arrival (*Wright*).

ver. 34. FOR EVERY SHEPHERD IS AN ABOMINATION UNTO THE EGYPTIANS] The monuments afford abundant evidence of this hatred of the Egyptians to shepherds. The artists of Upper and Lower Egypt vie with each other in caricaturing them. They are represented always as dirty and unshaven, and in some cases as a deformed and an unseemly race. Their figures were painted on the soles of Egyptian slippers as a token of contempt. Comp. Hengstb. *Eg.* p. 41; Wiseman, *Science and Rev.* II. p. 80. It is generally assumed that this hatred of shepherds had its origin in the cruel oppression of the Egyptians by a race of nomad or shepherd invaders; but it would seem to proceed from a deeper source, namely, religious rancour. "In Egypt, where the one pursuit was agriculture, and where everything was prescriptive, it was a doctrine of religion that every shepherd by occupation was unclean, and inadmissible within the precincts of her temples" (Osburn, *Isr. in Eg.* p. 96).—Joseph directed his brethren to introduce themselves as *shepherds*, not only in spite of the fact that shepherds were an abomination to the Egyptians, but *on that very account;* for in the occupation of his brethren there was the surest guarantee that their national and religious peculiarities would not be endangered or destroyed, and that they would not be absorbed by the Egyptians (*Kurtz*).

Chapter XLVII.

ver. 2. FIVE MEN] The number *five* seems to have had some peculiar significance with the Egyptians, as it is used repeatedly in connexion with them; comp. ch. xli. 34; xliii. 34; xlv. 22; xlvii. 26; Isa. xix. 18. What gave it this significance does not appear; it may have been derived from the same source as the five-day division of time among the Chinese, Mongols, and Aztecs.

ver. 6. IN THE LAND OF GOSHEN LET THEM DWELL] Pharaoh may not improbably have hoped that by the settlement of a devoted tribe in the border-province he would secure a desirable bulwark against the incursions of the Bedouin robbers of the desert, and also against the other nations of the East (*Kurtz*).

ver. 9. MY PILGRIMAGE] He thus speaks of his life, not so much in reference to the wandering nature of his existence, as to the better and heavenly country, which (Heb. xi. 8—16) he and his fathers had in view. Comp. ch. xxiii. 4; 1 Chron.

xxix. 15.—FEW] in comparison with the length of days that Abraham and Isaac attained to.—EVIL] Though in some respects prosperous, he had met with many sorrows. He had to fly from Esau, and serve twenty years; he fled from Laban; was afflicted in Dinah, Simeon and Levi, in Reuben, and on the score of Joseph (*Kidder*).

ver. 10. BLESSED PHARAOH] His presuming to bless the king of Egypt is to be accounted for, not merely from his greater age, but also from the impulse given to him by the consciousness that he was called of God to be a blessing to the nations (*Kurtz*).

ver. 11. LAND OF RAMESES] Goshen, of which the chief city was Rameses. There is no reason to suppose that the city was not in existence at the time of Joseph; for Ex. i. 11 does not refer to the first building, but to the fortification of the city (*Kurtz*).

vers. 13—26. The sacred narrative here records the great change which was effected in the political state of Egypt by Joseph. When the money of the Egyptians was exhausted in the purchase of food, he supplied them with grain, receiving in return first their cattle, then their lands and their persons. When all the people and all the land were thus at his disposal, he returned the land to the occupiers with grain sufficient for food and for seed, requiring in return an annual rent of one-fifth of the produce to be paid to the king. The priests, however, retained their lands rent free, because, being entitled to a daily supply of food from the king, they had not been compelled to barter their land and persons for food. This account is in its leading features corroborated by other sources of information. The monuments represent only kings, priests, and the military class, as landholders (Hengstenberg, *Eg.* p. 61). According to Strabo (XVII. p. 787), those employed in agriculture held their land subject to rent. According to Diodorus (I. 73), all the land belonged either to the priests or the kings or the military class. Herodotus (II. 109) attributes to Sesostris, to whom all the important deeds of the Pharaohs were by the ancients assigned, the division of the land among the Egyptians and the exaction of an annual rent. These notices, in representing the military class also to be exempt from taxation, do not essentially differ from the Scripture account. For, as we learn from Herodotus (II. 141, 168), the land of the military class was given by the king in lieu of pay, and was revocable at his will. Comp. Hengstenberg, *Eg.* 60; *Pent.* II. 445.

ver. 16. GIVE YOUR CATTLE] The monuments, not to speak of the testimony of classical writers, prove that although Egypt was especially adapted to agriculture, the breeding and care of cattle, including horses, oxen, cows, goats, asses, and sheep, were not neglected. For instance, in a tomb near the pyramids of Gheezeh bearing the name of Cheops, is the representation of a head-shepherd presenting himself to give an account of the 834 oxen, 220 cows, 3234 goats, 760 asses, and 974 sheep, intrusted to him. Yet Von Bohlen denies that there were asses in Egypt (Hengstenberg, *Eg.* p. 5).

ver. 18. THE SECOND YEAR] i.e. the year after they had parted with their cattle.

ver. 20. AND JOSEPH BOUGHT ALL THE LAND OF EGYPT FOR PHARAOH] The monarch's provident care and timely outlay had secured the people from the extreme consequences of their improvident neglect of the years of plenty. Joseph therefore took no unfair advantage of the necessities of the Egyptians, in causing the king to reap the fruits of his prudence and outlay. And in reference to the light in which Joseph's measures are to be regarded, the remark of Michaud is very important. "In order to shed its blessings over Egypt the Nile required a strong hand to turn it into canals, and thus to direct its fertilizing waters. This distribution of its waters required the assistance of public and sovereign authority. It was therefore necessary that government should interfere, and this necessity of interference must to some extent have changed and modified the rights of landed proprietors" (*Correspond. d'Orient par Michaud et Poujoulat*, VIII. 60).

ver. 21. HE REMOVED THEM TO CITIES] Diodorus remarks (I. 57) that Sesostris raised many great mounds, and upon them *transplanted the towns* which were situated too low. The fresh regulations in the country, and especially the new canals, necessarily created a great number of towns and villages for the management of the grounds which were portioned out, and were now partly cultivated for the first time. To that we may most naturally refer the remark that 'Joseph removed them to cities from one end of the borders of Egypt to the other end thereof' (Lepsius, *Chron. of the Egypt.* p. 482, ed. Bohn).

Ver. 22. FOR THE PRIESTS HAD A PORTION ASSIGNED THEM OF PHARAOH] Herodotus says (II. 37), "They consume none of their own property, and are at no expense for anything; but every day bread is baked for them of the sacred corn, and a plentiful supply of beef and goose's flesh is assigned to them, and also a portion of wine made from the grape."

Ver. 24. THE FIFTH PART] In a country so fertile as Egypt, where seventy per cent., it has been computed, is in modern times extracted from the tillers of the soil, twenty per cent. of the produce cannot be considered a heavy tribute to the monarch whose wise and laborious measures had preserved the Egyptians from the consequences of a seven years' dearth. Under the rule of Mehemet Ali every village was compelled to cultivate two-thirds of its lands with cotton and other articles solely for the Pasha; and also to render back to him, in the form of taxes and exactions in kind, a large proportion of the produce of the remaining third. Robinson, *Bib. Res.* I. 29.

Ver. 31. AND ISRAEL BOWED HIMSELF UPON THE BED'S HEAD] While speaking to Joseph he had sat upright on his bed (ch. xlviii. 2, xxvii.

19), but he now bent himself towards the upward end of it (*Knob.*), or prostrated himself on the bed (*Del.*), in order to thank God that his last wish was granted. Through the weakness of old age he could not rise up and prostrate himself on the ground. The Septuagint here translates, *worshipped [leaning] on the top of his staff*, though it translates the same sentence in 1 Kin. i. 47, *worshipped upon his bed*. It is impossible to find a reference to these words in Heb. xi. 21. The inspired writer is there speaking of what took place *after Jacob blessed his sons*, and "shows how strong Jacob's faith was, when his body was so weak that he was not able to bow himself and worship without the help of a staff" (*Patrick*).

Chapter XLVIII.

ver. 2. AND ONE TOLD JACOB,...AND ISRAEL STRENGTHENED HIMSELF] Delitzsch draws attention to the significant change of names (*Jacob* lies sick, but *Israel* raises himself), which also appears in ch. xlv. 27, 28.

ver. 5. THY TWO SONS ARE MINE; AS REUBEN AND SIMEON, THEY SHALL BE MINE] Jacob here constitutes Ephraim and Manasseh heads of tribes. As Joseph thus had a double portion given to him, he had the birthright transferred to him. Comp. 1 Chron. v. 1; Deut. xxi. 17.

ver. 6. THY ISSUE, WHICH THOU BEGETTEST AFTER THEM, SHALL BE THINE] Any children which Joseph might have after these two were not to be reckoned as heads or founders of tribes; they would only rank as portion of the tribes of Ephraim and Manasseh.

ver. 7. He thus adopts Ephraim and Manasseh for the sake of his beloved Rachel who died so prematurely. To honour her memory he treats these two grandchildren as if sons, and thus increases the number of her children (*Knobel*).—DIED BY ME] as she accompanied me on my journey (*Knob.*), or *died for me*, i.e. *to my grief* (*Rosenm., Gesen., Tuch, Wright*).

ver. 14. GUIDING HIS HANDS WITTINGLY] Lit. *he made his hands intelligent*, i.e. placed his hands thus designedly (*Luther, Gesen., Maur., Knob.*). The translation of most of the ancient versions (*Sept., Syr., Vulg., Jonath.*), *he crossed his hands*, is preferred by Tuch and Delitzsch.

ver. 16. THE ANGEL WHICH REDEEMED ME] See note on ch. xvi. 7.—LET MY NAME BE NAMED ON THEM] Let them be called by my name, i.e. considered as my sons (*Maurer*). May they be worthy of having their names coupled with my own, and those of Abraham and Isaac (*Raphall*). Knobel translates, *may my name be named through them*, and refers to ch. xxi. 12.

ver. 19. HIS YOUNGER BROTHER SHALL BE GREATER] Even so early as the time of the Judges Ephraim held a high rank in Israel, far above Manasseh; Jud. iv. 5, v. 14, viii. xii. After the revolt of the ten tribes from Rehoboam it held the highest rank among the revolted tribes, so that by the prophets the kingdom of Israel is repeatedly addressed as Ephraim.

ver. 22. I HAVE GIVEN TO THEE ONE PORTION ABOVE THY BRETHREN] Jacob prophetically glances over the interval of the sojourn in Egypt, and beholds the tribes conquering the promised land. As representing his descendants, he awards to Joseph a double portion, a portion beyond what the other brothers receive (*Tuch, Delitzsch*). This seems to be the most natural interpretation of this difficult passage. The explanation which makes Jacob allude to the taking of Shechem by Simeon and Levi is quite untenable. It represents Jacob to adopt as his own an act, which in the next chapter he speaks of with horror. Nearly as improbable is the explanation according to which *the portion* means the piece of ground near Shechem where Jacob dwelt for a time, ch. xxxiii. 19, 20. But this he possessed by purchase, not by conquest.

Chapter XLIX.

ver. 1. As Jacob draws near to death, not only is he enabled to look into the future with clearer eyes, but the spirit of prophecy comes on him from above, and in its light he sees the longings of his heart fulfilled, and the promised land in the possession of his descendants. His twelve sons are standing round his bed, the representatives and fathers of the tribes by which the land is to be taken. Before his mind there are gathered together in one living picture all the pleasing and painful events of which they have been the cause. With prophetic vision he traces the characters and dispositions of the fathers as they are transmitted, expanded or modified, through the history of their descendants; and aided by this insight, he allots to every one, on the authority of God, his fitting portion of that land, in which he himself has led a pilgrim life for more than a hundred years, and which now stands with all its natural diversities, and with its rich and manifold productions, as vividly and distinctly before his mind as the different characters of his own sons (*Kurtz*).—IN THE LAST DAYS] Lit. *in the end of the days*, an expression occurring fifteen times in the O. T., and there, as in the N. T., always indicating the Messianic era. The possession of the promised land was the first stage of the series of events which were to find their consummation and end in the Messiah's kingdom, and which were all preparatory to His coming. Just as was the case with all the prophets, the prophetic insight of Jacob enabled him to see in the attainment of the first stage of the promise the realization of its full completion, but did not give him such knowledge of the times and seasons as to make him see the length of distance which lay between them. Thus we find the prophets often speaking of the two advents of Christ, as if the one was in time immediately consequent on the other.

ver. 3. MY FIRSTBORN, AND THE BEGINNING OF MY STRENGTH] Comp. Deut. xxi. 17, 'For he is the beginning of his strength; the right of the firstborn is his.' Ps. lxxviii. 51, 'And smote all the firstborn in Egypt; the chief of their strength in the tabernacles of Ham.'—BEGINNING

OF MY STRENGTH] i.e. *the first-fruit of my vigour* (*Knob., Del., Wright*).

ver. 4. UNSTABLE AS WATER] Lit. *thou that boilest over like water* (*Wright*). It implieth both his sudden light affections which carried him to evil, and his sudden downfall from dignity (*Ainsworth*). The figure is taken from water in a boiling caldron, foaming and bursting over its bounds (*Knobel*).—THOU SHALT NOT EXCEL] The preeminence belonging to him as firstborn is taken from him; 1 Chron. v. 1.—HE WENT UP] The change from the second to the third person expresses Jacob's horror at the thought of the deed.

ver. 5. BRETHREN] i.e. brethren in the fullest sense, not by birth only, but by likeness of disposition.—IN THEIR HABITATIONS] The marginal translation, *are their swords*, is supported by most modern expositors.

ver. 6. THEIR SECRET] or *council*. He disclaims any participation in the murderous act of Simeon and Levi.—DIGGED DOWN A WALL] is better translated, *houghed* or *hamstrung* [*the*] *ox.*—A WALL] Heb. *shur*. The parallelism usual in Hebrew poetry has led many to prefer the reading *shor*, *an ox*. If this reading be adopted, the word must be taken either collectively, as meaning *oxen*, which were slain promiscuously with the inhabitants of Shechem (*Knob., Tuch, Wright, Del.*), or as a figurative appellation of Shechem himself (*Herder, Schumann, Maurer*). In Scripture, e.g. Deut. xxxiii. 17, and in the classical writers, Hom. *Il.* II. 440, the comparison of princes or heroes to oxen is not unusual.

ver. 7. I WILL DIVIDE THEM IN JACOB, AND SCATTER THEM IN ISRAEL] Fulfilled literally in both cases. The participation of a leading member of the tribe in the sin of Peor (Numb. xxv. 14), the great diminution in the number of the tribe at the close of the forty years' wandering (Numb. i. 23, xxvi. 14), the omission of the tribe in the blessing of Moses (Deut. xxxiii.), prove that Simeon earned the fulfilment of the curse in its fullest meaning by not receiving any separate territory in Canaan. The tribe of Simeon was allotted only nineteen unconnected cities within the bounds of Judah's portion. Levi, by devotion to the cause of the Lord, turned the curse into a blessing (Ex. xxxii. 26; Deut. xxxiii. 9). Levi was scattered indeed in Israel, but as the honoured priesthood of the Lord. It may be here remarked, that this passage presents strong internal evidence of the prophecy having been uttered by Jacob. Had it been composed after the exodus, when the tribe of Levi was exalted to the enviable post of ministering to the Lord, the writer could never have thought of representing its lot as a curse.

vers. 8—12. Jacob, in the prophetic spirit, sees all the blessings assigned to Judah as culminating and centring in the Messiah who is to spring from his tribe. In the person of the Messiah he sees Judah receiving the homage which his grateful brethren pay him as the vanquisher of their enemies, and the author of peace and rest for them. He sees the great Saviour, who had rushed down on his enemies with the resistless force of a young lion, and having vanquished them had returned to his throne on high, sitting in the majesty of a repose which no power can interrupt. He sees Judah sitting as ruler of his tribe with his sceptre of tribal sway resting between his knees, until the coming of the Saviour brings, as His name denotes, peace and rest to the nation; a sure proof that, though the other tribes may be broken, Judah shall remain unbroken and self-governed through all the storms until the Messiah comes to establish the kingdom, and give the blessings promised to Abraham. In Him the tribal sway of Judah shall terminate, only to be changed into that of universal dominion; for all nations shall flow to Him to be blessed by obeying Him. His kingdom shall be one of peace and rest and happiness; for He comes not in the array of earthly conquerors, but in peaceful guise; and He furnishes richly those blessings which alone can satisfy truly the craving heart of man.

ver. 8. JUDAH] The verb from which the name is derived refers, with only two apparent exceptions, to the *praise of God*. Hence Hengstenberg explains it, '*God* shall be praised;' and not, as it is generally explained, '*He shall be praised.*' Comp. ch. xxix. 35. "He whose very existence becomes the cause of exclaiming, 'Praise be to God,' will assuredly receive praise from his brethren."—THY HAND SHALL BE IN THE NECK OF THINE ENEMIES] Thou shalt put to flight all thine enemies, and press them hard when they are fleeing. Comp. Ex. xxiii. 27; Ps. xviii. 40. For the fulfilment, comp. the *acknowledged* Messianic predictions in the O. T., Ps. ii. 9, cx. 2, 6; Isa. lxiii. 2—6; in the N. T., Act. ii. 34; 1 Cor. xv. 25; Heb. ii. 14; Rev. vi. 2, xix. 10—21.—THY

FATHER'S CHILDREN SHALL BOW DOWN BEFORE THEE] Phil. ii. 9—11, 'Wherefore God also hath highly exalted Him, and given Him a name which is above every name: that at the name of Jesus every knee should bow,' &c. Comp. Ps. lxxii. 11. To Judah is transferred the blessing which Isaac had promised to Jacob: 'People shall serve thee ...thy mother's sons shall worship before thee.' The texts cited prove that it was intended to relate to the Messiah, the Immanuel, who was to spring from Judah.

ver. 9. A LION'S WHELP...AS A LION...AS AN OLD LION] In the young lion is represented the fearless might and impetuous resistless force, in the full grown lion, the awful majesty of might in repose which the champion of Judah was to possess, and which no enemy would dare to disturb.—THOU ART GONE UP] As the lion when he has made sure of his prey goes up to his mountain retreat; Song of Sol. iv. 8, 'Look from the top of Amana, from the top of Shenir and Hermon, from the lions' dens.' Ps. civ. 21, 22. For the application, comp. Eph. iv. 8, 'When He ascended up on high, He led captivity captive.'—HE STOOPED DOWN, &c.] The figure represents the perfect peace and repose which the deliverer of Judah was to enjoy after his complete victory over his enemy. That Jacob had *the Messiah alone* in view when he represented Judah as *a lion*, is proved by Rev. v. 5, 'Behold, the Lion of the tribe of Juda, the Root of David, hath prevailed to open the book.'

ver. 10. THE SCEPTRE] Heb. *shebhet*. Primary meaning *a rod;* hence rod or wand betokening office; hence the office itself, e.g. of king, Isa. xxxiii. 22, 'The Lord is our Judge' (*Shebhet*), or of ruler or head of tribe, 1 Sam. x. 19, 20, where the tribes were evidently represented by their leaders; hence, lastly, the tribe itself, Ps. lxxiv. 2, 'Remember the rod [tribe] of thine inheritance;' 1 Kin. xi. 13. In this passage it signifies the sceptre of authority over the tribe.—A LAWGIVER] Heb. *Mechokek;* properly *Governor*, as in Judg. v. 14. The parallelism of Hebrew poetry authorizes us to translate it here, 'the ruler's staff,' as in Num. xxi. 18.—THE SCEPTRE...FROM BETWEEN HIS FEET] Judah is represented as the head of his tribe, sitting with his sceptre or staff of tribal authority in his hand, and the end resting on the ground between his knees. On the ancient monuments of Persepolis kings are represented in this attitude. Each tribe of Israel had, even before the exodus, a certain organized form of self-government, by which its existence as a distinct tribe was maintained. Jacob foretells that, though the other tribes should be broken up and dispersed, Judah should as a tribe preserve its existence until Shiloh should come. It is proved that Judah, even during the Captivity and under the Roman government, continued as a distinct people under its own rulers and elders, and that thus as a tribe it existed until the destruction of Jerusalem by Titus.—SHILOH] Derived from the Hebrew *shalah, to be safe, secure,* " chiefly used of one who enjoys peace and prosperity" (*Gesenius*); it means *Peacefulness, Rest,* or *Security,* and implies the great blessing of the reign of the King Messiah, who is here foretold under the name Shiloh. The different derivations according to which the word was meant to signify, *he that is to be sent (Jerome), what is destined to him (Sept.), his son (Calvin),* are now with one accord rejected. But here the harmony of modern exposition ends; for even those who regard the prophecy as Messianic, and who derive the word Shiloh from *shalah* or a kindred root, differ widely as to the import of the word Shiloh, and the construction of the sentence in which it stands. There are five interpretations contended for: (1) *Until rest comes, and people obey him* (Vater, Gesenius, Knobel). (2) *Until he comes to rest, and people obey him* (Hofmann, Kurtz). (3) *Until he comes to Shiloh, and the people obey him* (Delitzsch). (4) *As long as they come to Shiloh* (Maurer). (5) *Until Shiloh comes, him shall the people obey* (Hengstb., Winer). But (1) and (2) are overthrown by the circumstance that, from its form, Shiloh must be a proper name (Hengstb., *Christol.* I. 60; Delitzsch, p. 589). Against (3) is the objection that sacred history shows no fulfilment of the prophecy. The arrival of the tribes at Shiloh (Josh. xviii. 1) was followed by no such change, either in the internal polity of Judah, or the outward circumstances of the tribe in relation to the other tribes or to foreign nations, as is intimated by the prophecy thus interpreted. For if we take the *sceptre* to denote *tribal sway*, the arrival at Shiloh made no alteration in the tribal constitution of Judah. If we take it to denote the sceptre of royal rule over the tribes, Judah possessed no *authority* over the other tribes until the reign of David, when Shiloh had long ceased to be the centre of worship for Israel.

In the wilderness Judah marched first of the tribes, but alike with the other tribes was ruled by Moses. After his death, Judah with the other tribes was ruled by an Ephraimite. On two occasions, in the time of the Judges, Judah is mentioned in such a manner as to show that it held no recognized authority over the rest of Israel (Judg. i. 1; xx. 18). But one of the Judges of Israel, Othniel, was of Judah. Against (4) is the objection that the particles translated, *as long as*, never have that meaning. The interpretation (5) alone is free from grammatical or historical difficulties, provided that the *sceptre* of Judah is taken to relate to *tribal* and not *royal* government. The tribe of Judah existed self-governed from the time that it became a tribe until the birth of Christ. The only objection is the difficulty of tracing a connexion between the name of the Messiah and the name of the city Shiloh. But (*a*) there is no absolute necessity of tracing any such connexion. The city may have been thus accidentally named by the Canaanites just as the city of Melchizedek was called *Salem, peace*. Or (*b*) it may have been named by the Israelites without any intentional reference to this prophecy, just as the founders of Nazareth never dreamed of the prophecy of the *Netzer* in Isa. xi. 1, and yet the coincidence was used by God to draw attention to Jesus the Nazarene, as Him in whom the prophecy was fulfilled. Just in the same way the Israelites may have named the city of the house of their God, Shiloh, in thankful remembrance of the rest which He had given them (Josh. xi. 23; xviii. 1), and yet never have thought of alluding to the Shiloh of prophecy. And the Lord may have arranged that thus they should name it in order to raise their minds from the present blessings of the earthly Canaan to those of the real kingdom of God; for when they reflected that this state of peaceful enjoyment was under an Ephraimite, Joshua, they might be reminded that this was not the true rest which the Lord promised His people, that it was still to come, when the Prince of Peace, the Lion of the tribe of Judah, should appear. A full discussion of the various interpretations will be found in Hengstenberg, *Christol.* I. 47—90; Kurtz, II. 35—88.— UNTO HIM] i. e. to Shiloh.— THE GATHERING] or more properly, *the willing submission.*—OF THE PEOPLE] The Hebrew word is that which always denotes the Gentiles. On this prediction of the share of the Gentiles in the blessing of Abraham, comp. Isa. ii. 2; xi. 10; xlii. 4; lx. 5; Ps. lxxii. 8.

ver. 11. BINDING HIS FOAL, &c.] The images here are all of peace and plenty. Shiloh, to whom the nations are to gather in willing submission, and whose strength is compared to the lion, is yet to come in peaceful guise. In His kingdom is to be the enjoyment of all the abundance that man can desire. Throughout the O. T. the horse is represented as the animal of warfare (Job xxxix. 19), and the great element of military strength (Isa. ii. 7; xxxi. 1; Hos. i. 7); but the ass is always represented as the animal for employment in time of peace. Thus when, in Zechariah, the peaceful nature of the Messiah's reign is described, He is represented as coming on an ass (ix. 9). That the *wine* and *milk* are images of the abundance of the blessings which man should desire, appears from Isa. lv. 1 and Song of Sol. v. 1.

ver. 13. HAVEN OF THE SEA] better translated, *shore of the sea*, i.e. of the Mediterranean sea.—HIS BORDER SHALL BE UNTO ZIDON] The western boundary was to be Phœnicia, here named from its chief city. This passage also supplies internal evidence of the antiquity of this prophecy. Tyre lay much nearer the border of Zebulun than Zidon did, and had it been in existence at the time must have been mentioned instead of Zidon. According to Josephus, Tyre was not built till the time of the Judges.

vers. 14, 15. These words give an account of Issachar's temper and lot. His land was *pleasant*, and its inhabitants lovers of *peace* and *rest*, and instead of wars and merchandise gave themselves up to the labours of husbandry (*Kidder*). The country allotted to Issachar included the most fertile and inviting portions of Canaan. Within its bounds were the valleys of Jezreel, Megiddo and Esdraelon, famous for their beauty and richness. Only once does the history of Israel make mention of Issachar as joining in the warlike exploits of the nation, and that when 'the princes of Issachar were with Deborah.'—
AN ASS] In the East, and especially in ancient times, the ass was much more highly thought of than at present it is in northern Europe. In Palestine and Arabia, Africa and the South of Europe, it is still remarkable for strength and beauty, so that the comparison implies nothing ignoble or mean. Homer compares Ajax to an

ass; and the Caliph Mervan obtained the sirname, *the ass*, on account of his great strength and daring in battle (Marigny, *Hist. of the Arabs*, II. 387). The comparison implies that the men of Issachar would be strong, hardy, patient, and enduring (*Raphall*).—COUCHING DOWN BETWEEN TWO BURDENS] or *between the stalls*, as in Judg. v. 16. It is a proverbial expression of husbandmen who abandon themselves to idleness and indulgence (*Gesen.*).—BECAME A SERVANT UNTO TRIBUTE] i.e. a tributary servant. Wright translates, *became liable to the service of a slave*, i.e. worked without receiving wages.

ver. 16. The children of the bondwoman were evidently not considered equal to the sons of Jacob's wives; comp. ch. xxxvii. 2. Jacob, in proceeding from the sons of Leah to the sons of the handmaids, takes care to declare that they were to be founders of tribes just as the children of the freeborn wives.—DAN SHALL JUDGE HIS PEOPLE] i.e. the people of the twelve tribes, as in Deut. xxxiii. 7 (*Knobel, Delitzsch*). It seems better to understand *his people* as denoting *the people of his own tribe*. The blessing then means that Dan, notwithstanding his low origin, or the small extent of territory allotted the tribe, should exist as an independent, self-governed tribe, like the others.

ver. 17. AN ADDER IN THE PATH] The Cerastes, a horned snake, still frequently found in Egypt. This snake is of the colour of sand, in which it lies buried on the road, and perceives by means of the horn-feelers the approach of the horseman. A sharp sting in the hoof causes the horse to throw the rider (*v. Gerlach*). The image represents the Danites as managing their wars more by craft and cunning than by open hostility. The prediction does not appear to have Samson particularly in view (*Patrick*).

ver. 18. I HAVE WAITED FOR THY SALVATION, O LORD] The thought of the trials he had himself passed through, and of those which he sees awaiting his descendants, draws from the patriarch this expression of his longing for the promised salvation of the Lord.

ver. 19. GAD] He makes a kind of play on the name Gad, which resembles *Gedud, a troop*. This tribe had its inheritance on the eastern side of Jordan, and was harassed by the Ammonites and other predatory tribes (Judg. x. xi.). By the defeat of the Ammonites in Jephthah's time, and the decisive victory over the Hagarenes (1 Chron.

v. 18—22), they procured a peaceful enjoyment of their inheritance until the time of the captivity.—A TROOP SHALL, &c.] This should be translated, *a troop shall attack him, but he shall attack their rear*, i.e. shall put the invading enemy to flight (*Maurer*).

ver. 20. A description of the fruitfulness of Asher's inheritance. Comp. Deut. xxxiii. 24. For the truthfulness of the prediction, see Stanley, *Sin. and Pal.* p. 358.—ROYAL DAINTIES] meat fit for the table of kings (*Wright*).

ver. 21. A HIND LET LOOSE] He compares Naphtali to a hind *roaming at large*, or, as some prefer translating, a *graceful* hind, which, "light-footed and swift, easily eludes its persecutors on the mountain-heights" (*Kalisch*).—GIVETH GOODLY WORDS] It would seem that this tribe excelled in eloquence or poetry. The only proof we have of this gift is the song of Deborah in Judg. v.

ver. 22. JOSEPH IS A FRUITFUL BOUGH, &c.] Lit. *Joseph is the son of a fruit-tree, son of a fruit-tree by the well, his branches spread over the wall.* The image is plain and elegant. Joseph is compared to the layer of a fruit-tree (probably of a layered vine; comp. Ps. lxxx.), which has the fairest prospect of thriving; beneath it is the well supplying moisture and nourishment, and over it the wall to protect it from wind and weather, and to afford support to its boughs (*Delitzsch*).

ver. 23. THE ARCHERS, &c.] An image of the persecutions which Joseph endured at the hands of his brethren and in Egypt, and which were repeated in the history of Ephraim, which suffered much from the jealousy of the other tribes (Judg. xii.), and also from the frequent attacks of the Syrians.

ver. 24. HIS BOW, &c.] Joseph is strengthened by God Himself so as to withstand his enemies.—THE ARMS OF HIS HANDS] It is through the strength of the arms that the hands can bend the bow, and so direct the arrow (*Delitzsch*). But Knobel and Kurtz translate, *the strength of his hands.*—FROM THENCE IS THE SHEPHERD, THE STONE OF ISRAEL] i. e. from the same divine power and mercy it was that Joseph became *the feeder* (shepherd), and *the stay and support* (stone) of Israel and his family (*Ainsw., Kid., Pat., Rosenm.*). The passage is better rendered, *the arms of his hands were made strong, or received strength, from the hands of the mighty God of Jacob, from thence, from the shepherd,*

v. 18—22), they procured a peaceful enjoyment of their inheritance until the time of the captivity.—A TROOP SHALL, &c.] This should be translated, *a troop shall attack him, but he shall attack their rear*, i.e. shall put the invading enemy to flight (*Maurer*).

ver. 20. A description of the fruitfulness of Asher's inheritance. Comp. Deut. xxxiii. 24. For the truthfulness of the prediction, see Stanley, *Sin. and Pal.* p. 358.—ROYAL DAINTIES] meat fit for the table of kings (*Wright*).

ver. 21. A HIND LET LOOSE] He compares Naphtali to a hind *roaming at large*, or, as some prefer translating, a *graceful* hind, which, "light-footed and swift, easily eludes its persecutors on the mountain-heights" (*Kalisch*).—GIVETH GOODLY WORDS] It would seem that this tribe excelled in eloquence or poetry. The only proof we have of this gift is the song of Deborah in Judg. v.

ver. 22. JOSEPH IS A FRUITFUL BOUGH, &c.] Lit. *Joseph is the son of a fruit-tree, son of a fruit-tree by the well, his branches spread over the wall.* The image is plain and elegant. Joseph is compared to the layer of a fruit-tree (probably of a layered vine; comp. Ps. lxxx.), which has the fairest prospect of thriving; beneath it is the

G.

well supplying moisture and nourishment, and over it the wall to protect it from wind and weather, and to afford support to its boughs (*Delitzsch*).

ver. 23. THE ARCHERS, &c.] An image of the persecutions which Joseph endured at the hands of his brethren and in Egypt, and which were repeated in the history of Ephraim, which suffered much from the jealousy of the other tribes (Judg. xii.), and also from the frequent attacks of the Syrians.

ver. 24. HIS BOW, &c.] Joseph is strengthened by God Himself so as to withstand his enemies.—THE ARMS OF HIS HANDS] It is through the strength of the arms that the hands can bend the bow, and so direct the arrow (*Delitzsch*). But Knobel and Kurtz translate, *the strength of his hands*.—FROM THENCE IS THE SHEPHERD, THE STONE OF ISRAEL] i.e. from the same divine power and mercy it was that Joseph became *the feeder* (shepherd), and *the stay and support* (stone) of Israel and his family (*Ainsw., Kid., Pat., Rosenm.*). The passage is better rendered, *the arms of his hands were made strong, or received strength, from the hands of the mighty God of Jacob, from thence, from the shepherd, from the stone* or *rock of Israel* (*Maurer, Delitzsch*). The insertion of 'from thence' points emphatically to the Shepherd and Rock of Israel as the source of Joseph's strength.

ver. 25. By a slight alteration the English version becomes more intelligible and nearer the original. *From the God of thy father—may He help thee!—and from God Almighty—may He bless thee!* [*may there come upon thee*] *blessings of heaven above, &c.* (*Maurer, Delitzsch*).— BLESSINGS OF HEAVEN ABOVE] i.c. fertilizing rains and dews.—BLESSINGS OF THE DEEP THAT LIETH UNDER] i.e. springs and abundance of water.—BLESSINGS OF THE BREASTS AND WOMB] productive cattle. For the reverse of these blessings, comp. Deut. xxviii. 23; Hos. ix. 14.

ver. 26. THE BLESSINGS OF THY FATHER HAVE PREVAILED ABOVE THE BLESSINGS OF MY PROGENITORS UNTO THE UTMOST BOUND OF THE EVERLASTING HILLS] For not only have the blessings of his progenitors been most prosperously fulfilled in him, surrounded as he is by his numerous descendants; but while his fathers could only bless individuals, he is in the act of blessing an entire, great, glorious, and imperishable people (*Raphall*). The present translation is supported by Delitzsch.—UNTO THE UTMOST BOUND OF THE EVERLASTING HILLS] The eminence and long duration of these blessings are metaphorically expressed by the height and duration of ancient hills; comp. Isa. liv. 10 (*Kidder*).—THAT WAS SEPARATE FROM HIS BRETHREN] These blessings belong to Joseph, who, being selected from the number of his brethren to a higher destination, was separated and consecrated, and whose descendants were to obtain a high importance in Israel (*Knobel*).

ver. 27. Benjamin is fitly compared to a ravening wolf for his warlike courage and success against his enemies; an account of which we have, Judg. iii. 15, xx. 21; Gal. ii. 5 (*Kidder*). —THE MORNING,...AT NIGHT] denoting the unceasing and unwearied boldness and ferocity of Benjamin; comp. Ps. xcii. 2; Eccles. xi. 6.

ver. 28. BLESSED THEM] Even Reuben, Simeon, and Levi received a blessing in being taken in as heads of tribes, and inheritors of the promised land (*Kidder*).

Chapter L.

ver. 2. HIS SERVANTS THE PHYSICIANS] i.e. those physicians in his service whose peculiar office it was to embalm. As we learn from Herodotus (II. 84) that in Egypt each distemper and each organ had its peculiar physician, it is not strange that Joseph should have had several in his service. Comp. Hengstb. *Eg.* p. 66.—TO EMBALM] The antiquity of the practice in Egypt is proved from some mummies bearing the dates of the oldest kings. Full descriptions of different modes of embalming are given by Herodotus, Book II. c. 86, and Diodorus, I. 91. However, "they are not justified in confining the modes of embalming to three, since the mummies show a far greater variety" (Wilkinson, *Herod.* Vol. II. p. 139).

ver. 3. AND FORTY DAYS] Diodorus states that the process of embalming lasted more than thirty days; I. 91. When Herodotus (II. c. 86) says that the body was kept in natron seventy days, he included in that period the whole time of mourning (Hengstb. *Eg.* p. 68; Wilkinson, *Herod.* Vol. II. p. 142).

ver. 4. JOSEPH SPAKE UNTO THE HOUSE OF PHARAOH] On every other occasion we find Joseph speaking directly to Pharaoh. But now he was in mourning; and, according to the Egyptian custom related by Herodotus, his hair and beard were unshorn; and, as is shown in note on ch. xli. 14, he could not, according to Egyptian notions of propriety, enter the royal presence.

ver. 5. LET ME GO] A man in Joseph's high position could not venture to leave his master's country without permission.

ver. 9. IT WAS A VERY GREAT COMPANY] "The custom of funeral trains (says Rosellini) was peculiar to all periods, and to all the provinces of Egypt. We see the representations of funeral processions in the oldest tombs at Eilethyas, and similar ones are delineated in those of Saqqarah and Gizeh; we also find others of a like nature in the Theban tombs, which belong to the eighteenth, nineteenth, and twentieth dynasties." When we behold the representations of the processions for the dead on the monuments, we seem to see the funeral train of Jacob (Hengstenberg, *Egypt*).

ver. 10. THE THRESHING-FLOOR OF ATAD, WHICH IS BEYOND JORDAN] As *Goren ha-atad*, 'the buckthorn threshing-floor,' is on the other side, i.e. the east of the Jordan, the procession did not take the nearest route, by Gaza and through the territory of the Philistines, but went by a long circuitous route round the Dead Sea, and so crossed the Jordan, and entered Canaan on the eastern side. The reason of this may be attributed to political circumstances, with which we are unacquainted (*Kurtz*).—BEYOND JORDAN] Lit. *across Jordan;* and the place was evidently on the *east* side of Jordan. An argument has been derived from this expression to prove the late authorship of the Pentateuch. Moses, it is argued, could not have described the situation of the place by a term which describes it relatively to a person in Canaan. But the use of this term here is to be explained from the necessity imposed on a writer circumstanced as Moses, of fixing on some ideal point of view in relation to which he might speak of localities far distant from himself. Regarding Canaan as his true home, Moses would naturally in such a case make it his centre. See Hengstb. *Pent.* II. p. 256; Keil. *Einl.* p. 132.—THERE THEY MOURNED] The great external demonstrations of sorrow which the Egyptians exhibited in their mourning are thus described by Herodotus (II. 85): "Lamentations and funerals were celebrated. When a man died in a house, that is, one of rank, all the females of the family, covering their faces with mud, and leaving the body in the house, ran through the streets, girded up, and striking their bare breasts, and uttering loud lamentations. All their female relations joined them. The men beat their breasts in like manner, and also girded up their dress."

ver. 11. ABEL-MIZRAIM] This name cannot mean *the mourning of the Egyptians*, which would be *Ebel-mizraim*, neither need we suppose it to mean, with Gesenius, Tuch, and Delitzsch, *the meadow of the Egyptians;* but it is best to consider *abel* as a verb in the third person singular pret., *Egypt mourns* (*Wright*).

ver. 13. HIS SONS CARRIED HIM INTO THE LAND OF CANAAN] unaccompanied, it seems, by the Egyptians. A peaceful company of mourning relatives might readily enter a strange land, but the armed escort of Egyptians would hardly be permitted to cross the frontier. And, besides, religious prejudices might deter the Egyptians from assisting at the interment of the patriarch of the shepherd tribe.

ver. 19. AM I IN THE PLACE OF GOD?] He acts as one who believes the truth, 'Vengeance is mine; I will repay, saith the Lord.'

ver. 20. See note on ch. xlv. 5.

ver. 23. THE CHILDREN OF MACHIR THE SON OF MANASSEH WERE BROUGHT UP UPON JOSEPH'S KNEES] i.e. were adopted by him, not to be founders of new tribes (see ch. xlviii. 6), but to inherit his special rights and property. Thus Kurtz.

ver. 26. IN A COFFIN] A wooden mummy-case, made generally of sycamore, and of shape resembling the deceased. See the passage of Herodotus in note on ver. 2. It is well remarked by v. Gerlach, that "this first book of Moses concludes with an act of faith on the part of the dying Joseph, which connects it with the second, and points to the fulfilment of the promises which now follows."

THE END.

Cambridge:
PRINTED BY C. J. CLAY, M.A.
AT THE UNIVERSITY PRESS.

www.ingramcontent.com/pod-product-compliance
Lightning Source LLC
Chambersburg PA
CBHW022101300426
44117CB00007B/544